FAMOUS TRIALS

A READER'S DIGEST BOOK

Produced by Andromeda Oxford Ltd.

The acknowledgments that appear on
page 188 are hereby made a part of
this copyright page.

Library of Congress Cataloging in Publication Data

McLynn, F. J.
    Famous trials : cases that made history / Frank McLynn.
        p.   cm.
    Includes index.
    ISBN 0-89577-655-3
    1. Trials—Popular works. 2. Trials—United States—Popular
works. 3. Trials—Great Britain—Popular works.   I. Title.
K540.M45 1995
347′.07—dc20
[342.77]
                                                    95-22728

Printed in Spain

FAMOUS TRIALS

CASES THAT MADE HISTORY

Frank McLynn

THE READER'S DIGEST ASSOCIATION, INC.
Pleasantville, New York / Montreal

CONTENTS

6   *Introduction*

10   **SPECIAL COURTS**

12   THE HIGH PRIEST CAIAPHAS *v.* JESUS OF NAZARETH

16   THE CROWN *v.* SIR THOMAS MORE

20   THE RUMP PARLIAMENT *v.* KING CHARLES I

26   THE COMMITTEE OF PUBLIC SAFETY *v.* GEORGES-JACQUES DANTON

30   THE SOVIET UNION *v.* NIKOLAI BUKHARIN

36   BROWN *v.* BOARD OF EDUCATION OF TOPEKA, KANSAS

42   THE STATE OF ISRAEL *v.* ADOLF EICHMANN

48   THE STATE OF PAKISTAN *v.* ZULFIKAR ALI BHUTTO

52   THE PEOPLE'S REPUBLIC OF CHINA *v.* THE GANG OF FOUR

58   **CHURCH COURTS**

60   THE COURT OF THE INQUISITION *v.* JOAN OF ARC

64   ST. JULIEN RESIDENTS *v.* LOCAL WEEVILS

68   THE HOLY OFFICE *v.* GALILEO GALILEI

74   THE COMMUNITY *v.* ALLEGED WITCHES

78   **MILITARY COURTS**

80   THE BRITISH ARMY *v.* WOLFE TONE

86   THE STATE OF VIRGINIA *v.* JOHN BROWN

92   THE FRENCH ARMY *v.* ALFRED DREYFUS

98   THE ALLIED NATIONS *v.* NAZI LEADERS

106   THE ALLIED NATIONS *v.* HIDEKI TOJO

112 JURY TRIALS

114 MELETUS *v.* SOCRATES

118 THE CROWN *v.* THE "TOLPUDDLE MARTYRS"

122 THE CROWN *v.* MADELEINE SMITH

126 JAMES MCNEILL WHISTLER *v.* JOHN RUSKIN

132 THE CROWN *v.* FLORENCE MAYBRICK

136 OSCAR WILDE *v.* THE MARQUESS OF QUEENSBERRY

142 THE STATE OF ILLINOIS *v.* LEOPOLD AND LOEB

148 THE STATE OF TENNESSEE *v.* JOHN T. SCOPES

152 THE PEOPLE *v.* JULIUS AND ETHEL ROSENBERG

156 THE CROWN *v.* WILBERT COFFIN

160 THE CROWN *v.* PENGUIN BOOKS LTD.

166 THE STATE OF SOUTH AFRICA *v.* NELSON MANDELA

172 THE U.S. GOVERNMENT *v.* DANIEL ELLSBERG

176 THE CROWN *v.* LINDY AND MICHAEL CHAMBERLAIN

180 THE ATTORNEY GENERAL *v.* HEINEMANN PUBLISHERS AND PETER WRIGHT

184 THE STATE OF MISSISSIPPI *v.* BYRON DE LA BECKWITH

188 *Bibliography & Acknowledgments*

190 *Index*

INTRODUCTION

WAS JUSTICE DONE?

Some of the most dramatic stories in human history have unfolded in the courtroom, many of them far more gripping than fiction. The trials that follow—from the earliest, in which the philosopher Socrates is condemned to death, to the most recent, in which the murderer of a civil rights activist is brought to justice some 30 years after committing the crime—reveal the ongoing search for justice in human societies. Over time, the struggle has continued with varying degrees of success. Some of these trials are tragic examples of justice subverted; but the sad tales stand alongside those of courage and persistence to create and uphold a just system enshrined in law.

DUE PROCESS: THE BACKBONE OF JUSTICE

The proper objectives of any legal trial are that it be conducted fairly and that the outcome be just. A judicial system cannot simply come to a fair decision without regard to the means; it must do so through fair procedure, which over time has come to be known as "due process."

The cornerstone of due process is the presumption of innocence, which means that the person accused must be proved guilty beyond reasonable doubt. In the United States, Britain, and across the present and former British Commonwealth, the defendant must also be given timely notice of the accusations against him or her. The body chosen to decide the issue of guilt must be impartial and independent. Where that body is separate from the judge (as in trial by jury), the judge must interpret the laws of the land and operate as an objective guardian of fairness. For both sides to be able to present their cases to the court, the judge may have to ensure that counsel is competent and that comprehensive advice is given to both parties. All these elements, working together, allow the legal process to serve a just outcome for both the individual on trial and society at large.

Much is offered to a defendant at the end of the 20th century, especially where human rights and individual freedom are protected by law, that would not have been offered even a hundred years ago. However, the concept of an evenhanded trial is not new. During the trial of the Greek philosopher Socrates in 399 B.C. both sides were given equal time to speak, a safeguard to justice that was lost in many trials during the centuries that followed. In any society, ancient or modern, confidence in the system of justice depends on knowledge that each citizen will have access to legal advice, to supportive witnesses, and to a fair and thorough process.

Two trials (State of Virginia *v*. John Brown and the Crown *v*. Wilbert Coffin) illustrate what may happen when due process is absent. In each case the defendant was executed following a trial in which he had neither access to expert advice nor the support of witnesses. In contrast, Leopold and Loeb, defendants who were both sons of millionaires, bought the expert advice of an exceptionally talented lawyer and so escaped the capital sentence that would certainly have been the fate of less privileged defendants.

PROCEDURE VERSUS JUSTICE

Although due process plays its part in a fair outcome, it can also get in the way of justice. In the third trial of Byron de la Beckwith for the murder of Medgar

Evers—30 years after the crime was committed—the evidence presented against Beckwith convinced the jury that he was guilty of a premeditated, racist murder. Yet Beckwith's lawyers argued with considerable force, right up to the Supreme Court of the United States, that a man who had twice before been charged with murder, but not convicted (because the jury had failed to agree), could not legally be tried again so long after the event. Both the U.S. Constitution and the constitution of the state of Mississippi (where Medgar Evers was murdered) guarantee a speedy trial and rule out repeated trials for the same crime—a situation known as double jeopardy. Beckwith could only be tried again because the other two cases had ended in mistrials, meaning that he had never been acquitted. Nonetheless, the Supreme Court of Mississippi affirmed by a bare 4 to 3 vote that it was lawful to try Beckwith a third time so long after the event. Had the third trial been prevented, a murderer would have escaped justice.

Any conflict between justice and due process of law may tempt authorities to take shortcuts to what they believe to be the right result. The conduct of the Nazis during World War II, particularly in pursuit of the "Final Solution," so horrified people at the time that few cared whether the court followed strict procedural rules. In fact, it is to the credit of the states that organized the Nuremberg war crimes tribunal that they conducted trials at all, rather than resort to summary executions. Nevertheless, the charges against the wartime leaders were actually questionable, since the leaders had violated no international law then in existence. The International Military Tribunal that convicted the German and Japanese defendants had to create new laws and then apply them retroactively.

The justice of these trials rests not only on whether it was fair to formulate new law after the event, but whether justice could be served when procedural disadvantages were inflicted on the defendants. These questions continue to be weighed against the evil of allowing war criminals to go unpunished. The fact that the Nuremberg Tribunal (staffed by distinguished lawyers of four nations) acquitted three defendants of the charges brought against them shows that, in spite of the irregularities of the proceedings, every attempt was made to judge each defendant fairly in the light of the evidence.

JUSTICE CORRUPTED

Shortcuts to justice become indefensible when the law itself is immoral, or the state that upholds it is corrupt. In 19th-century England, a group of agricultural laborers later known as the Tolpuddle Martyrs created a trade union to improve their working conditions by peaceful and lawful means. According to the law of the time, their actions amounted to a criminal conspiracy. Most people today would consider that law oppressive and wrong. The fact that the trial itself was not conducted fairly, even by the legal standards of the time, made an immoral conviction inevitable.

In the justice system of a totalitarian state, fair trials are rare or nonexistent. For example, the regime in the Soviet Union under Joseph Stalin is regarded today as no more than an apparatus of terror. Stalinists used the judicial system to bring trumped-up charges against Nikolai Bukharin and many others, then conducted the trials with complete disregard for due process. So too the military regime in Pakistan during the 1970s, which brought a murder charge against its former democratic leader, Zulfikar Ali Bhutto, as well as the apartheid government in South Africa that arrested and tried Nelson Mandela and other protesters.

While some unjust convictions rest on no satisfactory grounds (even under the laws of the state in question), others stem from cases where the law of the land was broken. Nelson Mandela and Wolfe Tone both admitted to illegal acts of sabotage and treason respectively. However, each argued that his actions were justified by the presence of a corrupt regime and an unjust legal system. Tone believed that the British had no right to govern Ireland, while Mandela saw sabotage as the only means to bring about the end of "many years of tyranny, exploitation, and oppression of my people."

JUSTICE AND THE WORLD OF IDEAS

Some of history's most intriguing trials were essentially battles of ideas. Religious loyalty is pitted against loyalty to the state in the case of Sir Thomas More. The established church tries to restrict freedom of thought in the case of Galileo. The state seeks similar restrictions on freedom of expression in the trial of *Lady Chatterley's Lover*. The perennial battle between national security and freedom of information erupts in the cases of Daniel Ellsberg and Peter Wright.

Racial, religious, or ideological prejudice lies at the heart of many landmark trials of ideas. In Brown *v.* Board of Education of Topeka, Kansas, the central issue was clearly the legality of differential treatment according to race. However, prejudice often plays a less overt role in legal proceedings. Race was certainly the root issue in Nelson Mandela's trial. Anti-Semitic feeling played a significant role in the unjust trial of Alfred Dreyfus, and perhaps also in the long delay in revoking the decision. With the benefit of hindsight, it seems likely that Florence Maybrick's conviction owed more to her extramarital affair than to any concrete evidence against her. While anti-Semitism may have played a role in the conviction of Julius and Ethel Rosenberg, the main focus of attention during their trial was their avowed communist sympathies.

THE FUTURE OF JUSTICE

No human system can ensure that the innocent are never convicted, the guilty never acquitted. Yet, where due process is respected and trials are conducted openly and fairly, human error can be substantially reduced. Judges, lawyers, and jurors must carefully balance a just result with the means used to reach it. When democratic law is carefully applied, particularly by ordinary citizens, without fear of partiality to either prosecution or defense and without prejudice against individuals because of their color, creed, or politics, there is no better guarantee of justice.

Many of the cases described in this book were conducted in the full glare of media attention. While publicity can serve as a check to injustice, it can also exact a heavy price on the judges, lawyers, defendants, and particularly the citizens who make up the juries—as the recent trial of O.J. Simpson clearly demonstrated. However difficult the pursuit of justice may be, it is vital to the continued health and steady improvement of the justice systems throughout the world that ordinary citizens continue to believe that it is worth pursuing.

Above Florence Maybrick in the dock defending herself on a charge of murder, August 1889.

SPECIAL

*S*ometimes a case is so complex, or the political issues surrounding it so far-reaching, that the state must refer it to the highest judicial authority in the land, usually a court consisting of several senior judges and no jury. Under the best conditions a case tried by this kind of special court enjoys the full protection of due process of the law, and the verdict establishes a precedent for new legislation. However, many so-called special courts are scarcely courts at all, but rather ad hoc tribunals conducted outside the normal rules of due process. Typically they are set up to try high-profile political prisoners and intended to reach a preordained verdict, by fair means or foul. Such special courts rarely have any authority beyond the crude principle that might is right. In the worst cases they bring charges that are inconsistent with the law of the land and impose severe and unprecedented punishments on their victims.

A special court may be the court of last resort, set above the trial-by-jury process, or it may be specially adapted to try a particular case. In either instance, it serves a political purpose that may bring changes to the existing law of the land. In a period of rapid political change, for example in the aftermath of revolution or a military coup, special courts often bear the burden of legitimizing the new political regime. Part of that task may be to dispose of political enemies of the new regime—usually by execution—in a series of aggressive "show trials."

Danton, Bukharin, Bhutto, and the Gang of Four all suffered "show trials," though in widely different circumstances. Their trials were intended both to teach a lesson to potential troublemakers and to act out the triumph of "good," as embodied by those in political power, over "evil," as represented by the accused. One observer of Bukharin's trial commented that it had many of the features of a medieval morality play. The trial of the Gang of Four— conducted in Communist China in the early 1980s— staged a symbolic degradation of the old guard, rendered the more powerful by being presented in carefully selected "sound bites" to a worldwide audience through the international media.

COURTS

By their nature, special courts often make painful rulings on matters of religion, conscience, and morality. In the case of Sir Thomas More, though his conviction for treason was questionable, the new law that attended the charges, requiring an oath of allegiance, was valid according to the terms set out by the English Parliament. More defended his refusal to obey the new legislation on grounds that it contradicted the laws of God and the Catholic Church, of which he was a minister; he could not be loyal to the king and God at the same time. The question of who wielded ultimate authority was also the central moral and legal problem in the trial of Charles I. If the courts of England were the king's courts and the monarch was the fount of justice and the object of all allegiance, how, then, could he commit treason against himself, or be tried by his own court?

The trial of Adolf Eichmann raises even more fundamental questions about the authority of a special court as moral adjudicator. Serious legal problems surrounded Eichmann's trial in a state that did not exist at the time of his alleged committed crimes, and the Israeli court's right to punish him has never been universally recognized.

12 THE HIGH PRIEST CAIAPHAS *v.* JESUS OF NAZARETH

16 THE CROWN *v.* SIR THOMAS MORE

20 THE RUMP PARLIAMENT *v.* KING CHARLES I

26 THE COMMITTEE OF PUBLIC SAFETY *v.* GEORGES-JACQUES DANTON

30 THE SOVIET UNION *v.* NIKOLAI BUKHARIN

36 BROWN *v.* BOARD OF EDUCATION OF TOPEKA, KANSAS

42 THE STATE OF ISRAEL *v.* ADOLF EICHMANN

48 THE STATE OF PAKISTAN *v.* ZULFIKAR ALI BHUTTO

52 THE PEOPLE'S REPUBLIC OF CHINA *v.* THE GANG OF FOUR

Are You King of the Jews?

THE TEMPLE AUTHORITIES v. JESUS OF NAZARETH

CIRCA A.D. 30

Above The gospel writers relate that a crown of thorns was placed on Jesus' head at his crucifixion by the Roman soldiers, who mocked him as the "King of the Jews."

The only certain fact about the trial of Jesus of Nazareth is that he was condemned to death by the Roman governor of Judea, Pontius Pilate, around A.D. 30. Almost every other aspect of the case—the crime he was alleged to have committed, the procedure by which he was tried, and the reason for the savage sentence of death by crucifixion—has been a long-standing subject of debate among scholars trying to sort out the various viewpoints described in the four Gospels of the Bible's New Testament. These accounts were written some decades after the events took place. But the facts would have been known to many who had been eyewitnesses or had heard firsthand accounts of the proceedings. It is not surprising, therefore, that the Bible writers give vivid accounts of what happened. What remains to be understood is why these events took place: what were the motives behind the arrest and trial of Jesus?

THE PRETEXT FOR JESUS' ARREST was his behavior in Jerusalem during the week preceding the great festival of Passover. Some 300,000 pilgrims had already converged on the city and were beginning seven days of prayer and purification when Jesus rode through one of the city's gates on a borrowed donkey while a cheering crowd threw cloaks and palm branches on the ground before him. (Later, Jesus' disciples would identify his action as a fulfillment of Zechariah's prophecy, made centuries before, describing the arrival of the Messiah. This man, chosen by God to deliver the people of Israel, would establish God's kingdom on earth.) The crowd's enthusiasm was not so excessive that it put the people or Jesus in immediate danger of arrest, but it alerted the Temple authorities, responsible for keeping the peace in Jerusalem, to Jesus' presence. They already knew that his actions throughout Judea had won him a remarkable popular following. This not only threatened their authority but also risked inviting unwanted Roman attention to the region.

During the following week Jesus visited the Temple, where he taught about "the Kingdom" and answered questions. This was bad enough in the eyes of the Jewish leaders, but Jesus also made them his enemies when he destroyed the busy stalls of the merchants and moneychangers who crowded the Temple's outer courts. Everything that Jesus did and every word that he said were reported to the

Jewish Law Under Roman Rule

At the time of the trial of Jesus, Judea was under Roman occupation; but most towns were administered by Jewish elders in the traditional way. Jerusalem was governed by the Jewish high priest, Caiaphas, and the Temple court, or Sanhedrin, a council of 70 members. Judea's Roman governor (*praefectus*), Pontius Pilate, had the power to sentence anyone, even a Roman citizen, to death without a trial of the kind necessary in Rome. The non-Roman people of Judea were at his mercy, and a direct appeal to the emperor would have been their only recourse.

After Jesus was arrested, he was taken before a group of priests from the Sanhedrin—headed by Caiaphas—and interrogated. According to the Gospel of St. John, he was questioned first by Caiaphas's father-in-law, Annas, an elder of the Temple. The hearing determined the grounds for referring Jesus' case to the Roman governor.

The Sanhedrin accused Jesus of blasphemy—"diminishing the honor of God"—an offense in Jewish law punishable by public stoning to death. According to St. Mark's Gospel, Jesus was then formally condemned to death, but St. Luke records no verdict, and whether there was a consensus of opinion is not clear. Historians have not established that the Temple authorities at this time possessed the power to carry out executions, even if the hearing had constituted a legal trial; certainly in most cases, that right lay exclusively with the Roman governor. It would, in any case, have been unwise to carry out such a sentence in the presence of a huge, volatile crowd without the knowledge and protection of the Roman military.

high priest of the Temple, Joseph Caiaphas, an experienced administrator. It was his duty to arrest troublemakers without provoking any disturbance that might necessitate the intervention of the Roman military. Caiaphas could see that Jesus might well inflame the crowd—he was dangerous.

ARRESTING THIS POPULAR TEACHER AND PROPHET within the precincts of the Temple would have caused the kind of riot that Caiaphas was anxious to avoid. Fortunately for him, his agents had discovered that one of Jesus' band of disciples, Judas Iscariot, could be bought. They paid Judas thirty silver shekels, the price of a low-grade slave, to guide officers of the Temple and soldiers one night to the quiet garden of Gethsemane, well outside the city walls, where Jesus had often met with his closest followers to pray. Jesus did not fight the arrest, and he insisted that his friends not fight it either. The fact that not one of his disciples was taken away probably indicates that Caiaphas knew that Jesus was not planning to lead an armed insurrection. For the time being, Caiaphas just wanted to question him.

Above Jesus before the high priest, Caiaphas, charged with "diminishing the honor of God." Caiaphas asked, "Are you the Christ, the Son of the Blessed One?" When Jesus replied, "I am," Caiaphas said it was blasphemy and tore his robe as a sign of grief.

"We found this man perverting our nation, forbidding us to pay taxes to the emperor, and saying that he himself is the Messiah, a king."

THE MULTITUDE ACCUSES JESUS
Luke 23 : 2

*"Where are you from?
…Do you refuse to speak to
me? Do you not know that I
have power to release you, and
power to crucify you?"*

PONTIUS PILATE
John 19 : 9–10

PONTIUS PILATE

The writers of the Bible and the Roman historian Tacitus (A.D. 55–120) state that the founder of the Christian religion was crucified while Pontius Pilate was governor of Judea (A.D. 26–36), and in this context his name has been preserved in the creeds of the Christian Church. According to tradition, Pilate belonged to the Samnite clan of the Pontii (hence the name Pontius). He became governor of Judea through the intervention of Sejanus, a favorite of the emperor Tiberius. Most of the time, Pilate lived in his luxurious villa in Caesarea. He visited Jerusalem only for major festivals to ensure that peace was maintained.

During his 10-year term as governor, Pilate offended the Jews by displaying images of Tiberius on top of legionary banners throughout Jerusalem, even though the law of Moses forbade such images. This caused such unrest that Tiberius eventually ordered Pilate to remove the images from the city. Around A.D. 30 Pilate presided at the trial of Jesus. In A.D. 36 he was ordered back to Rome after the people of Samaria (the region between Judea and Galilee) complained that he had used excessive cruelty in preventing the followers of one of their prophets from accompanying the prophet up Mount Gerezim. In Rome he faced an imperial commission of inquiry and was sentenced to exile in Vienne, France. According to a fourth-century account, he killed himself on the orders of the emperor Caligula in A.D. 39.

Above The trial of Jesus took place in the city of Jerusalem, viewed here from the southwest.

AFTER QUESTIONING JESUS, CAIAPHAS SENT HIM TO PILATE. Knowing that the Roman would not be interested in a Jewish religious dispute, Caiaphas phrased the charge in deliberately political terms: Pilate was told that Jesus had claimed to be "king of the Jews." This could be construed as treason; it labeled Jesus as a zealot and a rebel against Rome. Pilate's subsequent behavior suggests that he found the accusation unconvincing.

When he heard that Jesus was from Galilee, Pilate decided to send him before Herod Antipas, the son of Herod the Great, who ruled Galilee as a puppet king under Roman authority. Herod was in Jerusalem for the feast of Passover; he had heard of Jesus and wanted to see him, until he discovered that the reputed miracle worker would not perform to order. In fact, Jesus refused to speak. Angered, Herod ordered his soldiers to mock Jesus, dress him in a "royal robe," and return him to Pilate. The Roman governor, unlike Herod, found his prisoner an enigma worthy of exploration:

PILATE: Are you the king of the Jews?
JESUS: Do you ask this on your own, or did others tell you about me?
PILATE: Your own nation and the chief priests have handed you over to me. What have you done?
JESUS: My kingdom is not of this world.
PILATE: So you are a king?
JESUS: You say that I am a king.…Everyone who belongs to the truth listens to my voice.
PILATE: What is truth?

Whether Pilate meant to launch a philosophical discussion with his mysterious prisoner or simply expressed his own skepticism is unclear. Jesus fell silent.

It was Pilate's custom, according to the Gospel of St. Mark, to acknowledge the Passover festivities by releasing one prisoner held under his jurisdiction. At the time of Jesus' arrest, Pilate had in his custody a man named Barabbas, a known insurrectionist who had already committed murder during the course of an armed uprising. Pilate announced to the crowd of Jews who had gathered that he found no fault with Jesus, but he offered them a choice: did they want him to release Barabbas or Jesus? The Gospel of St. John records that Pilate was actually afraid of being responsible for Jesus' death. At the same time, he dared not set free a man who claimed to be a king and could therefore pose a threat to the Roman authority of Caesar. If Pilate was trying to help Jesus escape death, however, his attempt failed. The crowd yelled for the release of Barabbas. Pilate called for a bowl of water, washed his hands as a gesture that he accepted no responsibility for the affair, and handed Jesus back to the Temple authorities for execution.

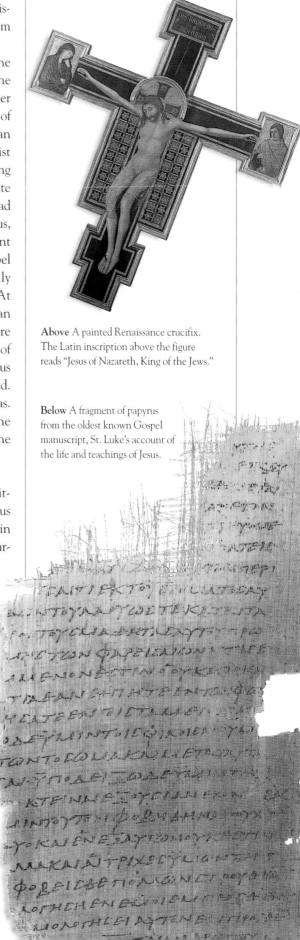

Above A painted Renaissance crucifix. The Latin inscription above the figure reads "Jesus of Nazareth, King of the Jews."

Below A fragment of papyrus from the oldest known Gospel manuscript, St. Luke's account of the life and teachings of Jesus.

JESUS WAS GIVEN THE ROMAN SENTENCE FOR TREASON by non-Roman citizens, death by crucifixion, a punishment reserved for the most serious crimes. The sentence guaranteed that the Roman military would be in charge of the execution, fulfilling Caiaphas' wish to avoid any public disturbance. In accord with normal practice, Jesus was stripped and scourged, an event that usually weakened prisoners enough to shorten their agony on the cross. He then had to carry the heavy wooden crossbar of his own cross through the streets to a hill outside the city walls, where a permanent upright post waited; once there, he lay on the ground beneath the post while nails were driven through his hands into the crossbar. The beam was then hoisted by soldiers into place across the upright, forming a T-shape, and Jesus' feet were nailed to the post. Jesus' ordeal on the cross lasted from nine in the morning until three in the afternoon, when he was finally pronounced dead. Later his friends were given permission to take away the body for burial.

The Gospels record, and Christians believe, that after three days Jesus came back to life. Their experience of his resurrection and belief in their own future of eternal life with God transformed Jesus' disciples and friends into people willing to proclaim his teaching throughout the world and, if necessary, to die themselves for their faith in him. This most famous trial in history and its aftermath continues to reverberate throughout the world today, almost 2,000 years later.

A Double-Edged Sword

THE CROWN *v.* SIR THOMAS MORE

JULY 1 – JULY 6, 1535

Above The ax and execution block kept at the Tower of London and used in the time of King Henry VIII for the public beheading of political prisoners.

By 1534 England's King Henry VIII had been battling the Catholic pope for eight years, unsuccessfully petitioning to divorce his first wife, Catherine of Aragon. Finally, Henry took the only route open to him—he proclaimed himself head of the Church of England. On March 23, 1534, Parliament passed the Act of Succession, declaring Henry's marriage to Catherine void and validating his second marriage to Anne Boleyn. The act carried with it a stiff penalty for any who challenged it: it called for a charge of treason and a sentence of death. To ensure total support, Henry ordered that all adult subjects take an oath of allegiance.

A SUMMONS WAS ISSUED ON MARCH 7, 1534, requiring Sir Thomas More, a prominent statesman and author, to take the oath the following day at Lambeth Palace. More was privately opposed to Henry's split with Rome and had resigned as lord chancellor in 1532. When he arrived at Lambeth Palace, he found the archbishop of Canterbury, the lord chancellor, the king's chief adviser, Thomas Cromwell, and other friends of the king waiting to see what he would do. They strongly urged More to take the oath and showed him a list of influential people who had already signed it. More insisted that although Parliament had the right to name Henry's successor, it was wrong to declare Henry's first marriage invalid. He could not in good conscience take the oath. When More was offered a second opportunity to swear allegiance in April 1534 and once again refused, he was imprisoned in the Tower of London along with another leading churchman, Bishop John Fisher.

More had been in prison without trial for seven months when Parliament passed a series of acts intended to force any still hesitant about the oath to a decision. The Act of Supremacy, which finalized the break with Rome, declared that the king was the "Supreme Head" of the Church of England, but omitted the former conditional clause "so far as the law of Christ allows." The Second Act of Succession enshrined the controversial oath of allegiance in the statute books. The Act of Treasons extended the definition of treason to include words either spoken or written against the king, the queen, or their heirs. Finally, the Act of Attainder—which was specifically designed to put pressure on More, Fisher, and five other recalcitrant churchmen—proclaimed that those refusing to take the oath of allegiance forfeited all their possessions.

Oyer and Terminer

In the 11th century, following the Norman conquest of Britain, the British monarch began to delegate his judicial powers to trusted members of court. By the 14th century, these courtiers had become itinerant justices authorized to deal with judicial matters of two sorts: "Oyer and Terminer," in which they listened to all the evidence in a particular case, then made a final judgment; and "Gaol Delivery," in which they tried or released all the prisoners in a particular prison.

More was tried before a commission of Oyer and Terminer made up of 18 of his peers, with the right of appeal to the king alone. These 18 men, many of them More's enemies, acted as both prosecutors and advisers to the accused. More knew the law in great detail; he chose to conduct his own defense. Despite his skilled refutation of the evidence against him, it became clear that he had no chance of acquittal. In fact, he was convicted on the testimony of a single lying witness, Richard Riche. Twelve years later the law was changed to require the evidence of at least two hostile witnesses for conviction in a capital case.

BIOGRAPHY

Sir Thomas More (1478–1535) was born in London, the son of a judge. As a young man, More trained as a lawyer and in time became one of the most distinguished authors and politicians of the Renaissance era. In 1516 he published *Utopia*, his eloquent view of an ideal society. Two years later he produced *The History of King Richard III*, England's first work of scholarly historical distinction. During

Henry VIII's early years on the throne, More made rapid progress up the political ladder, first becoming chancellor of the Duchy of Lancaster in 1525, then lord chancellor in 1529, following Cardinal Thomas Wolsey's dramatic fall from power. Wolsey had failed to gain the pope's permission for Henry VIII to divorce his wife, Catherine of Aragon. As did other leading churchmen, More watched with

Above Thomas More and his family, by Rowland Lockey circa 1527. More is seated second from left, wearing a large gold chain.

silent disapproval the successive steps that led the king finally to break away from the Church of Rome. This attitude, and More's refusal to deny it, led to his imprisonment, trial, and execution in 1535. Four hundred years later he was canonized by the Catholic Church.

MORE WAS BROUGHT FOR INTERROGATION before Thomas Cromwell and other members of the ruling council on April 30, 1535. They informed More that the king wanted to know his opinion on the new statutes, particularly the Act of Supremacy. When More was unable to give a satisfactory answer, Cromwell warned him that Henry would let the law take its course. Meanwhile, word came from Rome that the pope had made Bishop Fisher a cardinal. "Let the pope send him a hat when he will," King Henry stormed, "…head he shall have none to set it on." Now Henry was determined that More and Fisher be trapped into explicit treasonable denial of the Act of Supremacy. On June 3 a gathering of king's men—including Cromwell, Cranmer, and Thomas Boleyn, the new queen's father—interrogated More in the Tower. Cromwell told More that the king commanded him to answer plainly: he must either acknowledge Henry as supreme head of the Church or "utter plainly his malignity." More replied that he was a loyal servant of the king, but added: "for if it were so that my conscience gave me against the statutes (wherein how my mind giveth me I make no declaration)…it were a very hard thing to compel me to say either precisely with

"Yet unto the oath that there was offered unto me I could not swear, without the jeopardizing of my soul to perpetual damnation."

THOMAS MORE,
in a letter to his daughter,
Margaret Roper,
1534

17

it against my conscience to the loss of my soul, or precisely against it to the destruction of my body." In other words, if he spoke out, it would cost him dearly whether he told the truth or a lie. Unable to trap More, they asked him why, if he was prepared to die for his beliefs, he would not condemn the statute. More replied: "I have not been a man of such holy living as I might be bold to offer myself to death, lest God for my presumption might suffer me to fall."

Infuriated by More's refusal to cooperate, Cromwell sent Sir Richard Riche, an agent provocateur who had already trapped Fisher into an explicit denial of the Act of Supremacy. Riche tried to corner More:

Above The Tower of London, where More was imprisoned and put to death in 1535. It was used as a royal residence until the death of Henry VII in 1509. His son Henry VIII, who preferred to live in the more fashionable Palace of Whitehall, used the Tower as a jail and place of execution for his most important enemies.

RICHE: "Admit there were, Sir, an act of Parliament that all the realm should take me for king. Would not you, Master More, take me for king?"
MORE: "Yes, sir, that would I."
RICHE: "I put the case, further, that there were an act of Parliament that all the realm should take me for pope. Would you then, Master More, take me for pope?"
MORE: "Suppose Parliament should make a law that God should not be God. Would you then, Master Riche, say that God were not God?"
RICHE: "No Parliament may make any such law."

More fell silent, leaving Riche to draw the obvious conclusion. Still lacking an outright statement from More, Cromwell and the king decided that this exchange with Riche would form the basis of an indictment against him. On June 17, 1535, More received the news that Fisher had been tried and convicted. Fisher was beheaded five days later.

"I verily trust and right heartily pray, that though your lordships have now here in Earth been judges to my condemnation, we may yet hereafter in heaven all merrily meet together, to our everlasting salvation."

THOMAS MORE,
to the members of the court,
July 1, 1535

MORE'S TRIAL TOOK PLACE IN WESTMINSTER HALL ON JULY 1. The formal indictment stated that More had "traitorously and maliciously, by craft imagined, invented, practiced, and attempted wholly to deprive our sovereign lord the king of his dignity, title and name of Supreme Head on Earth of the Church of England." Four pieces of evidence were offered to the court: More's silence when interrogated by Cromwell, Cranmer and Boleyn; his correspondence with Fisher, which had been burned; an allegation that he wrote to Fisher that the Act of Supremacy was a two-edged sword; and his conversation with Richard Riche on June 12.

More, speaking in his own defense, made short work of the first point: "Your statute cannot condemn me to death for such silence, for neither your statute nor any laws in the world punish people except for words or deeds." Any discussion of his correspondence with Fisher could only be speculation, but More denied that he had written that the statute was "like a sword with two edges, for if a man answer one way it will confound his soul, and if he answer the other way it will confound his body." He had, he said, only written conditionally: "If the statute cut both ways like a two-edged sword, how could a man behave so as not to incur either danger?"

Riche was called in to give evidence on the final count. He described the exchange, but added a fictional, damning sentence: "No more than Parliament could make a law that God were not God could Parliament make the king Supreme Head of the Church." More addressed the jury: "If I were a man, my lords, that did not regard an oath, I needed not, as it is well known, in this place, at this time, nor in this case, to stand here as an accused person....And if this oath of yours, Master Riche, be true, then pray I that I never see God in the face, which I would not say were it otherwise to win the whole world." More then gave his own version of the conversation. He accused Riche bluntly of perjury and, turning to the bench, asked his accusers: "Can it therefore seem likely unto your honorable lordships, that I would in so weighty a cause so unadvisedly overshoot myself as to trust Master Riche, that I would unto him utter the secrets of my conscience touching the king's Supremacy?"

Above A posthumous painting of More in prison, holding the red wooden cross that he carried to his execution. This is one of two portraits that form a diptych celebrating the life of Sir Thomas More.

THE JURY TOOK JUST 15 MINUTES TO FIND MORE GUILTY. They were unanimous in their verdict. The lord chancellor rose to pass sentence, but More interrupted him with the reminder that every prisoner should be asked why judgment should not be given against him. Granted permission, More spoke freely at last. He argued that sentence should not be passed because he had been found guilty by a statute that was not valid. "This indictment is grounded upon an Act of Parliament directly repugnant to the laws of God and his Holy Church...it is therefore, in law among Christian men, insufficient to charge any Christian man."

More was condemned to death. Although the penalty for high treason was to be hanged, drawn, and quartered, More's sentence was commuted by the king to beheading by the ax, widely considered to be a more noble end. Early in the morning on July 6, 1535, he walked to his death on Tower Hill, not dressed in cloth of gold, as he had wished, but in a coarse gray gown and carrying a red wooden cross. After giving a short address to the onlookers, in which he asked the people to pray for him and bear witness that he suffered death for the Catholic faith, he knelt at the block and told the executioner to be of good cheer: "Pluck up thy spirits man and be not afraid to do thine office; my neck is very short; take heed therefore thou strike not awry, for saving of thine honesty." His head was severed with a single stroke.

HENRY VIII's DIVORCE

In order to cement a political alliance in Europe, Henry VII of England and the Spanish monarchs, Ferdinand of Aragon and Isabella of Castille, arranged a marriage between England's 14-year-old heir, Prince Arthur, and the 16-year-old Spanish princess, Catherine of Aragon. Their wedding took place in 1501, but six months later the prince died. Loath to lose the political advantages of the match, Henry VII obtained a papal dispensation to allow his second son, the future Henry VIII, to marry the widowed Catherine.

Despite frequent pregnancies, Catherine bore only one surviving child, Princess Mary. The king was desperate for a male heir and worried for the future of the Tudor dynasty.

The issue came to a head in 1526, when Henry fell in love with Anne Boleyn, one of his wife's ladies-in-waiting. He appealed to the pope for permission to divorce Catherine on the grounds that he had broken God's law in marrying his brother's widow. He had been punished, he claimed, by the death of all his male children.

The pope was understandably unwilling to declare the royal marriage unlawful, so in 1531 Henry took the law into his own hands and put aside the wife recognized by Rome. He married Anne Boleyn and crowned her queen in 1533. Having rejected Rome's authority, Henry made his break with the pope final by establishing himself as the supreme head of a new Protestant Church of England.

Divine Right of Kings

THE RUMP PARLIAMENT v. KING CHARLES I

JANUARY 20–27, 1649

Above The orb and scepter, the monarch's symbols of temporal and spiritual power. They are still used as part of the coronation ceremony when a new monarch is crowned.

The trial of King Charles I brought England to a crisis of government that had been in the making for half a century. During the seven years prior to the king's trial in January 1649, England had endured a state of civil war, with the king's Royalist supporters fighting toe-to-toe against Parliament's New Model Army—the Roundheads—in a series of bloody battles. Although no single interpretation can explain the complex causes of the war, at the heart of it lay two fundamentally opposed ideologies: The king held that it was his "divine right," invested by God and independent of Parliament, to exercise absolute power as monarch; Parliament believed—and fought to ensure—that as a representative body, it had the right to control, among other things, England's economy and militia. Given so wide a breach in viewpoints, it is hardly surprising that after his defeat in the civil war, Charles came to trial as a political prisoner, in proceedings that sidestepped the accepted system and code of justice of the day.

TWO MONTHS EARLIER, THE ROYALISTS HAVING BEEN DEFEATED, two-thirds of Parliament's House of Commons—the Presbyterian majority—had wanted to make peace with the king. They hoped to establish, with the help of the Scots, a Presbyterian regime and had already entered into negotiations with the king on the Isle of Wight, where he was being held prisoner. But the army no longer trusted Charles. Earlier that year, Charles had encouraged the Scots to rise against the army and invade England. In early December the commissary general of the army, Henry Ireton, and his troops marched into London. When the Presbyterian members of the House of Commons arrived on December 6 and 7 to take their seats, Ireton gave orders to have them forcibly turned away. Those who resisted were arrested. His purpose was twofold: to shape Parliament into a force against the king, and to see that Charles, "the capital and great author of our troubles," was "brought to justice" for having personally launched the second phase of the civil war. Although the members of Parliament were convinced that Charles had been in league with the Scots, they possessed no evidence to support the accusation.

ON JANUARY 2, 1649, PARLIAMENT accused "Charles Stuart, the now King of England" of "a wicked design…to introduce arbitrary and tyrannical government," in pursuit of which aim he had "levied and maintained a cruel war

Absolute Monarchy

Until the execution of Charles I, the British commonly believed that the king derived his authority directly from God and that he could not be held accountable by any earthly authority. This unwritten doctrine—known as "the divine right of kings"—effectively gave the king absolute power.

At his trial Charles disputed the jurisdiction of Parliament on this basis. As king, he argued, he was answerable only to God, not to the people. Parliament, in turn, argued that when Charles took his coronation oath, he promised to uphold the liberties of the people; he had broken his promise by

waging a "cruel war against the Parliament and the kingdom." Anticipating the ideas of John Locke and Thomas Jefferson, the prosecution asserted that if the king broke his contract with the people, the people had the right to punish him. By trying the king when no precedent existed for such an action, Parliament flirted dangerously with totalitarianism, in which the state sets itself above the law and arbitrarily creates new laws to consolidate its own power. The monarchy was re-established in England in 1660. After the Revolution of 1688, however, the doctrine of divine right disappeared from British politics.

BIOGRAPHY

Charles I (1600–49) was the third child of James I of England, who was also James VI of Scotland. The sudden death of Charles's brother Henry in 1612 made him heir to the throne at the age of 11. He became king in 1625 and in the same year married the French princess Henrietta Maria. Friction over domestic and foreign policy surfaced between the king and Parliament, but for the first three years of his reign, Charles cooperated with Parliament, guided by his close friend, George Villiers the duke of Buckingham. After the duke was assassinated in 1628, Charles suspended Parliament and ruled alone until 1640. During this period he levied unpopular taxes to finance his foreign policy and in 1637 attempted to force Presbyterian Scotland to accept a new Anglican prayer book, an action that exacerbated years of resentment against the established church. With Scotland ready to rebel, Charles had to recall Parliament in April 1640 to raise money. When Parliament renewed its attacks on royal prerogatives, civil war broke out. Charles was defeated in the conflict that raged from 1642 to 1646, and again in 1648. In January 1649 he was tried for tyranny, treason, and murder, found guilty, and executed.

Right Charles I on horseback, painted by Van Dyck in the late 1630s.

in the land against the Parliament and kingdom." The House of Lords rejected the charge. The king could not, they said, be condemned for treason against himself. The ordinance was amended to state that "the people are, under God, the original of all just power" and "the Commons of England, in Parliament assembled, being chosen by and representing the people, have the supreme power in this nation." Having armed itself with this sovereign authority, Parliament voted to set up a High Court of Justice, composed of 135 commissioners, to try the king. Chief among them was Lieutenant General Oliver Cromwell, the army's most distinguished commander. As late as the end of December, Cromwell had wanted to spare Charles's life. But once the High Court was established, he threw himself with energy into the proceedings.

A two-week delay followed, while the king's accusers reached an agreement on the terms of the indictment, found a qualified judge, and prepared Westminster Hall. It was there that the king's trial opened to the public on January 20, 1649. Only 68 of the 135 commissioners attended; many refused to take part—including the illustrious parliamentarian general,

> *"I will rather choose to wear a crown of thorns with my savior, than to exchange that of gold, which is due to me, for one of lead."*
>
> CHARLES I
> declares his determination
> to overcome parliamentary forces
> on the eve of civil war,
> January 10, 1642

Above The chair on which Charles sat during his trial in Westminster Hall.

Thomas Fairfax, the most distinguished lawyers in the land, three chief justices, the Master of the Rolls, and the Speaker of the House of Commons—because they believed that the court had no historical validity or moral justification. One Roundhead officer expressed the underlying problem: although he was sure that putting the king on trial was just, "yet I know not how it may justly be done."

PROCEEDINGS BEGAN WHEN JOHN BRADSHAW, LORD PRESIDENT of the court, ordered the prosecutor to read the charges. John Cook—a religious zealot and a republican—solemnly declared that Charles was "a tyrant, traitor, murderer, and a public and implacable enemy to the Commonwealth of England" and "had maliciously levied war against the present Parliament and the people therein represented."

Charles replied, "I would know by what power I am called hither." The court, he insisted, had no jurisdiction. Furthermore, he had been arrested while in the process of negotiating with Parliament for a constitutional settlement and had been brought to London by force. He was, he argued, their lawful king by "divine right"; no one had the authority to put on trial a divinely anointed king. It was sacrilege, and they would answer for it on the Day of Judgment. To the king's first point, Bradshaw replied that the court's authority was "the people of England, of which he was the elected king." Charles retorted that England had never had an elected king. England had been a hereditary monarchy for a thousand years, and he, Charles, had been chosen to govern, not by the people but by God, entrusted by Him with "the care of the Liberties of the People."

Plainly the loser in this debate, Bradshaw adjourned the court until Monday, January 22. As the new day of proceedings began, Cook warned Charles that if he refused to plead his case, he would be treated as guilty, according to a well-established legal precedent, and sentenced. The king replied that he would not answer charges in a court whose authority he rejected. The argument over the court's authority continued for some time, but eventually Bradshaw silenced Charles and had the clerk read the

THE ENGLISH CIVIL WAR

The civil war in England was fought in two distinct phases: four years of bitter fighting (1642–46) between the Royalist Cavaliers and Parliament's New Model Army, the Roundheads, led by Oliver Cromwell; then a united Royalist and Presbyterian uprising against the New Model Army in 1648. Charles suffered a decisive defeat in 1645 at the Battle of Naseby, and in 1648 his supporters were crushed again by Cromwell at Oxford.

The war grew out of complex and interwoven tensions. Underlying the constitutional quarrel between king and Parliament was a religious division

between the radical Puritans (Cromwell and the Roundheads) and the more moderate Protestants, represented by the Church of England. After his capture, Charles maintained in his private letters that he was dying to protect the Anglican Church and its bishops. Had he agreed to the abolition of the bishoprics, he would have broken his coronation oath to uphold the Church of England.

Some historians have tried to explain the war in the context of class conflict, but no clear pattern of economic interest emerges. The parliamentary party was composed, in

modern terms, of right-wing capitalists and left-wing radicals, and the Royalists included both progressives and reactionaries. Some historians have argued that the gentry was on the rise; others, that it was declining. Still others see the struggle as one between the "Court"—those dependent on royal patronage—and the "Country"—those who paid the expenses of central government without reaping any benefit. Whatever the causes, the "English Revolution" was without question a genuine civil war, in which brother killed brother, father fought son, and parents disowned their children.

Above A contemporary engraving of the trial of Charles I. The king sits with his back to the public, facing the clerks of the court and, behind them, Parliament.

charges once more. Charles again refused to plead, and the lord president ordered him to be taken away. Charles demanded the reasons for his treatment. "Sir, 'tis not for prisoners to require," replied Bradshaw. *"Prisoner, Sir! I am not an ordinary prisoner,"* replied the king in so commanding a tone that even the trial's official scribes recorded the words in italics. Bradshaw stood his ground, however, and the king was led back to confinement.

TWO DAYS LATER THE COURT RECONVENED WITHOUT THE PRISONER and heard from 33 witnesses, who placed the king at the battles of Edgehill, Naseby, and other major engagements of the civil war. On January 25 these depositions were read aloud at a public session—the due process—and on the afternoon of January 27, Charles was escorted into Westminster Hall to

> *"I say, sir, by your favor, that the Commons of England was never a Court of Judicature."*
>
> CHARLES I
> arguing with Bradshaw,
> lord president of the court,
> January 22, 1649

Above John Bradshaw, lord president of the court that tried the king "as a tyrant, traitor, and murderer." In his private life Bradshaw was a fierce republican and a devout Puritan.

> *"For the charge, I value it not a Rush. It is the liberty of the People of England I stand for."*
>
> CHARLES I
> to the court,
> January 23, 1649

Above The death warrant of Charles I, signed and sealed by the members of the court. The first signature (bottom left) is Bradshaw's, followed by Thomas Grey's and Oliver Cromwell's. General Ireton's signature is in the second column.

hear his sentence read. He stood before the 67 judges and Bradshaw, the lord president, robed in scarlet. Knowing that once a man had been sentenced to death he no longer had the right to address the court, Charles asked to be allowed to speak first. Bradshaw replied, "You disavow us as a court, and therefore for you to address us is not to be permitted." Charles persisted, and Bradshaw eventually silenced him by striking a bargain to let him speak before the sentence was passed if Charles would agree not to interrupt the proceedings.

THE CHARGES WERE READ ONCE MORE, and once more the king refused to plead. Instead, since the judges were proposing regicide, he requested permission to speak on behalf of "the peace of the kingdom and the liberty of the subject" before a joint session of both Houses of Parliament, the Lords

Left An anonymous 17th-century painting of the execution of Charles I. The central image is surrounded by four medallions: the king (top left); the king being led to his death (bottom left); the executioner with the severed head (top right); people dipping cloths in the king's blood (bottom right).

> *"I go from a corruptible to an incorruptible crown, where no disturbances can be, no disturbances in the world."*
>
> CHARLES I
> to his chaplain, Bishop Juxon,
> shortly before his execution,
> January 30, 1649

and the Commons. The judges retired to discuss the king's request. Some of their number, especially John Downes, were quite sympathetic to Charles's appeal. When a heated argument broke out on the issue, Cromwell ended it with a menacing hiss at Downes: "Art thou mad? Can't thou not sit still and be quiet?" After tempers had subsided, the court reconvened. Bradshaw told the king that it had been decided unanimously that no delay would be tolerated; he must hear his sentence. In a speech that lasted forty minutes, Bradshaw maintained that the members of Parliament were "the sole Makers of the Law" and that "the law was his [Charles's] master." Bradshaw instructed the clerk to read out Parliament's sentence, which concluded with these words: "The said Charles Stuart, as a tyrant, traitor, murderer, and a public enemy to the good people of this nation, shall be put to death by the severing of his head from his body."

The judges rose to signify their assent. The king asked to be heard, in accordance with Bradshaw's promise, but was denied. He was forcibly removed by the guards and carried in a sedan chair to Whitehall. Before he left he managed one parting comment. "Poor souls," he said of his judges. "For sixpence they will say as much of their own commanders."

THE KING WAS SUMMONED TO HIS EXECUTION on Tuesday, January 30, a bitterly cold day. Anxious that if he shivered from the cold, onlookers would think that he was shivering from fear, Charles wore two shirts to keep him warm. Mounting the scaffold, he addressed the crowd with the words he had prepared in prison: "I fear not death. Death is not terrible to me." However, the guards had been instructed to keep the people well back, and the king's words were lost in the wind. His chaplain, Bishop William Juxon, reported that as Charles laid his head on the block, he uttered a last, cryptic word: "Remember!" The executioner, whose identity has never been discovered, severed his head in one clean blow.

POSTSCRIPT

Parliament, after it had tried and executed the king, set up a Council of State to govern the new republic, with Oliver Cromwell as its head. One of Cromwell's first actions was to take control of the rebellious Scots, who in February 1649 had declared that Charles's son should be Charles II of Scotland. In 1651 Cromwell defeated Charles II at the battle of Worcester, and the king fled to France in disguise. Two years later Cromwell sought a constitutional basis for his rule and assumed a new title—lord protector. One of his generals, John Lambert, drew up a document called The Instrument of Government, which declared that "the supreme legislative authority...shall be and reside in one person and the people assembled in Parliament. The style of which person shall be the lord protector of the Commonwealth of England, Scotland and Ireland." Parliament did not approve the document, and the dispute dominated Cromwell's Protectorate. By January 1658, Cromwell had lost patience with Parliament and dissolved it. He died in September of that year. His son, Richard, took over as lord protector but was ousted by the army. To prevent anarchy, the army turned to Charles II. If Charles would assume England's throne, he could issue a general pardon, ensure liberty of conscience, and resolve all disputes "in a free Parliament, by which, upon the word of a King, we will be advised." In May 1660 Charles II was proclaimed king of England and returned to London amid great rejoicing.

Let Us Be Terrible

THE COMMITTEE OF PUBLIC SAFETY *v.* GEORGES-JACQUES DANTON

APRIL 3 – APRIL 5, 1794

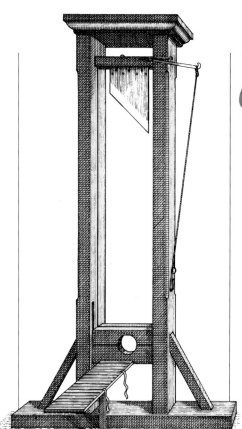

Above The guillotine was used by Robespierre's Committee of Public Safety to execute thousands in the center of Paris during 1793 and 1794.

When, in 1794, Georges-Jacques Danton came to trial before revolutionary France's Committee of Public Safety, he was, like Aesop's eagle, shot down with an arrow fledged with one of his own feathers. As one of the more radical architects of the French Revolution, Danton himself had set up the committee in an effort to contain the violence sweeping the country. "Let us be terrible," he had resolved, "so that we can prevent the people from being terrible." Established on April 6, 1793, the committee held emergency executive powers to deal with, in the words of its founding decree, "all offenses against liberty, equality, and indivisibility of the republic…and of all plots tending to reestablish the monarchy." Now Danton stood accused as an offender.

Danton was deposed as head of the committee by Maximilien Robespierre, a man far more bloodthirsty than his predecessor. While civil war raged, and Austria and Prussia stood ready to intervene on the side of the growing number of royalist exiles, Robespierre initiated "the Terror." Aimed at quashing any resistance to the committee, its central symbol was the guillotine in the Place de la Revolution (now Place de la Concorde). One of its first victims, on October 16, 1793, was Queen Marie Antoinette.

DANTON DID THE UNFORGIVABLE WHEN HE CRITICIZED THE TERROR. Warned of Robespierre's malice, Danton made a thinly veiled reference to this in a speech to the National Convention. "Perhaps 'the Terror' once served a certain purpose," he declared, "but it ought not to strike at innocent people. No one wishes to see an individual treated as a guilty person because he doesn't happen to have sufficient revolutionary vigor." His enemies launched a campaign to undermine his influence.

On December 1, 1793, Danton informed the revolutionary radicals that their role was ended. They in turn criticized him for lack of commitment to the revolution. He defied his enemies to prove their vague allegations. Robespierre filled the Committee of Public Safety with his own followers, who proceeded to compile a list of charges against Danton. Some of the charges reflected Robespierre's personal disapproval of Danton's "reprehensible life style": Danton surrounded himself with rascals, alleged Robespierre, and openly tolerated immoral living. Danton said that public opinion is a whore and posterity is nonsense. Danton laughed at virtue as though it were a joke.

This time Danton refused to counterattack. "It would only mean the shedding of more blood," he said. "There has been enough. It is better to be guillotined than to guillotine." He

Left The indictment accusing Danton of crimes against the state, signed by members of the Committee of Public Safety.

Georges-Jacques Danton was born in 1759 near Troyes into a middle-class, provincial family. He followed his father into the legal profession, becoming a successful lawyer in Paris and a member of France's representative assembly, the States-General, in 1789. He was a large man with a resonant voice, whose fame as an orator reached its high point in September 1792 after the violent overthrow of the monarchy. As Prussian armies advanced into the heart of France to aid the king, Danton made a rallying speech the French people would never forget: *"Pour les vaincre, pour les aterrer, que faut il? De l'audace, encore de l'audace, et toujours de l'audace."* ("What do we need to defeat the enemy? We need daring, more daring, and still more daring.") He was elected deputy for Paris to the newly formed National Convention and voted for the execution of Louis XVI in January 1793. He went on to crush his political opponents, the moderate Girondists, and in April 1793 created the Committee of Public Safety to help stop the bloodbath in the wake of revolution. His control of the government lasted only three months before his fellow revolutionary, Maximilien Robespierre, orchestrated his downfall. When Danton attempted to recover his power, he was arrested, tried, and, like so many others before him, sent to the guillotine.

Right An anonymous pencil sketch of Danton, dated April 5, 1794, the day of his execution.

offered no resistance even when he was arrested on the night of March 30, 1794. He and five of his supporters were incarcerated in the Luxembourg prison for two days. On April 2 he was taken to the Conciergerie to hear the formal indictment against him.

The trial was a sham from the beginning. Both the public prosecutor, Antoine Fouquier-Tinville, and the president of the court, Antoine Herman, had been warned by the Committee of Public Safety that they would pay with their own lives if they failed to secure a conviction. The jury was composed of a scant seven men—the only ones who could be counted on to return a verdict of guilty. No official record of the trial was kept. Historians have had to rely on eye-witness reports and the partial transcript made by one of the jurymen. He began by copying down all Danton's words, but could not keep up with the outpouring of eloquence. All accounts agree, however, that Danton raged into court like a mad bull. When asked his place of residence he replied: "My residence will soon be in the Great Beyond, but you will find my name in the Pantheon of History."

FROM THE START OF THE TRIAL, DANTON MANAGED TO OUTPOINT both Fouquier-Tinville and Herman. When an old comrade of Danton's, François-Joseph Westermann, insisted on being indicted alongside him, Herman tried to brush him aside by saying that the actual process of the indictment was "only a formality." Danton caused an uproar among observers by replying: "Our whole presence here is just a formality."

Disruption followed disruption in the packed courtroom before the charges were finally read out. Danton was accused of plotting to restore the monarchy and put the duc d'Orleans on the throne, and of conspiring with the traitor Dumouriez (a revolutionary general who had defected to the

A People's Court

Before the revolution, most criminal and civil cases concerning France's privileged class were heard by 13 judicial courts, or *parlements*. Each was made up of 50 to 130 noble judges or magistrates, who had purchased their office. During the revolution, a decree of the Constituent Assembly replaced these with elected tribunals, including, on April 6, 1793, the Committee of Public Safety. This was composed of nine (later 12) revolutionary activists elected by the National Convention for one month (they were then eligible for reelection). The committee was set up to provide for the defense of the nation against foreign and civil war. From April to July Danton dominated the committee. But on July 10 he lost his position to his political rival, Maximilien Robespierre. From September 1793 to July 1794 the committee acted as a "people's court." Some 300,000 suspected counterrevolutionaries were arrested and condemned in groups; 17,000 went to the guillotine and countless others died in prison without trial.

Austrians). Then Danton addressed the crowded courtroom. With his booming voice, he showed an uncanny instinct for theatrical performance: "My voice," he roared, "which has so often been heard speaking in the people's cause, will have no difficulty in thrusting this calumny aside. Will the cowards who have slandered my name dare to meet me face to face? Let them show themselves and I will cover them with their own ignominy." Though Herman, the president of the court, tried to quiet Danton, his voice was so powerful and charged with such passion that crowds outside the Palais de Justice, and even across the river Seine, could hear him.

Danton went on to denounce the conspiracy against him and to attack the "untouchable" committee. "I am in full possession of all my faculties when I summon my accusers to come forth," he cried. "I demand the right to pit my strength against theirs." At this the audience burst into applause.

THE FRENCH REVOLUTION

Many date the start of the French Revolution to July 14, 1789, when a mob stormed the Bastille—the prison that had come to symbolize the despotic Bourbon monarchy. Others, however, point to May 5, 1789, when France's ancient representative assembly, the States-General, met for the first time since 1614. The French king, Louis XVI, was forced to reinstate this body to solve France's acute financial crisis. Long periods of warfare and aid given to the American colonists during the American Revolution (1775–83) had drained the French coffers. The poor of the land had been squeezed dry, and the only source of fresh revenue was the nobility, protected from taxation by ancient privileges. After a bitter wrangle in the States-General, the nobility was forced to pay its way. When the king agreed to this demand, the Assembly went one step further, demanding political sovereignty in the form of a National Constituent Assembly. So began the momentum that would end in revolution.

Having achieved remarkable financial and political advances, the more radical members of the Assembly, known as the Jacobins, pushed for social overhaul as well. Growing fervor eventually boiled over into bloody insurrection on August 10, 1792, and culminated in 1793 with the execution of the king. Civil war erupted between the royalists and the revolutionaries; France's royalist neighbors, Austria and Prussia, joined in to support the monarchy. In 1793 Maximilien Robespierre introduced an emergency measure to deal with "enemies of the revolution" that was so bloody that it came to be called the Reign of Terror. Thousands died in prison or under the guillotine before July 1794, when a violent counterrevolution finally sent Robespierre himself to the scaffold, and thus brought the Terror to an end.

Left The storming of the Bastille, sketched as it happened by one of the mob of captors on July 14, 1789.

DANTON ADDRESSED THE PUBLIC, RATHER THAN THE JUDGE AND JURY. "People, you will judge me when you have heard me," he said. "My voice will not only be heard by you but throughout all of France." He proceeded with arguments that convinced the crowd that the charges against him were unsustainable; rumors spread throughout Paris that he would have to be acquitted. Herman and Fouquier-Tinville were desperate. Their own lives depended on delivering Danton's death sentence. As Danton transformed the trial into his stage, his every flight of oratory applauded by the crowd, Herman wrote in panic to Fouquier-Tinville, telling him that they needed to suspend Danton's defense. Otherwise he would clear himself of the charges with the full approval of the people.

This hurried change of plan tore away the last shred of legality attached to Danton's trial. He was outraged: "I am not allowed to call witnesses?" he cried out in despair. "I might as well resign my defense." The flustered Herman was obliged to promise him a further hearing the next day (April 4), when Danton's codefendants also launched spirited defenses. In despair at the growing anarchy in the courtroom, Fouquier-Tinville wrote to the National Convention for advice.

One of Robespierre's close associates on the Committee of Public Safety, Louis Antoine Saint-Just, persuaded the committee that Danton and his fellow prisoners were fomenting insurrection against the court. In light of this the committee allowed Fouquier-Tinville to forbid the defendants to plead. On hearing the decision, Danton leaped to his feet, fixed his eyes on Robespierre's supporters, and shouted: "You are murderers." In his final words to the court Danton painted himself in the role of a public hero: "During the past two days the court has got to know Danton. Tomorrow he hopes to sleep in the bosom of glory. He has never asked for pardon and you will see him fly to the scaffold with his usual sincerity and the calm of a clear conscience."

The president and prosecutor had the prisoners removed from the court, and the jury retired. Even with seven handpicked enemies of Danton on the jury, Herman and Fouquier-Tinville still feared acquittal. In a final act of panic, they illegally entered the jury room, ready to threaten any waverers. The jury returned the required verdict, and Herman pronounced the sentence of death, ordering that it be read to the prisoners: they were to be guillotined the next day. On April 5, 1794, Danton and his associates went to their death, composed and dignified. He was just 34 years old. Three months later Danton's prophecy against his persecutor, made during his trial, came true. Robespierre followed his adversary to execution on the guillotine.

"Murderers! Look at them! They have hounded us to our deaths! Vile Robespierre! You too will go to the scaffold. You will follow me, Robespierre."

DANTON
in his own defense,
April 4, 1794

Above An engraving showing Danton and his friends appearing before the *Tribunal Revolutionaire* in April 1794. Danton, standing in the box on the right of the picture, points accusingly at his judges.

A Show of Justice

THE SOVIET UNION v. NIKOLAI BUKHARIN

MARCH 2 –12, 1938

Above Bukharin and Trotsky, characterized in the Soviet periodical *Izvestia* as bloodthirsty mad dogs being reined in, 1938.

Below Lenin's funeral in 1924. Both Stalin and Bukharin, elite members of the Party's inner circle, carried his coffin. Stalin is on the far left of the picture, looking down, and Bukharin partially hidden on the far right.

*I*n 1938 Nikolai Bukharin became one of the last of the Russian Revolution's leading figures to be toppled by Joseph Stalin in the wave of "purges" known as the Great Terror. Bukharin had been a trusted lieutenant and close friend of Vladimir Lenin, the chief Bolshevik ideologist, during the early days of revolutionary activity between 1905 and 1917. Yet sterling political credentials were no protection under the Soviet Union's new leader. Once the "darling of the Party," Bukharin joined his Bolshevik contemporaries, Marshal Mikhail Tukhachevsky (commander-in-chief of the Red Army), Grigori Zinoviev, and Lev Kamenev as a victim of Stalin's show trials conducted from 1936 to 1938.

Other Soviet officials appeared in the dock alongside Bukharin: Genrikh Yagoda, the people's commissar for internal affairs and former head of the NKVD (the secret police); Alexei Rykov, one of Stalin's major opponents during the 1920s; and Nikolai Krestinsky, the former vice-commissar for foreign affairs. By the time Stalin had accused these high-ranking communists, the last remaining pillars of the Bolshevik revolution, of conspiring against the state, the machinery of his purges had become virtually unstoppable. So arbitrary was the cycle of arrest and punishment, designed to eliminate existing and potential rivals, that Stalin himself lost sight of his real enemies and executed most of his friends.

THE RUSSIAN REVOLUTION

The turbulent history of the Soviet Union, which ended in 1991 with the collapse of the Communist state, began 74 years earlier with the revolutions of February and October 1917. These outbreaks were the culmination of years of secret activity against the czars, which had been gathering strength since the 1870s.

Before the revolutions, various political factions had pressed for political and social reforms through both propaganda and violence. But the movement for change found no single focus until Vladimir Ilyich Ulyanov (Lenin), steeped in the theories of Karl Marx, rose to preeminence in the early 1900s as the leader of the Russian Social Democratic Labor Party. In 1903 this party split into two factions: the Mensheviks ("the minority") and

the more militant Bolsheviks ("the majority"), led by Lenin. Under the banner of "peace, land, and bread," Lenin won the support of industrial workers in the Russian capital, St. Petersburg, and of disaffected members of the Russian army, who had been thrown by the czar into a world war that they did not want to fight.

With populist backing the Bolsheviks staged a bloodless coup in 1917, then went on to fight a civil war against czarist forces and other anti-Bolshevik groups. For this purpose Lenin's right-hand man, Leon Trotsky, created the Red Army that eventually defeated the counterrevolutionaries in 1921. After Lenin's premature death in 1924, a power struggle developed between Trotsky and another of Lenin's allies, Joseph Stalin. Trotsky

Above The insignia of the Soviet secret police, who arrested Bukharin on Stalin's orders and brought him to trial.

was exiled from the Soviet Union and eventually assassinated in Mexico in 1940 by agents acting for Stalin. Meanwhile, Stalin proceeded to build a new Soviet empire that ultimately became even more oppressive than the czarist one that it replaced.

BUKHARIN'S TRIAL OPENED ON MARCH 2, 1938, after a year of careful preparation by the Soviet Union's chief prosecutor, Andrei Vyshinsky. He intended to incriminate Bukharin in a conspiracy of espionage, sabotage, murder, and high treason and to accuse him of masterminding an ambitious plot against Stalin and the Soviet economy that was intended ultimately to reinstate capitalism. To support his argument, Vyshinsky coerced false confessions from Yagoda, Rykov, Krestinsky, and 20 other less prominent party officials. There was nothing to link the accused to one another except their status in the hierarchy, and the charges covered every kind of antigovernment activity. Several small fry officials readily admitted to doctoring butter with nails and powdered glass, destroying truckloads of eggs, engineering a peasants' revolt by killing tens of thousands of pigs and horses, and even deliberately spreading epidemics of disease among livestock.

Associating Bukharin with these activities and suggesting that he was hatching a master plot against the state was patently ridiculous, but the prosecution proceeded on Stalin's instructions. Vyshinsky needed to transform Bukharin's image from that of revolutionary fighter and Marxist theoretician to arch-traitor. To emphasize the picture he sought to paint, Vyshinsky regularly addressed Bukharin's fellow-accused as "vermin," "mad dogs," and "carrion"—language intended to brand them as common criminals, murderers, and spies. Following lengthy interrogation, and in some cases torture, the

> *"One has to remember Comrade Stalin's instruction that there are sometimes periods, moments in the life of a society and in our life in particular, when the laws prove obsolete and have to be set aside."*
>
> ANDREI VYSHINSKY,
> writing in 1937

The Stalinist Purges

During the 1930s the Soviet police instituted a network of spies, informers, prisons, and labor camps in response to increasing pressure from the country's leader, Joseph Stalin. They were instructed to round up enemies of the state, who were tortured, imprisoned, and executed without due process of law. To demonstrate how traitors would be punished, Stalin brought high-ranking suspects to trial before an audience that included Western diplomats and members of the international press. The trial of Nikolai Bukharin was the last of three major staged trials conducted during the Stalinist purges of 1936–38.

Making a mockery of the post-revolutionary "people's courts" that had been set up in November 1917, prosecutors rehearsed their witnesses and scripted large parts of Bukharin's trial to create the impression of a forceful and effective government. One eyewitness, the British diplomat Fitzroy Maclean, wrote that the trial was a cross between a "medieval morality play and a modern gangster film." Throughout the purges, millions of Stalin's "enemies" died in summary executions or were sent to labor camps in Siberia (a common punishment under the czarist regime) without even the pretense of justice.

"I plead guilty to…the sum total of crimes committed by this counterrevolutionary organization, irrespective of whether or not I knew of, whether or not I took a direct part in, any particular act."

NIKOLAI BUKHARIN
at his trial,
March 1938

Below One of Stalin's propaganda posters, published in 1939 and intended to show his personal strength and military power.

witnesses incriminated themselves with outrageous tales of villainy and claims of preeminence as enemies of the people. Each in turn also incriminated Bukharin. Where contradictions appeared in their testimony, Vyshinsky dismissed the inconsistencies as ploys in a diabolical plot by the Trotskyists and their "fascist" helpers in the West to confuse the tribunes of the people. The murmurs of horror and disgust that arose from the audience made it clear that the prosecutor's tactics were working.

BY THE TIME BUKHARIN APPEARED IN THE DOCK ON MARCH 5, 1938, Vyshinsky claimed to have established a damning list of crimes. Bukharin had planned to murder Lenin in 1918, said Vyshinsky. He had intended to dismantle the entire social structure of the Soviet Union; he had plotted with Marshal Tukhachevsky to open the western front of Russia to the Germans in the event of war; he had conspired with Yagoda to murder Sergei Kirov and the writer Maxim Gorky; and he had instructed his minions to make contact with and pass information to the secret services of Britain, Germany, and Japan, with pro-czarist counterrevolutionaries and with Leon Trotsky, who was living in exile in Mexico.

Below Moscow workers outside the courthouse during March 1938 demand the death penalty for Bukharin and his fellow defendants by raising their hands as a sign of agreement.

Looking out over a vast, 500-seat courtroom that had once been the ballroom of the Czarist Nobles' Club, Bukharin—out of duty to the party—pleaded guilty as charged. Then, to the astonishment of the court, he went on to defend his "errors," subtly redefining himself as a man on trial for disagreeing with Stalin, rather than a common criminal guilty of numerous trumped-up crimes and misdemeanors. To the general charges of belonging to a "rightist Trotskyist bloc" Bukharin pleaded guilty; he added that even if he had not committed the treasonable acts mentioned in the indictment, it was a logical consequence of his "erroneous" political stance that he might have done so. That he had been the agent of a foreign power he categorically denied. Neither had he plotted to murder Lenin, to dismantle the Soviet Union, nor to open the front to the Germans.

Bukharin's eloquence visibly affected Vyshinsky. "You're hiding behind a torrent of words," the prosecutor declared, "quibbling over details, wandering off into politics, philosophy, theory, and so on, which you should forget once and for all." He tried to unsettle Bukharin by recalling some of the other prisoners, but as one "star" witness after another took the stand, Bukharin tore their evidence to shreds. Desperate, Vyshinsky produced his trump card—three of Bukharin's associates from 1918, when he was supposed to have plotted to assassinate Lenin. Bukharin proved conclusively that he had been in Petrograd (St. Petersburg), not Moscow, on the alleged date of the conspirators' meeting.

BIOGRAPHY

Nikolai Ivanovich Bukharin (1888–1938) was the son of a Moscow schoolteacher. He studied economics in Moscow and Vienna and joined the Bolshevik Party in 1906. When he was banished to Siberia in 1910 for his political activities, he escaped to New York, where he lived until after the October Revolution of 1917. He returned to a changed Russia and soon became one of Lenin's closest comrades, despite disagreements over Russia's withdrawal from World War I in 1918. Bukharin also became the Bolshevik Party's leading thinker—he was editor of *Pravda* from 1918 to 1929, a member of the Politburo in 1924, and head of the Comintern (an international communist organization) in 1926. After Lenin's death, Bukharin opposed Stalin's policy of collectivization during the late 1920s. Despite the fact that he joined the "right-wing" opposition to Stalin in 1928, he was still called on to draft the so-called Stalin Constitution in 1936 (intended to improve the appearance of democracy in the Soviet Union), and he remained a member of the Central Committee until his arrest in 1937. In 1987, 50 years after his execution, the Soviet Union granted Bukharin a posthumous pardon and reinstated him as a member of the Communist Party in 1988. This process, known as rehabilitation was also applied to other victims of the purges, as a new generation of Soviet leaders sought to de-Stalinize the U.S.S.R.

Above Andrei Vyshinsky, chief prosecutor of the Soviet Union from 1935, presided over Stalin's show trials from 1936 to 1938.

Vyshinsky concluded his cross-examination of Bukharin and brought Yagoda back to the stand. Yagoda, whose physical appearance suggested torture, handed Vyshinsky the damaging admissions the prosecutor sought, including the information that he had plotted with Bukharin to infiltrate the secret police and seize the Kremlin. On March 11, Vyshinsky was ready to sum up for the prosecution. He recapitulated the details of the crimes committed by the Trotskyists and their collaborators in the foreign intelligence agencies. He emphasized Bukharin's alleged role as the leader of "a foul-smelling heap of human garbage" and likened Bukharin to Al Capone and Judas Iscariot, a "cross between a fox and a pig." Working up to a crescendo he declared: "Our country only asks one thing: crush the accursed reptile! Time will pass. The weed and the thistle will grow on the graves of these execrable traitors. But on us and our happy country, our glorious Sun will continue to shed his serene light. Guided by our beloved Leader and Master, Great Stalin, we will go forward to Communism along a path that has been cleansed of the sordid remnants of the past."

The accused were given an opportunity to speak in their own defense. Most of them simply reiterated their guilt and threw themselves on the mercy of the court. Bukharin's opportunity came on March 12. He made a formal confession of guilt to all the plots, sabotage, and assassinations that had ever been mentioned in the indictment, whether he knew about them or not. He added that he hoped his execution would serve as "the last severe lesson" to those disloyal to the state.

The psychology of pleading guilty to charges that were patently absurd has puzzled historians. Some have speculated that Bukharin's faith in communism under Stalin was so completely shattered that his life had become meaningless to him. His last desperate act of hope in the ideology he had

"What matters is not the personal feelings of the repentant enemy but the flourishing progress of the U.S.S.R. and its international importance."

Nikolai Bukharin,
his final statement,
March 1938

Below Judge Ulrich sums up in the Bukharin case, March 1938.

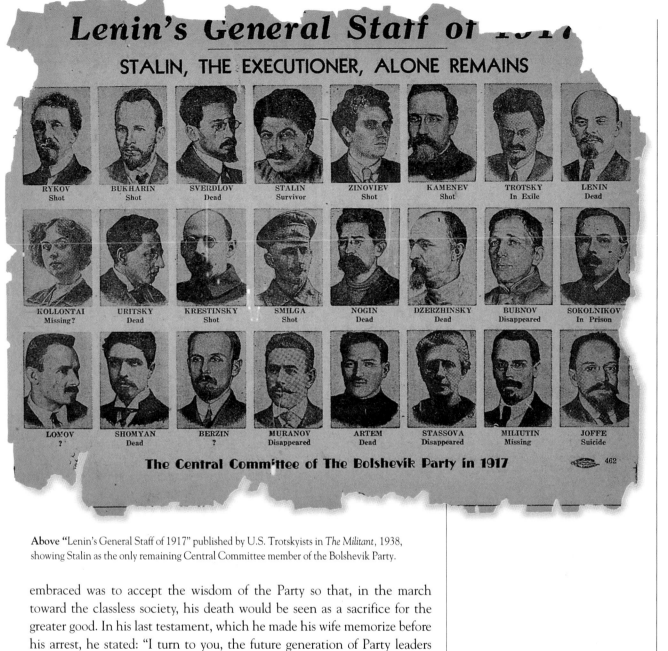

Lenin's General Staff of 1917

STALIN, THE EXECUTIONER, ALONE REMAINS

RYKOV Shot	**BUKHARIN** Shot	**SVERDLOV** Dead	**STALIN** Survivor	**ZINOVIEV** Shot	**KAMENEV** Shot	**TROTSKY** In Exile	**LENIN** Dead
KOLLONTAI Missing?	**URITSKY** Dead	**KRESTINSKY** Shot	**SMILGA** Shot	**NOGIN** Dead	**DZERZHINSKY** Dead	**BUBNOV** Disappeared	**SOKOLNIKOV** In Prison
LOMOV ?	**SHOMYAN** Dead	**BERZIN** ?	**MURANOV** Disappeared	**ARTEM** Dead	**STASSOVA** Disappeared	**MILIUTIN** Missing	**JOFFE** Suicide

The Central Committee of The Bolshevik Party in 1917

462

Above "Lenin's General Staff of 1917" published by U.S. Trotskyists in *The Militant*, 1938, showing Stalin as the only remaining Central Committee member of the Bolshevik Party.

embraced was to accept the wisdom of the Party so that, in the march toward the classless society, his death would be seen as a sacrifice for the greater good. In his last testament, which he made his wife memorize before his arrest, he stated: "I turn to you, the future generation of Party leaders whose historical mission includes an obligation to disentangle the ghastly tissue of crimes which in these terrible days is spreading on a grand scale, burning up like a flame and choking the Party....I am certain that sooner or later the filter of history will inevitably wash the filth from my head....I ask the new, young, and honest generation of Party leaders to have my letter read out at a plenary session to vindicate my name and restore me in the eyes of the Party."

The trial ended at 9:30 P.M. on March 12, and at 4:00 A.M. on March 13 the judges pronounced the death sentence on Bukharin, Krestinsky, Yagoda, Rykov, and 14 others. On March 15 Bukharin was shot by a firing squad, after writing a final note to Stalin in which he addressed the leader by his familiar name: "Koba, why do you need me to die?"

КОПИЯ

СПРАВКА

Военная Коллегия
Верховного Суда
Союза ССР

«09» февраля 19 88 г.
№ СП-002/37

121200, Москва, ул. Воровского, д. 15

Дело по обвинению Бухарина Николая Ивановича, до ареста 27 февраля 1937 г. - Главный редактор газеты "Известия" пересмотрено Пленумом Верховного Суда СССР 4 февраля 1988 года.

Приговор Военной коллегии Верховного Суда СССР от 13 марта 1938 года в отношении Бухарина Н.И. отменен и дело прекращено за отсутствием в его действиях состава преступления.

Бухарин Николай Иванович реабилитирован посмертно.

НАЧАЛЬНИК СЕКРЕТАРИАТА ВОЕННОЙ
КОЛЛЕГИИ ВЕРХОВНОГО СУДА СССР
ПОЛКОВНИК ЮСТИЦИИ

А. НИКОНОВ

A Nation on Trial

BROWN *v.* BOARD OF EDUCATION OF TOPEKA, KANSAS

JUNE 25, 1951 – MAY 17, 1954

Above Linda Brown (back row, fourth from the right) with her classmates in the fourth grade at Monroe School, Topeka, Kansas, in 1951, the year that the trial began.

*T*here are occasions when an individual case puts an entire culture on trial, and the verdict makes history. Brown *v.* Board of Education of Topeka, Kansas, was such a case, and it drew the finest legal minds of its day into the battle for equal rights in the United States.

In the spring of 1951, the Reverend Oliver Brown's nine-year-old daughter, Linda, was in the fourth grade in Monroe School, Topeka, Kansas. Traveling to Monroe involved an inconvenient bus journey of nearly five miles and a walk through a dangerous area of town. Her parents would have liked her to attend Sumner School, just four blocks away. But Sumner was an all-white school, and Linda was black. Since 1867 a Kansas statute had permitted cities with a population of more than 15,000 to maintain racially separate elementary schools. In 1951 seven Kansas cities, including Topeka, had set up segregated elementary schools. Topeka had four grade schools for black children and 18 for white children.

Oliver Brown sought the aid of the National Association for the Advancement of Colored People (NAACP), which was already bringing lawsuits against the system of segregated schools in other states. At this point Brown's aim was to protest against the distance that his child had to

Segregation and the Supreme Court

The U.S. Civil War led to three constitutional amendments that provided the foundation of equal rights for black Americans. The 13th Amendment (1865) abolished slavery; the 14th Amendment (1868) guaranteed due process and equal protection of the laws for all persons born or naturalized in the United States; and the 15th Amendment (1870) guaranteed the right to vote for all persons born or naturalized in the United States. But in practice, these amendments proved difficult to enforce. While states in the North and West continued to legislate against racial discrimination, the Southern states reinforced segregationist policies with a series of what became known as the Jim Crow laws (named after a black vaudeville character). These laws introduced segregation in schools, parks, restaurants, theaters, and even segregated burial plots in cemeteries.

The case of Plessy v. Ferguson, decided in the Supreme Court in 1896, was a landmark in segregationist policy-making. A black man named Homer Adolph Plessy, who was traveling by train from New Orleans to Covington, Louisiana, had seated himself in a railroad car reserved for whites only. When he refused to move, he was arrested. In the trial that followed, the U.S. Supreme Court supported segregation by upholding the concept of "separate but equal" facilities for blacks, laid down by state law in 1890. Not until the late 1940s and early 1950s did the growing and vociferous campaign for equal rights, led by the NAACP, expose the inherent inequality in the "separate but equal" policies and challenge them as ultimately unconstitutional.

Above Robert Carter, the NAACP lawyer who presented the case for the Brown family in the U.S. District Court for Kansas during June and July 1951.

travel, not to take the lid off a seething political issue. Lena Burnett of the NAACP recalled Brown as a diffident man, quiet, hardworking, and withdrawn, an unlikely lightning rod for the anger that his case would arouse. The NAACP agreed to take the case and filed it with the U.S. District Court for Kansas on February 28, 1951. Its title was Brown v. Board of Education of Topeka, Kansas. The NAACP appointed one of its most prominent lawyers, Robert Carter, to handle the case, assisted by Jack Greenberg. By the time the case came to court, the NAACP had solidified its purpose not only to win the right for Linda Brown to attend the school of her parents' choice, but to build a record for a case before the Supreme Court in Washington, D.C., that would challenge segregation as a denial of the equal rights upheld by the U.S. Constitution. Behind Carter's ambitious plan lay the NAACP's belief that segregation inevitably produced inequalities between whites and blacks in educational facilities and curriculum.

THE TRIAL OPENED ON JUNE 25, 1951, before a three-judge panel led by Walker Huxman. At the outset Kenneth McFarland, representing the board of education, pointed out that the state provided a free bus service for black children, but not for white children, and provided two "health rooms" for feeding undernourished children in its four black schools, but only the same number of "health rooms" for the 18 white schools. Most of Carter's witnesses were other black parents who wanted to register complaints about the distance that their children had to travel; they did not tackle the NAACP's central issue. When Oliver Brown took the stand, he was nervous and failed to speak up for the court even after repeated urging by Judge Huxman. He made errors of fact and left out basic information, such as which school his daughter currently attended. Linda Brown was not even in court, nor was the case explained to her by her parents, who preferred to shield her from the proceedings. The lead prosecutor, Lester Godell, simply made the point that many white children made long journeys to school, and Oliver Brown was dismissed. Only the last witness, Silas Hardrick Fleming, addressed the issue of segregation. He asked Judge Huxman if he

"The more I think about this case, the more importance I think it will have on our main objective of securing legal support for our attack on segregation."

ROBERT CARTER,
in a memo to his NAACP colleague
Thurgood Marshall,
May 1951

could make a voluntary statement about why he had come to court. Silencing objections from the prosecution, Judge Huxman agreed, and Fleming declared: "It wasn't to cast any insinuations that our teachers are not capable of teaching our children…the entire colored race is craving light, and the only way to reach the light is to start our children together in their infancy and they come up together."

THE DEFENSE CALLED AS ITS FIRST EXPERT WITNESS Professor Hugh W. Speer, an educational psychologist. Speer gave lengthy testimony that white and black teachers received equal training and comparable teaching loads, and that auditorium and gym facilities were about equal in black and white schools. However, he continued, "If the colored children are denied the experience in school of associating with white children, who represent 90 percent of our national society…then the colored child's curriculum is being greatly curtailed."

The defense called nine expert witnesses in all, and Speer's sentiments were echoed by the rest. Wilbur B. Brookover, a social psychologist from Michigan State College, further testified that segregation persuaded black children that they were "a subordinate, inferior kind of citizen." The final expert witness, Louisa Holt, was a staff member at the Menninger Foundation, a psychiatric clinic in Topeka. She emphasized that feelings of inferiority among the black community were reinforced by the law, which gave official and legal sanction to imposed segregation. These feelings of inferiority also impaired black children's motivation to learn. Arguing on the other side of the case, Harold R. Fatzer, attorney general for Kansas, stated that facilities were equal in black and white schools in the state, and upheld the rule of separate but equal as a practical working solution.

Five weeks later the Kansas court gave its unanimous verdict. It did not overturn the precedent established in Plessy v. Ferguson in 1896, but stated that whether segregation itself constituted inequality was another matter, and appended nine "findings of fact" to the verdict. In particular the findings reflected the testimony of Louisa Holt on the demotivating effect that segregation had on black children. Greenberg wrote to Hugh Speer that "Judge Huxman's opinion, although ruling against us, puts the Supreme Court on the spot, and it seems to me that it was purposely written with that end in view."

BROWN'S LAWYERS APPEALED to the Supreme Court in Washington, D.C. By 1952 Brown v. Board of Education was one of five school segregation cases (the others were from the District of Columbia, Delaware, South Carolina, and Virginia) scheduled to come before the Supreme Court. The cases were grouped together, and Brown appeared

first on the alphabetical list. The NAACP considered this a boon, because the fact that the Browns lived in Kansas showed that segregation was not just a Southern problem. The NAACP had raised $100,000 to fight the campaign and hired a team of lawyers that included Thurgood Marshall, later the Supreme Court's first black judge. The Supreme Court did not rule at once but handed the cases back to the lawyers with the request that they find grounds for overthrowing the separate-but-equal doctrine.

This latest request was a stalling device; the Supreme Court was split on the issue of desegregation. Four of the nine judges (Hugo Black, Harold Burton, William Douglas, and Sherman Minton) wanted to overrule Plessy *v.* Ferguson; three (Tom Clark, Stanley Reed, and Chief Justice Fred Vinson) favored

CHIEF JUSTICE EARL WARREN

Born and raised in Los Angeles, Earl Warren (1891–1974) trained as a lawyer and began his career in the Alameda County district attorney's office. He served as California's attorney general from 1939 to 1943 and presided over the controversial internment of Japanese Americans after Pearl Harbor. He was elected three times as governor of California between 1943 and 1953, and was Thomas Dewey's running mate in the failed 1948 Republican campaign to oust Harry Truman from the White House.

Appointed chief justice to the Supreme Court in 1953 by President Eisenhower, Warren disappointed his Republican supporters by sponsoring liberal reform, developing ideas that were years ahead of Congress and public opinion. In 1964 he presided over the much-quoted Warren

Commission, which investigated the assassination of President Kennedy. Four years later, after he had served for 15 years as chief justice, he resigned on the grounds of age. Many experts consider Earl Warren the greatest chief justice in American history since John Marshall, the founder of U.S. constitutional law.

upholding it; two (Felix Frankfurter and Robert Jackson) supported desegregation but could find no rationale for overturning the Plessy ruling.

Under Chief Justice Vinson, it is unlikely that the Supreme Court would have overruled the Plessy verdict. But in September 1953 Vinson died. He was replaced by Earl Warren, a liberal Republican and former governor of California, who was convinced that justice demanded an end to the separate-but-equal policy. Warren wanted segregation in schools to be ruled unconstitutional, and he knew that in a case with such momentous consequences, the Supreme Court would have to speak with one voice. Over the next few months he worked with determination in frequent discussions with his colleagues to achieve unanimity on the Brown case.

ON DECEMBER 12, 1953, THE COURT HELD ITS FIRST CONFERENCE on the Brown case. Warren delivered his opinion that the Plessy decision was unsustainable unless one allowed the premise that blacks were inferior to whites. He would not allow that premise: therefore schools should be desegregated. His arguments convinced Clark and Frankfurter, but Jackson and Reed, still skeptical, barred the way to a unanimous decision. Chief Justice Warren, "first among equals," proved himself a worthy leader. Acting with energy and courtesy he circulated his draft opinions personally to the other justices. When Jackson spent some time in the hospital, Warren went every day to collect the justice's annotated comments on the latest drafts.

In the meantime he worked out a shrewd strategy whereby the Court would deliver an opinion declaring segregation unconstitutional, but would postpone the decree implementing the decision. This would give those states affected by the decision the chance to participate in framing the

"I always felt that colored children ought to have the same opportunity in school that any other child had. But it was my duty as attorney general to support the laws of the state as they were constituted."

HAROLD R. FATZER,
State's attorney general for Kansas,
speaking to the *Kansas City Star*
on May 17, 1964,
about the events of 1952–53

Above The team of attorneys acting for the families in the case of Brown v. Board of Education of Topeka, Kansas, stand outside the Supreme Court Building in Washington, D.C., on May 17, 1954. From left to right they are George E. C. Hayes; Thurgood Marshall, special counsel for the NAACP; and James Nabrit.

"We conclude, unanimously, that in the field of public education the doctrine of 'separate but equal' has no place. Separate educational facilities are inherently unequal."

CHIEF JUSTICE EARL WARREN, summing up on May 17, 1954

decree. He hoped to gain their support in upholding the decision in their own courts. In February Warren took a formal vote. Eight of the judges were in favor of overruling Plessy v. Ferguson; only Reed, a Southerner, still held out. Warren lunched with Reed more than 20 times in pursuit of agreement. In the second week of May 1954, Warren had a crucial conversation with Reed, reported by one of Reed's law clerks. "Stan, you're all by yourself in this now," said Warren. "You've got to decide whether it's really the best for the country." On May 15 formal unanimity was secured.

ON MONDAY, MAY 17, 1954, a day some called "Black Monday," Warren read the Supreme Court's decision to a group of reporters. In the 28-minute statement, he set out the points at issue: "Does segregation of children in public schools solely on the basis of race, even though the physical facilities and other 'tangible' factors may be equal, deprive the children of the minority group of equal educational opportunities? We believe that it does....To separate them from others of similar age and qualifications solely because of their race generates a feeling of inferiority as to their status in the community that may affect their hearts and minds in a way unlikely ever to be undone."

This landmark decision brought about a compromise. The judgment required the federal courts to "take such proceedings and enter such orders and decrees consistent with this opinion as are necessary and proper to admit to public schools on a racially nondiscriminatory basis with all deliberate speed the parties to these cases." The phrase, "with all deliberate speed," was suggested by Justice Frankfurter and was interpreted by Southern politicians as permitting much deliberation and very little speed. Change was painfully gradual, and integration met enormous resistance. Antisegregationists claimed that the Court had exceeded its brief, since equality of opportunity was not enshrined in the Constitution. James Keston of the *New York Times* wrote that the judges had relied "more on social science than legal precedents" and that the ruling was more like "an expert paper on sociology than a Supreme Court decision."

But Brown v. Board of Education was, nevertheless, a milestone that made it possible to declare segregation unconstitutional in many other areas. Champions of the decision said that for the first time in its history the Supreme Court had fulfilled the role envisioned for it in the Constitution, as an active promoter and enforcer of justice. The *Washington Post* published in an editorial on May 19 that "abroad as well as at home, this decision will engender a renewal of faith in democratic institutions and ideals."

POSTSCRIPT

Southern Congressmen attacked the Supreme Court decision as an affront to states' rights and a flagrant abuse of judicial power that could lead to the destruction of the Anglo-Saxon race. Violence spread in the South when certain state governors refused to support integration. In 1957 Gov. Orval Faubus of Arkansas called in units of the National Guard to prevent the integration of students at Little Rock High School. In response, President Dwight D. Eisenhower reluctantly sent in 500 paratroopers from Kentucky to enforce the federal district court's integration order. In 1962 a young man named James Meredith, denied entry to the University of Mississippi, was reinstated only after President John F. Kennedy ordered in 3,000 federal troops; Meredith was protected from racial violence by a federal marshal throughout his four years of study, but such measures did little to change the hearts and minds of Southern leaders.

In 1963 Gov. George Wallace of Alabama pledged to "stand in the schoolhouse door" to block enrollment of black students at the University of Alabama. He kept his pledge to white voters in the face of mass protests led by Martin Luther King, Jr. But federal pressure throughout the state's business community forced him to give way, and federal-controlled national guards escorted black students onto the campus.

Segregation in public places was effectively ended in 1964 with the case of Mary Hamilton, a black woman in Alabama, when the U.S. Supreme Court ruled by a majority decision that she was entitled to the same facilities on public transport as a white woman. The 1964 Civil Rights Act and the 1965 Voting Rights Act followed soon after, and the Supreme Court ruled that both acts were constitutional. By the mid-1960s, the struggle for civil rights, inaugurated by Brown v. Board of Education of Topeka, Kansas, was well on its way.

Above Central High School, Little Rock, Ark., became a battleground in 1957, when Gov. Orval Faubus defied the directive to integrate.

Above Governor George Wallace stands "in the schoolhouse door" at the University of Alabama in June 1963.

The Man in the Glass Booth

THE STATE OF ISRAEL v. ADOLF EICHMANN

APRIL 11 – DECEMBER 15, 1961

In the spring of 1961, Adolf Eichmann waited in Jerusalem for his trial to begin. He stood accused of 15 counts of war crimes and crimes against humanity. Twenty years earlier he had served as one of the Nazi functionaries in the "final solution," Hitler's plan for the systematic destruction of the Jewish people. After World War II ended he escaped to Argentina, avoiding the arrest and trial many of his comrades underwent at Nuremberg. But the Israeli Secret Service tracked him down in 1959, and the following year, by order of Prime Minister David Ben-Gurion, Eichmann was kidnapped. He arrived in Israel on a diplomatic plane on May 22, 1960. Seven days later there began a long series of police interrogations, to which Eichmann submitted voluntarily from May 29, 1960, until February 2, 1961. Based on the resulting dossier, Israel's attorney general indicted Eichmann for crimes against the Jewish people.

THE TRIAL BEGAN ON APRIL 11, 1961. On the topmost tier of a raised platform, three Jewish judges—Benjamin Halévi, Yitzhak Raveh, and presiding judge Moshe Landau—sat facing the court. Just below them sat the interpreters, who translated the Hebrew proceedings into French, English,

Above The yellow Star of David, an emblem sewn onto the clothes of Jewish citizens in every Nazi-occupied country. This star originated in occupied Holland and is marked *Jood*, the Dutch word for Jew.

BIOGRAPHY

Above Eichmann in Argentina, where he lived from 1950 until his abduction in 1960.

Karl Adolf Eichmann (1906–62) was born at Solingen in the Rhineland, one of five children. After the death of his mother in 1916, the family moved to Linz, Austria, the town where Hitler went to school. During his youth he was often mistaken for a Jew, and (perhaps as a result) developed a fascination with the language and culture of the Jewish people, even teaching himself to speak and write Yiddish. Eichmann did not finish high school, but worked as a salesman in Austria before joining the Nazi Party in 1932. He was recruited into the SS (the *Schutz-Staffel*, or "protective squadron"), the powerful Nazi elite corps, where his talent for administration and insight into Jewish culture was rewarded with special responsibility for what the Nazi regime referred to as "the Jewish question." When fellow Nazis accused him of being a Jewish spy, which led to a full investigation of his background by the party, he became overtly anti-Semitic. By his own admission he was subsequently responsible for the "cleansing" or forced emigration from Austria of almost 150,000 Jews, and after 1942 he served as a key administrator of Hitler's "final solution," the systematic execution of some 6 million Jews. Captured after the war by American troops, he concealed his identity, escaped, and hid in Germany. In 1950 he made contact with ODESSA, a clandestine organization established by SS veterans in Germany, probably in early 1947, to move former SS men safely to South America. In May of the same year he escaped to Argentina under the name Richard Klement and sent for his family. He was kidnapped 10 years later in Buenos Aires by Israeli "Jewish Volunteers." He was then taken to Israel and tried for war crimes and crimes against humanity. Found guilty, he was executed on May 31, 1962.

Above Jewish children in the Warsaw Ghetto, circa 1943. Most went to the death camps.

and German. Another tier down, Eichmann sat to the left, enclosed in a bulletproof glass booth intended to protect him from hostile observers. To the right was the witness box. At the bottom of the platform, with their backs to the public, sat the prosecutor (the attorney general of Israel, Gideon Hausner), his staff of four assistants, and the defense counsel, with a single temporary assistant. The proceedings began when the court usher cried out, "*Beth Hamishpath*" ("The House of Justice").

FROM THE START, THE TRIAL PROVOKED international controversy. The objections were straightforward: Eichmann had been illegally abducted and Israel had no right to hold him; he was being tried for crimes that did not exist in the law books at the time he committed them; and his trial was being conducted by a nation-state that did not exist during World War II. Strictly speaking, the entire proceedings were illegal. Israel justified its actions to the rest of the world by saying that the murder of 6 million Jews was so evil that the new Jewish state was compelled to bring Eichmann to trial at whatever cost; in fact, Israel assumed the right to act for the Jewish community worldwide. Because it could not extradite Eichmann from Argentina by legal means, the Israeli government had resorted to force. Significantly, Israel's spokespeople pointed out, West Germany had not requested the return of its citizen. The legal adviser to the Israeli Foreign Ministry, Shabtai Rosenne, added that other European countries also had the right to try Eichmann and they would be free to do so after an Israeli verdict had been put on record. To counter charges that Eichmann's trial in

Israeli Retribution

The Agreement of London in 1945, the legislation behind the Nuremberg trial of the same year, outlawed the systematic destruction of the Jewish people during the Nazi regime as a "crime against humanity." Eichmann was officially named in the judgment at Nuremberg, but his later abduction by "Jewish Volunteers" and his illegal removal from Argentina posed political and legal problems on an international scale. The president of the World Jewish Congress suggested to Prime Minister Ben-Gurion that Eichmann should be turned over to an international court and tried by one judge from each of the nations whose citizens had perished in the Holocaust. Ben-Gurion refused, insisting that Eichmann be tried in Jerusalem under the Nazi and Nazi Collaborators Punishment Law 5710 of 1950. Although international opinion was hostile to Eichmann, Israel's position was also unpopular: a new state, founded in 1948, Israel had not been the scene of the crimes in question, and it had no right in international law to try Eichmann for crimes committed across Europe between 1938 and 1945.

Below Eichmann giving evidence from his bulletproof glass booth, constructed to prevent an assassination attempt during the trial. Eichmann's evidence was given in German and relayed to the court in Hebrew, French, and English; questions and proceedings were translated back into German through headphones.

Jerusalem was no more than a show trial under a kangaroo (mock) court, the Israeli authorities provided funds for Eichmann's defense counsel. The person chosen for the job was Dr. Robert Servatius of Cologne, who had been one of the defense lawyers at Nuremberg; he was assisted by Dieter Wechtenbruch of Munich.

THE PROSECUTION'S OPENING ADDRESS lasted for three sessions and outlined the entire history of Jewish persecution since the time of the pharaohs. The international media criticized the exposition, declaring that this hardly squared with the prosecution's argument that the Holocaust was a unique event calling for exceptional punishments. The media also felt that this approach diverted attention from Eichmann. However, the prosecution then narrowed its scope and proceeded to call witnesses. One hundred and twenty survivors of the Nazi regime testified, each describing different aspects of the horrors of persecution during the Nazi years. Many of their stories focused on Eichmann: Eichmann's beating a Jewish youth to death; Eichmann's direct orders (documented in an official note) to shoot Jews. Eichmann's personal culpability was established with incontrovertible evidence. The prosecution showed members of the court vast amounts of official documentation and reminded them of the numerous references to Eichmann during the Nuremberg trials and of his own admissions about organizing transportation to the death camps. The prosecutor, Gideon Hausner, claimed that there were actually 6 million prosecutors accusing Eichmann in court, for whom Hausner was only a living representative.

> *"The trial of the criminal Eichmann will be the Nuremberg of the Jewish people, which since the liberation has been deprived of the right to bring its butchers to justice."*
>
> DAVID BEN-GURION, Israeli prime minister, in an interview to the press, April 1961

NAZI HIERARCHY

The SS (*Schutz-Staffel*) was an armed paramilitary organization through which the Nazi Party achieved totalitarian control in Germany during the 1930s. When war broke out in 1939, the security service of the SS, led by Heinrich Himmler, was joined to the regular German police, including the *Gestapo* (secret police), to form a central security office, the *Reichssicherheitshauptampt* (RSHA).

Section IV of the RSHA was the bureau of the *Gestapo* headed by Heinrich Müller. Its duties were to eliminate opposition to the Nazis within Germany and its occupied territories and to round up Jews throughout Europe for deportation to extermination camps. Subsection IV-A handled "opponents," accused of communism, sabotage, liberalism, and assassinations; subsection IV-B dealt with "sects"— Catholics, Protestants, Freemasons, and Jews. In 1941 Eichmann was appointed head of subdivision IV-B-4, which dealt

with the deportation of Jews. He had already used his knowledge of Jewish customs gained in his youth to spy for Reinhardt Heydrich, RSHA's chief until 1942. In this new capacity, Eichmann administered the railroads used to transport and deport Jews. In the early days of the war he arranged mass emigrations; later he ran the trains to the death camps and managed other logistical aspects of the wholesale slaughter of Jews and other "enemies" of the Nazi state. In all these activities he reported to Müller.

Technically and organizationally Eichmann occupied a relatively low position in the Nazi hierarchy; even the commanders of the *Einsatzgruppen* (the mobile killing units of the SS) had a higher rank than he. He was in fact the most junior functionary invited to the Wannsee Conference of January 1942. As such, he nevertheless played a central role in planning and assigning the details of mass genocide.

Above Heinrich Müller, head of the *Gestapo*, or Nazi secret police, who issued Eichmann's orders.

Above Crowds outside the courthouse listen to the day's proceedings on the radio. Many were survivors of the death camps or their descendants, and felt a deep personal interest in the outcome.

"It is my profound conviction that I must suffer for the acts of others and carry the burden imposed upon me by Fate."

ADOLF EICHMANN'S
final plea to the court,
December 1961

Eichmann had only one defense: he was carrying out the orders of his superiors—Heinrich Müller, Reinhardt Heydrich, Ernst Kaltenbrunner, and ultimately, Heinrich Himmler. Hausner dismissed this excuse. Far from being a cog in the Nazi machine, he claimed, Eichmann had fulfilled a central role in the apparatus of slaughter, even though he ranked below Müller and the others. He was guilty of criminal conspiracy and war crimes as defined at Nuremberg, Hausner declared, and the court should also find him guilty of a conspiracy to commit crimes against the Jewish people and against humanity. He asserted that Eichmann should be held responsible not only for his own acts but for those of others who took part in the conspiracy.

THE COURT ADJOURNED ON AUGUST 11 and reconvened three days later to hear Robert Servatius's summation for the defense. Servatius pointed emphatically to the fact that Eichmann had acted on orders from above, a line of defense known as "superior orders." He also detailed the weakness of the state's case in international law: Israel had abducted the accused; the trial was not being conducted in a neutral venue or by neutral judges; the Israeli press's virulent campaign against Eichmann amounted to contempt of court; the specific counts of the indictment did not follow the Nuremberg judgment but rather Israeli law, which, among other things, established the death sentence for all Nazis and their collaborators; much of the written evidence was inadmissible by strict canons of law, and the reliability of the oral evidence about events so far in the past was suspect; and international law demanded at least one direct link between the accused and the punishing state, which was ruled out by Israel's nonexistence before 1948. Finally, Eichmann could not receive a fair trial, when any potential witnesses called in his defense might themselves be arrested and put on trial for war crimes.

Servatius finished with an earnest plea that the Israeli court not make Eichmann a scapegoat. Do not, he said, aim at "revenge on the accused for deeds which were in fact committed by Germany's political leaders. His conviction cannot serve as expiation for the atrocities committed. This trial can only determine what happened and serve as a warning for history."

THE PRESIDING JUDGE ADJOURNED THE COURT pending a judgment to be delivered in November. It was not until December 11 that the court was finally reconvened and the judgment given. The three judges took five sessions over three days to read the 244 sections of their judgment. They found Eichmann guilty of crimes against the Jewish people and against humanity, of war crimes, and of membership in the Nazi Party—a criminal organization as defined by Article 10 of the Nuremberg Charter. The next day Hausner made a long speech requesting the death penalty. Servatius asked for leniency, and Eichmann himself made a final address in which he apologized for his part in the Holocaust and formally asked the Jewish people for forgiveness. He insisted that whatever he had done, he had done on the orders of the German head of state. At 9 A.M. on December 15, 1961, the court sentenced Eichmann to death by hanging. He lodged an appeal, and the case was reexamined by the Israeli Supreme Court in March 1962, but the original verdict was upheld on May 29. Denied clemency by President Itzhak Ben-Zvi, Eichmann was hanged on May 31, 1962.

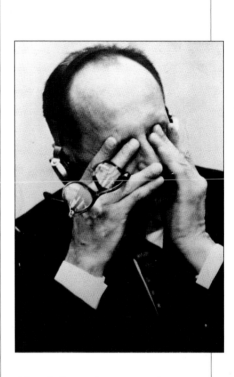

Above Eichmann showing signs of strain during the lengthy trial proceedings. Nearly two years passed between the initial police interrogations and the final judgment.

POSTSCRIPT

President Itzhak Ben-Zvi refused to grant Eichmann clemency at 10 P.M. on May 31, 1962. The Israelis hanged Eichmann just two hours later. By acting so quickly, they were able to prevent Eichmann's defense counsel, Robert Servatius, from arranging for West Germany to extradite its citizen.

The death sentence provoked as much international controversy as had the initial decision to hold a trial. Some critics said that Israel had demeaned itself by making a public display of the war crimes and the trial, when the proper action would have been to assassinate Eichmann in Buenos Aires. Others accused the authorities in Jerusalem of elevating the biblical "eye for an eye" to a principle of international law. Still others argued that "hanging was too good for him" and that Eichmann should have been sentenced to hard labor for life. The Jewish theologian Martin Buber considered the sentence a "mistake of historical dimensions" that lifted the burden of guilt for the Holocaust from the Germans. The Jewish philosopher Hannah Arendt deplored the "victim mentality" of the Israelis but thought the death sentence justified. She summed up the horror of the Nazi functionaries who killed as if it were simple office administration. It was, she said, a sobering picture of "the banality of evil."

"We find that no one... no member of the human race, can be expected to share the earth with you. That is the reason, and the only reason, you must hang."

HANNAH ARENDT,
Jewish political philosopher,
in *Eichmann in Jerusalem, a Report on the Banality of Evil*,
1963

If I Am Assassinated...

THE STATE OF PAKISTAN *v.* ZULFIKAR ALI BHUTTO

OCTOBER 24, 1977 – MARCH 24, 1979

Above A commemorative stamp of Bhutto, who won a seat in Pakistan's cabinet at the unprecedented age of 30 and went on to lead the nation. His meteoric rise and fall made him a legend in Pakistan's history.

Rough Justice

The trial of Zulfikar Ali Bhutto marked a first: a modern head of state, tried by a civil court for an alleged murder committed while in office.

Pakistan's judiciary was trained in the Anglo-Saxon tradition, which presupposed the accused's innocence until guilt was proven. Many of the trappings of Bhutto's trial were leftovers from the days of the raj, when the British legal system was imposed on its colonies. However, when General Zia, a zealous Muslim, seized power in July 1977, he imposed martial law and introduced a new legislative code enforcing traditional Islamic justice. Initially, Zia and the members of his junta wanted to try Bhutto before a court of martial law; but protests both at home and abroad forced him to capitulate and allow a civilian trial. Nevertheless, the sections of the Pakistani penal code under which Bhutto was charged left no doubt about the desired outcome. All but the last carried the death penalty.

The trial of Zulfikar Ali Bhutto for murder, which opened on October 24, 1977, was no ordinary criminal trial. As the former president (1971–73) and prime minister (1973–77) of Pakistan, Bhutto might have hoped for fair treatment before the law. But as in many volatile political situations, the law was about to be used against him.

As Pakistan's leader, Bhutto had made powerful enemies among right-wing Islamic parties. He had founded his own Pakistan People's Party (PPP) in 1967 to work for social and economic reform and especially to curb the power and influence of Pakistan's wealthiest families. In January 1977 he announced his intention to hold elections in March under a new democratic constitution. His victory provoked civil unrest and allegations from the fundamentalist right of election rigging. In July, Bhutto was forced aside in a coup led by General Zia ul-Haq, who suspended Bhutto's democratic constitution. Zia promised elections within 90 days; meanwhile, he kept Bhutto in "protective custody" for three weeks, then released him. By this time Zia had already formed a plan to destroy Bhutto in the eyes of the entire country. He would have him put on trial for murder.

The previous March, a 35-year-old minor politician named Ahmad Raza Kasuri—a former PPP member who had changed sides and made many political enemies—tried to run as a PPP candidate in the elections. The party rebuffed him as a turncoat. In response Kasuri raked up an old grievance against Bhutto. Three years earlier he and his family had been ambushed while traveling. His father, the highly respected Nawab Mohammad Ahmad Khan, was killed in the attack, but Kasuri claimed that he had been the intended target. When he filed a police report to that effect, he put the blame squarely on Zulfikar Ali Bhutto. He also claimed that he had been the victim of 15 assassination attempts, but in a subsequent inquiry, Pakistan's High Court cleared Bhutto of any involvement.

Even while General Zia was releasing Bhutto from "protective custody," he was setting up a team to investigate the Kasuri murder and the allegations against Bhutto. Zia arrested Bhutto for murder on September 3, 1977. The judge before whom the charges were presented found the evidence "contradictory and incomplete" and freed Bhutto on bail 10 days after the arrest. Three days later Zia arrested him again on the same charges, this time under "martial law." When the PPP organized demonstrations among Bhutto's many supporters, Zia canceled the upcoming elections.

Bhutto's case should have first been heard in Pakistan's lower courts, but instead Bhutto was arraigned before the High Court of Lahore, which automatically deprived him of one level of appeal. The judge who had granted him bail was removed from the bench and replaced by five of Zia's hand-picked judges, headed by Chief Justice Maulvi Mustaq, who canceled bail. Throughout the entire five-month trial, Bhutto appeared in court only in a specially built dock; and on Zia's orders, he remained in custody.

When proceedings opened on October 24, the court, with its judges bewigged in the British manner, recalled the impartial justice of the British colonial raj. However, it soon became apparent that the defendant could hope for neither due process nor a fair hearing. The only testimony linking Bhutto to the alleged conspiracy to murder came from Masood Mahmood, the director general of the Federal Security Force (FSF). Mahmood had been arrested immediately after Zia's coup. Two months' imprisonment at the mercy of the army had convinced him to take the stand and "confess" that he was party to the crime, after which he would be pardoned in return for testifying. Mahmood claimed that Bhutto had ordered him to have Kasuri murdered, that four members of the FSF had organized the ambush on Bhutto's orders, after which they had been arrested and confessed.

The four alleged assassins from the FSF were ushered into court as "co-accused," but one of them recanted his testimony, declaring that it had been extracted from him under torture. These events caused a sensation in the national press, and the following day the witness was not present in court; the prosecution claimed that he had suddenly "fallen ill."

Above On April 30, 1977, Bhutto and his army escort prevented a protest march in Islamabad by millions of Pakistanis who accused his party of election rigging in the March general election. Just two months later the army turned against Bhutto and staged a military coup, led by General Zia.

Indo-Pakistani War

As the subcontinent of India prepared for independence in 1947 after more than 200 years of British rule, centuries of racial and religious tensions flared into violence between Hindu, Muslim, and Sikh. Under the last British viceroy of India, Lord Mountbatten, the subcontinent was partitioned: the northwestern and northeastern sections were formed into a new nation called Pakistan, with a Muslim majority; the rest of the country became the predominantly Hindu republic of India.

Political tensions between West and East Pakistan bred instability and culminated in civil war and the secession of East Pakistan in 1971 to become a new country, Bangladesh. West Pakistan's attempt to halt secession ended in a catastrophic defeat at the hands of India. In the aftermath of the Bangladeshi debacle, Zulfikar Ali Bhutto, president of what had become simply Pakistan, initiated a series of moderate reforms, most notably the taxation of landowning families. This brought him into collision with religious fundamentalists, the old aristocracy, and right-wing army leaders. By 1973 the Pakistani right was waiting for a chance to bring Bhutto down.

Above General Zia ul-Haq, photographed shortly after he seized control of Pakistan in the military coup of July 1977.

THE DEFENSE CHALLENGED THE PROSECUTION WITH PROOF from an army logbook that the prosecution itself had submitted. It showed that the jeep allegedly driven during the attack on Kasuri was not even in Lahore at the time. The prosecution had the logbook disregarded as "incorrect." During the defense's cross-examination of witnesses, the bench repeatedly interrupted, causing the witnesses to whittle down or change their answers. The 706-page official transcript contained not one of the objections or inconsistencies in the evidence pointed out by the defense. Ramsey Clark, the former U.S. attorney general, who attended the trial, wrote: "The prosecution's case was based entirely on several witnesses who were detained until they confessed, who changed and expanded their confessions and testimony with each reiteration, who contradicted themselves and each other, who, except for Masood Mahmood…were relating what others said, whose testimony led to four different theories of what happened, absolutely uncorroborated by an eyewitness, direct evidence, or physical evidence."

During his trial Bhutto was housed in a cell with a dirt floor and a trickle of running water; outside he could hear other prisoners being lashed. When he began his testimony on January 25, 1978, Chief Justice Maulvi Mustaq—who had promised the world's press that the trial would be conducted in the full light of public scrutiny—closed the courtroom to all observers. In other words, although the prosecution's case was reported worldwide, the defense would be heard in camera. Bhutto responded by refusing to say any more. The chief justice apparently spent much of the time insulting Bhutto's home province of Sind. Bhutto demanded a retrial, accusing the chief justice of bias. The court refused his demand.

On March 18, 1978, Bhutto was found guilty of murder and sentenced to death. Appeals for clemency flooded in from all over the world; Bhutto

BIOGRAPHY

Zulfikar Ali Bhutto was born in 1928 in Sind Province, then part of British-ruled India. After a brilliant academic career at the University of California at Berkeley and Oxford University in England, he returned to Pakistan in 1953 to practice law. In 1958 he entered politics and rose quickly to be foreign minister (1963–66) under Ayub Khan. In 1967 Bhutto established the Pakistan People's Party (PPP), intended to introduce economic reform and democratic elections. After Pakistan's military defeat by India in 1971, Bhutto became president (1971–73) and prime minister until 1977. That year General Zia seized power and tried Bhutto for murder. Bhutto was executed on April 4, 1979. In 1988, after a decade of martial law under General Zia, Bhutto's daughter, Benazir, succeeded her father as prime minister of Pakistan.

Above Bhutto with his wife Nusrat (left) and children—Benazir is on the right—during his first appeal to the Supreme Court in July 1978. The verdict of guilty was reached on February 6, 1979.

Right Following Bhutto's execution, supporters throughout Pakistan mourned his death in public displays of grief. Here mourners hold up the PPP flag and pictures of their lost leader.

himself did not want to appeal only to face a prolonged farce in Zia's courts. With his health deteriorating rapidly, he was transferred to a death cell in Rawalpindi central jail. Meanwhile his family appealed on his behalf, and a hearing before the Supreme Court commenced in May. Bhutto was given just one week to prepare. Zia's soldiers hindered his family and the PPP by seizing documents and arresting PPP workers, but Bhutto somehow managed to issue a thorough rejoinder to the charges. Zia prevented its publication. It transpired that five of the nine appeals court judges were willing to overrule the Lahore verdict. Chief Justice Anwar ul-Haq reacted by adjourning the court until the end of July 1978, when the most clearly pro-Bhutto judge was due to retire.

That Chief Justice Anwar ul-Haq presided over Bhutto's appeal is perhaps the greatest injustice in the case. He was a Zia appointee, so close to Zia that he served as acting president while the dictator was out of the country. Defense lawyers battled successfully to win Bhutto the right to conduct his own defense before the Supreme Court. On December 18, 1978, Bhutto finally made his appearance in public before a packed courtroom in Rawalpindi. By this time he had been on death row for nine months and had gone without fresh water for the previous 25 days. Yet he addressed the court lucidly for four days, speaking without notes, to expose the absurdities of the prosecution's case.

THE APPEAL WAS COMPLETED BY DECEMBER 23. On February 6, 1979, the Supreme Court issued its verdict, guilty, a decision reached by a bare 4 to 3 majority between the four Punjabi judges from the military heartland of Pakistan and the three judges from minority provinces. The Bhutto family had seven days in which to appeal. The court granted a stay of execution while it studied the petition. By February 24, when the next court hearing began, appeals for clemency were arriving from heads of state around the world. Zia commented cynically: "All the politicians are asking to save a fellow politician but not many nonpoliticians have asked me for clemency." It amounted, he said, to mere "trade union activity."

All that legal minds could do was done on Bhutto's behalf. On March 24 the Supreme Court dismissed the appeal but unanimously recommended that the sentence be commuted to life, a decision that Zia would have to approve. Despite appeals from heads of state the world over, Zia upheld the death sentence. On April 4, 1979, Bhutto was hanged. Zia continued to rule Pakistan until August 17, 1988, when the plane in which he was traveling exploded. Bhutto's rejoinder to the charges against him was published in New Delhi, India, in 1979 and became the bestseller, *If I Am Assassinated.*

CHRONOLOGY

1967 Bhutto founds the Pakistani People's Party (PPP).

1974 Kasuri, a minor politician, is the victim of an ambush in which his father is killed. He blames Bhutto.

March 1977 Kasuri is rejected as a candidate for the PPP. He revives his old murder charge against Bhutto.

September 3, 1977 Zia has Bhutto arrested under civil law. Bhutto is released 10 days later.

September 17, 1977 Bhutto is rearrested under martial law.

October 24, 1977 Bhutto's trial begins. Witnesses begin to "disappear."

March 18, 1978 Bhutto is found guilty and condemned to death.

December 1978 Bhutto's appeal to the Supreme Court is rejected.

February 1979 Petitions for clemency pour in from heads of state. The Supreme Court recommends that the sentence be commuted to life.

April 4, 1979 Bhutto is hanged.

Enemies of the State

THE PEOPLE'S REPUBLIC OF CHINA *v.* THE GANG OF FOUR

NOVEMBER 1980 – JANUARY 1981

Above A political cartoon showing the crushing of the Gang of Four after their fall from power in 1976.

Justice and Politics

While the trial of the Gang of Four was not a political show trial, neither did it meet the standards of the post-Maoist Chinese legal system, established in 1980 and modeled on the legal systems of the Soviet Union and Western Europe. The proceedings exposed the sufferings of thousands of people who were persecuted during the Cultural Revolution of Mao Zedong's regime. In fact, the criminal acts outlined by the prosecution took place at a time when Mao had suspended the legal system, and the state did not recognize the acts as criminal. So great was Chairman Mao's continued popularity, that the prosecution sought to keep his reputation unblemished throughout, though it was obvious that he had been aware of (if not in favor of) Jiang Qing's misuse of power. The only evidence against the defendants was obtained under duress from frightened and reluctant witnesses, who were rehearsed in their parts. Completely at odds with any just system, the accused were allowed no defense. Jiang Qing in particular loudly asserted that they had only been following orders, but in this court such a statement was no defense.

After the death of Mao Zedong on September 9, 1976, a great political struggle erupted in the People's Republic of China. By December 1978 it had brought to power a modernizing, revisionist faction in the Communist Party led by Deng Xiaoping. In an attempt to discredit Mao's so-called Cultural Revolution, the new regime brought to trial four individuals closely associated with the turbulent events of those years. Deng inaugurated a new legal system on January 1, 1980; with the trial of the Gang of Four, as the accused came to be known, he hoped to legitimize the new criminal code and to break decisively with the "mistakes" of the Cultural Revolution.

THE FOUR PEOPLE BROUGHT TO TRIAL ON NOVEMBER 20, 1980, in Beijing were prime targets for Deng's plan: Chairman Mao's widow, Jiang Qing, a former actress and drama teacher who aspired to be Mao's successor as the leader of China; Zhang Chunqiao, the former party vice-premier and leading member of the politburo; Yao Wenyuan, a talented journalist who had masterminded Mao's propaganda campaign during the Cultural Revolution; and Wang Hongwen, a Korean War veteran, former politburo member, and political commissar in charge of the notorious Red Guards—the fearsome, slogan-shouting zealots whom Mao had recruited from elite student bodies and the families of party leaders.

The trial itself was legally questionable. Because no official transcript was kept, the only surviving records come from excerpts of the trial broadcast on Chinese television. The high court proceedings, held in open session before 35 judges, were viewed daily by about 800 members of the public, who entered free of charge on a rotating basis. The nature of the recorded dialogue reveals that this was not a scripted show trial. But the Four stood trial for political offenses, which when committed had been regarded as great acts of patriotism. They were charged, in an indictment 20,000 words long, with being personally responsible for wrongfully persecuting 750,000 people, 34,380 of whom died as a result.

By the time Deng's government brought the Gang to trial, many alleged witnesses against them had died or disappeared, and the testimony given was inadequate and incomplete. The prosecution went to extraordinary lengths to present whatever evidence it could. One witness, dying of cancer, barely alive, and on an intravenous drip, was interrogated 21 times in 27 days. No such effort organized the defense. No witnesses were called on the defendants' behalf, and the Gang of Four learned the details of the charges against them just three weeks before the start of the trial. Prosecution witnesses could not be cross-examined; in fact, most of the evidence took the form of recordings or audiovisual projection of documents on a screen. When Jiang Qing challenged the legality of the court itself, she was held in contempt.

BIOGRAPHY

Jiang Qing (also written Chiang Ch'ing), third wife of the Communist leader Mao Zedong, was born in about 1914 in Shantung Province, China, and named Luan Shu-Meng. She joined a theatrical troupe in 1929, took the stage name Lan P'ing, and soon became active in Communist politics. In the 1930s she played minor roles in films, and in 1937 she met Mao while working as a drama teacher in a school where he gave a political lecture. At the time he was married to his second wife, He Zizhen, one of the few women to survive the Long March of 1934, and a tireless party worker, who had borne Mao five children. He Zizhen could see that Mao was infatuated with the younger woman. An emotional breakdown led to He's hospitalization, at which point Mao announced his intention to marry Jiang Qing. He created a storm of opposition within his own party, but permission was finally granted in 1939 on condition that Jiang Qing would play no active role in party politics.

For years she kept a low profile. But in 1963 she spearheaded a movement to replace traditional Peking (Beijing) opera and ballet with works based on proletarian themes. As her ideas swept the country, they triggered what was soon dubbed the Cultural Revolution and made her a national hero. She reached the height of her influence in 1966, when she addressed mass rallies to explain her political philosophy and became closely associated with Mao's ruthless Red Guards.

As Mao's health deteriorated over the next decade, Jiang Qing controlled access to him, preparing the way for herself as the next national leader. However, by 1977, the year after Mao's death, her political enemies had already arranged to expel her from the Communist Party. They brought her to trial in 1980 with three other leading party officials for crimes against the state. In 1981 she received a suspended death sentence, which in 1983 was commuted to life imprisonment. She died by her own hand, while under house arrest, on May 14, 1991.

Above Mao Zedong and Jiang Qing, photographed together in the late 1930s, shortly after they first met.

ALL FOUR DEFENDANTS WERE TRIED BY THE SAME COURT, though different indictments were entered against each defendant. Wang Hongwen was charged with causing the deaths of 800 people in riots in Shanghai during the Cultural Revolution, with trying to organize a mutiny after Mao's death, and with poisoning Mao's mind against Zhou Enlai and Deng Xiaoping. He confessed to his crimes, cringing and apparently repentant.

Zhang Chunqiao was charged with conspiracy. Unlike Wang Hongwen, he refused to speak, and barely looked up from his seat. The judge read to him Article 35 of the new criminal code, which stated that if an accused remained silent, the evidence would be allowed to speak for him. Most of this evidence was given at sessions of which no public record is available.

The list of charges against Yao Wenyuan exceeded those of the other two male defendants. It included conspiracy to denounce Zhou Enlai and Deng Xiaoping to Mao in 1974; fomenting a leftist plot in 1975 and 1976 to get rid of Deng Xiaoping; suppressing media reporting of Zhou Enlai's funeral in 1976; falsifying the status of political leaders by tampering with press photographs; and gathering incriminating material on Deng and the rightists. Most of the evidence against Yao came from the views he had expressed in newspaper articles or in conversations with witnesses. Yao Wenyuan neither pleaded guilty nor remained silent; he tried to defend himself. Stammering, muddled, and often inarticulate, he still managed to challenge the prosecution's case by stating that he was merely following

"To rebel is justified."
BATTLE CRY OF THE RED GUARDS,
1966–67

"Fight selfishness, criticize revolutionism."
KEY SLOGAN
OF THE CULTURAL REVOLUTION,
1966–76

"I was the Chairman's dog. When he said bark, I barked, and when he said bite, I bit."

JIANG QING,
during the trial,
November 1980–January 1981

Below Jiang Qing, defiant, in the witness box on December 29, 1980. This was the last time that she appeared in court. Shortly after this picture was taken she was dragged out by bailiffs, still screaming.

government orders. The prosecution responded that the accused were on trial for crimes defined in the 1980 criminal code, not political "errors." In reality the defendants were being tried for their part in the Cultural Revolution, but the prosecution had to tread carefully to avoid implicating that era's leader. The enormous respect that Mao still commanded could put the case—perhaps even the government—at risk.

What made this trial stand out from those of other party members was the sensational clash between the prosecution and Jiang Qing. Arrested in October 1976, one month after her husband's death, Jiang Qing seemed stupefied that such a thing could be happening to her. She appeared genuinely amazed to discover that she was hated for her arrogance and lavish lifestyle. When she was arrested, her erstwhile sycophants spat in her face and shouted abuse, like "Now you'll get yours, you old bitch."

An intensive press campaign of denigration followed her arrest, preparing public opinion for the trial. Published reports claimed that she had said it would be good for China to have a new empress (herself, of course) and accused her of the "cult of personality." Some of the accusations against her were ludicrous. Because she had praised the Great Wall of China, for example, it was alleged that she supported the "Soviet revisionist imperialist" view that the wall was China's true frontier.

JIANG QING FACED CHARGES that she had attempted to turn Mao against Zhou Enlai and Deng Xiaoping; that she was involved in framing Liu Shaoqi (then head of state) and his wife; that she led the Gang of Four, who denied others access to Mao; that she ordered illegal house searches and the destruction of material that might compromise her; and that she persecuted old friends and acquaintances, even her former housemaid. She replied that since anything she had done before 1976 had Mao's authorization, her trial was also the trial of Chairman Mao, whom the party still venerated. The prosecution's response was not documented.

The first of many clashes between the judge and Jiang came when he asked whether in July 1968 she had demanded a list of the party members who had attended the 1959 plenary session of the Central Committee, with the aim of eliminating those she disliked and substituting her own nominees. Jiang replied that she knew nothing of such a list, at which the judge shouted: "I'm asking you whether it's true or not!" Jiang replied defiantly: "It's true, but you've put it wrongly." In another heated exchange between the judge and Jiang, she pushed beyond the court's tolerance:

JUDGE (shouting): You're not allowed to speak!
JIANG (to a witness for the prosecution): I had the right to expose you to the Chairman!
JUDGE (hammering the table with his gavel and shouting): You're not allowed to speak. Accused, Jiang Qing, you're not allowed to speak!
JIANG: If I do, what will you do?

THE CULTURAL REVOLUTION

The Chinese Communist leader Mao Zedong believed in the idea of "permanent revolution." He was convinced that post-Revolutionary society had gone wrong in Russia, becoming ossified and dominated by a new privileged class of bureaucrats. To keep China in the kind of ferment that would prevent stratified and hierarchical privilege from reappearing, as it had in the Soviet Union, Mao instituted a radical breakdown in the division of labor. Peasants must become decision-makers, while intellectuals must be set to work in the fields. Millions of young people were encouraged to challenge existing authority.

The most concentrated period of revolutionary fervor lasted from May 1966 to October 1976, a decade known today as the Cultural Revolution. During this time Mao commissioned his watchdog force, the Red Guards, to humiliate all those whom the Chairman suspected of aspiring to a cozy middle class: writers, teachers, managers, provincial governors, and city mayors. During massive rallies the Red Guards, who were usually students and militant young supporters, spat on their elders, shouted abuse, kicked them, forced them to kowtow with arms wide apart (the "jet-plane position"), and crowned them with dunces' caps. In a total reversal of traditional Chinese values, youth was hallowed while the old were persecuted, killed, or driven to suicide. According to the news agency, Agence France, which had correspondents in Beijing throughout the 1960s and 1970s, 400,000 people lost their lives. The political upheaval created such anarchy and tension that the Chinese urban economy was virtually paralyzed.

Above Chinese ballet from the 1960s, portraying the Red Guards as heroes and demigods. Banned from mainstream politics, Jiang Qing devoted herself to revolutionizing the arts, and doing away with traditional ballet and opera.

In the *Resolution on Party History*, published by Deng Xiaoping, national leader of China from 1981 to 1984, the Cultural Revolution is condemned as the "most severe setback and the heaviest losses suffered by the party, the state, and the people since the founding of the People's Republic." The *Resolution* ascribes responsibility to Mao, but carefully distinguishes his misguided action from the "counter-revolutionary Lin Biao and Jiang Qing cliques." Mao is portrayed as a tragic figure, the Gang of Four as corrupt enemies of the state.

JUDGE: If you go on committing crimes…
JIANG: You're the one who's committing crimes (Jiang laughs).
You call these renegades and rotten eggs here to speak and I want
to make it clear that—
JUDGE: To go on slandering people is to go on committing crimes!
JIANG: What crimes! You…
JUDGE: Take her away!

At this point a struggling and shouting Jiang was escorted from the court.

Jiang Qing was charged with persecuting Liu Shaoqi and his beautiful wife Wang Guangmei, whom she denounced as an American spy. Much was made of the fact that Jiang's treatment of Liu Shaoqi contravened the 1954 constitution concerning the honors to be given a head of state, though the ransacking and bullying of which she was accused occurred in 1966, after Mao had suspended the constitution and given his tacit approval to this and other acts of violence. Nevertheless, at the trial she claimed to remember nothing of her brutality to Liu (who died of neglect in jail in 1969) and of his wife (who was physically and mentally abused). The prosecution played a recording of one of her own speeches made on September 18, 1968, in which she could be heard speaking the following words: "I am now responsible for the first major case. I've been working on it for five or six hours a day. I can tell you now that Liu Shaoqi is a five poisons type of [Jiang screaming] big counterrevolutionary, traitor, renegade, secret agent, and villain….He sacrificed who knows how many good comrades. Who knows how many he sold out, that big traitor [still yelling]. I think he should die the death of a thousand little cuts—ten thousand!"

By the end of the trial, the prosecution had succeeded in exposing the architects of the Cultural Revolution to public scorn, subtly uncoupling China from the Maoist legacy without criticizing the Chairman. But they were less successful in their attempt to vindicate the new constitution. The pretense that the Gang of Four was being tried solely for crimes defined by the new criminal code fooled nobody. Everyone knew that the actions for which they were condemned had taken place in a legal vacuum deliberately created by Mao. He had suspended the courts that had sat since 1949, and had reviled the lawyers and legal systems as "bourgeois counterrevolutionary obscurantism." Even after 1971, when Mao permitted the courts to sit again, many offenses were dealt with summarily by the police. So how could the Four be condemned for criminal acts, when the party and media of the time had lauded their deeds? The prosecution never provided a convincing answer.

Deng Xiaoping's government managed to preserve the fiction of continuity with

> *"Arresting me and bringing me to trial is a defamation of Chairman Mao…I have implemented and defended Chairman Mao's proletarian revolutionary line."*
>
> JIANG QING,
> during the trial,
> November 1980–January 1981

Below Mao as benevolent father figure, in a poster launching the Cultural Revolution in 1966. During the trial of the Gang of Four this image of Mao was carefully preserved, while the other architects of the Revolution were held up to public scorn.

篡党夺权 按 既 定 方 针 办

Chairman Mao by pointing out that Jiang Qing and Mao were estranged in the final years of his life. It was clear that Mao must have supported her excesses, since he made no move to rescind her powers; but enough circumstantial evidence existed of his misgivings about her methods to maintain the illusion necessary for the stability of the state.

THE JOINT CIVILIAN AND MILITARY TRIBUNALS of the special court in Beijing gathered to hear the sentencing of the defendants on January 25, 1981. They had listened to two months of virtually nonstop testimony from the prosecution describing the villainous characters and practices of the Gang of Four. The court president, Jiang Hua, pronounced the death sentence on Jiang Qing, who was dragged from the court by police, screaming abuse at the president. She was not present when he announced that a two-year reprieve had been attached to the sentence, but with permanent deprivation of civil rights—such as the right to vote or receive a fair trial. Zhang also received the death sentence and a two-year reprieve; Yao was condemned to 20 years' imprisonment and deprived of political rights for five years; Wang received life imprisonment and permanent deprivation of political rights. Two years later, on January 25, 1983, Jiang Qing and Zhang's sentences were commuted to life imprisonment.

Above A political cartoon drawn by an unknown artist on a public wall in Beijing. The caption is a Chinese aphorism: "When the map was unrolled the dagger was revealed," meaning that in the course of time the Gang of Four's secret plotting against the party came to light.

CHURCH

Most church courts are set up to defend the religious orthodoxy of a specific sect. Ecclesiastical judges examine a prisoner's views and rule on whether or not these views conform in a way acceptable to the court. The inquisitorial system of justice forms the basis of most ecclesiastical trials. The centuries of notorious abuse by the Holy Office, an ecclesiastical court established by the Catholic Church, cast an undeserved shadow on an otherwise legitimate procedure.

The most important aspect of the inquisitorial system is that it ascribes a far more active role to the decision makers in the trial—whether judge or jury or a combination of the two. It is their task to discover what really happened. The trials of Joan of Arc and Galileo were conducted entirely along inquisitorial lines; both trials demonstrate the non-religious—in these cases, political—purposes such

a system often served. The cruelties and excesses with which the Catholic Court of the Inquisition is particularly associated eventually led to that court's demise, but such practices are not a necessary element of inquisitorial procedures. In particular, the private interrogation of suspected heretics under actual torture, or the threat of it, bears no resemblance to inquisitorial processes presently in use within civilian systems of law in countries such as France and Germany.

The primary purpose of the Court of the Inquisition was the suppression of heresy and the punishment of heretics. The authority of the Catholic Church had to be protected, and heresy by definition challenged church doctrines and teachings. The trial of Galileo for writing a book that supported the theory that the Earth revolved around the Sun and not vice versa may seem ludicrous today. Yet, scientific inquiry that challenged religious orthodoxy could not be tolerated in the climate of opinion at the time. The Catholic Church held as religious doctrine that the Earth was at the center of God's creation. To modern eyes, Galileo cuts an unimpressive figure, giving his inquisitors the capitulation they wanted in return for a quiet and secure old age. But once

COURTS

released from the rigors of the Holy Office, he expressed, in words later echoed by Thomas Jefferson, the notion that minds created free by God should not be compelled to submit to the will of others. In the case of Joan of Arc, Joan's effective self-defense led the Inquisition to threaten torture, a power sufficient to break all but the strongest will. After a heroic defense of her position, Joan recanted. Her subsequent attempt to reclaim her original position was fatal.

The extraordinary case of the Salem witches shows a society in the grips of paranoia, in which accusation came to equal guilt. Procedural fairness and careful consideration of the evidence gave way to the imaginings of children and, possibly, the ill will of neighbors. Most remarkably the trials at Salem and later at Boston were not conducted according to the criminal law applicable to the British colony of Massachusetts. Instead they employed the inquisitorial system, one that was wholly alien to that culture. In nations that adopt the accusatorial system today every potential case must be prosecuted according to the ordinary law of the land.

60 THE COURT OF THE INQUISITION *v.* JOAN OF ARC

64 ST. JULIEN RESIDENTS *v.* LOCAL WEEVILS

68 THE HOLY OFFICE *v.* GALILEO GALILEI

74 THE COMMUNITY *v.* ALLEGED WITCHES

A Modest Enquiry Into the Nature of Witchcraft, AND How Persons Guilty of that Crime may be Convicted: And the means used for their Discovery Discussed, both Negatively and Affirmatively, according to SCRIPTURE and EXPERIENCE. By John Hale, Pastor of the Church of Christ in Beverley, Anno Domini 1697.

Voices From God

THE COURT OF THE INQUISITION *v.* JOAN OF ARC

FEBRUARY 21 – MAY 17, 1431

Above A miniature portrait of Joan of Arc, from a richly illustrated rhyming history of Charles VII's reign by Martial d'Auvergne, 1484.

For just over a year Joan of Arc, dressed in a suit of white armor and flying her own standard, led French armies to victory against the English invasion intended to seize the crown of France. In 1431 on the heels of her success, she stood trial for heresy before an ecclesiastical court at Rouen. The trial is well documented in a Latin copy of a transcript made for the chief prosecutor. Based on this document, and with more than 500 years of hindsight, it seems clear today that Joan's real crime in the eyes of her English accusers was that she rallied the cause of French nationalism at a time when France was almost defeated by its enemies. It took little persuasion by the English to convince French clerics—who feared Joan's remarkable popularity—to put her on trial.

JOAN WAS CAPTURED BY BURGUNDIAN SOLDIERS ON MAY 23, 1430, and sold to the English for 10,000 francs. The English were determined to discredit her claims to divine inspiration. They hoped in the process to tarnish the cause of the dauphin, the future Charles VII, and promote the English heir Henry V. To demonstrate that Joan was inspired not by God but by the devil, they enlisted the support of the Inquisition, paid the expenses of her trial, and gave guarantees to the judges against harmful consequences from the prearranged verdict of heresy.

The Inquisition operated within a society that believed in the powerful existence and cunning of Satan and his servant demons. Its priority was to protect the church's absolute authority, and its members would not tolerate a 17-year-old peasant girl wielding political power. In particular they objected to Joan's claim that she had heard the voices of St. Michael, St. Catherine, and St. Margaret urging her in God's name to take up arms in support of the dauphin, France's rightful heir. Canon law at the time held that heavenly beings did not take on earthly shape; but it was believed that demons did. If the prosecution could establish that Joan had both seen and touched corporeal beings, she could be accused of allying herself to the devil.

The trial began in Rouen Castle on February 21, 1431. Joan's chief accuser was Pierre Cauchon, bishop of Beauvais. He claimed the right to try Joan because she had been captured in his diocese. Some of the assessors objected to the way she was interrogated. Yet she seemed able to defend herself, sometimes simply refusing to answer a question by saying, "Pass over that."

The Court of the Inquisition

As the Roman Catholic Church extended its power across Europe, it became preoccupied with the prosecution of anyone who threatened its absolute authority. In 1231 Pope Gregory IX set up the court of the Inquisition to deal with dissent from official church doctrine. Because the inquisitors never revealed the reasons why a defendant had fallen under suspicion and did not bring formal charges, there was no possibility of presenting a defense. In addition, heresy trials did not adhere to the normal rule that a person was innocent until proven guilty. An accused heretic was assumed guilty until proven innocent, and torture was often used to obtain "confessions" from those who stubbornly protested their innocence.

Cases of heresy were supervised by a bishop or other senior cleric, who presided over a court of "assessors"—in this case clerics from nearby abbeys or from the University of Paris. These onlookers were entitled to come and go constantly and to put questions freely. The relentless pressure of their questioning did much to wear down defendants, and the additional threat of torture was enough to make most prisoners confess.

Once found guilty, a heretic was forced to recant and could be given any punishment, from public penance and fasting to life imprisonment. Those, like Joan, who finally refused to recant were handed over to the civil courts, which had the power to impose a sentence of death.

THE STRUGGLE TO RULE FRANCE

The sovereignty of France had been the central issue of the Hundred Years War between England and France since its beginning in 1337. In 1422, after the death of the French king, Charles VI, France's monarchy hung in the balance. The dauphin was a weak man whose legitimacy was in doubt. Seven years earlier the English king, Henry V, had defeated the French at the battle of Agincourt. He had married Charles VI's daughter Catherine, and in the Treaty of Troyes in 1420 had named their son, the future Henry VI, king of England and France. Henry V died when his son was a boy, but the English nobles asserted this claim over the timorous dauphin. They were helped by the duke of Burgundy, who had made an alliance with Henry V.

Under Joan's leadership, the French armies rallied, and the dauphin became a heroic figure. Joan's victory in Orléans in May 1429 shifted the balance between the two armies. The dauphin joined his forces to Joan's, and they won a series of battles, culminating with the dauphin's coronation as Charles VII, on July 17, 1429.

Right The boy king, Henry VI of England, claimant to the throne of France, in the arms of his protector the earl of Warwick.

JOAN DENIED THE COMPETENCE OF THE COURT on the grounds that she was engaged in a divine mission. When Cauchon asked her, on February 22, about her "voices," she replied fiercely: "You say you are my judge. Take care as to what you do, for in truth I am sent by God and you are putting yourself in great danger." Cauchon tried a trick question to trap her: "Do you believe you are in a state of grace?" Either Joan must admit she was not, or she must admit to the sin of blasphemy by claiming to know God's mind. Her reply was masterly: "If I am not, may God put me in it; and if I am, may God keep me in it." Joan's accusers next focused on her male dress, and this became a crucial factor in the case against her. On February 27 she insisted, "All that I have done is by the commandment of the Lord, and if He had commanded me to take another dress I should have taken it, because it would have been by God's command."

By the end of the first phase of the trial (March 3), Joan was defending herself well. She impressed listeners by her total recall of previous replies, and Cauchon, aware that he was making no progress, adjourned the court until March 10, when questioning was resumed in Joan's cell. Asked again about wearing men's clothes, Joan was ordered to submit on this matter to the authority of the church. She replied that she would submit to God or the Holy Father in Rome, but not to the assessors, who were her enemies.

> *"You are not the Church; you are only my enemy."*
>
> JOAN to her accuser Bishop Cauchon, 1431

> *"St. Catherine*
> *told me that I should*
> *have help....Several times my*
> *voices told me that I shall*
> *be delivered by some*
> *great victory."*
>
> JOAN
> at her trial,
> March 14, 1431

ON MARCH 27 THE FIRST 30 OF AN EVENTUAL 70 CHARGES were read to Joan and answers demanded. When the remaining 40 charges were read shortly afterward, a sympathetic priest warned her to say that she would submit to the church's authority. At the next session she made this submission but refused to cooperate any further. Joan finally snared herself when she tried to escape by jumping from a high tower in her prison. Her captors accused her of attempted suicide, a mortal sin in the eyes of the Catholic Church. When asked if her voices had urged this violation of God's law, Joan replied that the voices had forbidden her to jump. This was a fatal admission, her disobedience delighting those who believed her to be a heretic. A new list of 12 "articles" or charges was drawn up, based on her self-incriminating replies.

The ideal outcome of the trial for those who opposed her would have been for Joan to recant. To force this end, Cauchon had her taken to the dungeon and shown the torture instruments, but she displayed such courage that the assessors thought better of torturing her. They turned to threats instead. On May 23 they warned Joan that she would be burned at the stake if she held to her existing testimony. She made a calm reply: "If I were to be condemned and saw the fire lit, the wood prepared, and the executioner or the man whose duty it was to light the fire ready to do so, and if I myself were in the fire, I would nevertheless say nothing different and would maintain what I have said during the trial until my death." With this the trial ended. Joan was found guilty of heresy. The absurd charge of witchcraft had been dropped. The pressure of disloyalty, exerted on any assessor who showed himself sympathetic to Joan, made the outcome certain.

BIOGRAPHY

Joan of Arc (c. 1412–31) was born the daughter of peasants at Domrémy, on the borders of Lorraine and Champagne. In her teens she claimed to hear voices ordering her to rescue France from domination by the English. Her leadership was instrumental in raising the siege of Orléans in 1429, but while trying to relieve Compiègne she was captured by her countrymen and sold to the English. The English convinced a French ecclesiastical court to try her for heresy and witchcraft. She was burned at the stake in Rouen in 1431. In 1920 Joan was canonized by the church that had martyred her. During two World Wars she became a heroic symbol to the French resistance and has sometimes been celebrated as the first martyr to die for the ideal of nationalism.

Above The coat of arms alleged to have been granted by Charles VII to "Jehanne de la Pucelle" on June 2, 1429, after Joan had helped to win a series of victories against the English.

Below An account of the raising of the siege of Orléans, describing Joan's heroism against the English and decorated with a cartoon of her in the margin. The account is part of the register of the Paris parliament, May 10, 1429.

Above A miniature portrait of an idealized Joan being burned at the stake dated circa 1484.

JOAN HEARD HER SENTENCE READ OUT in the churchyard of St.-Ouen Abbey on May 24. At the last moment she broke down and recanted, signed a deed of abjuration, and was condemned to life imprisonment. Back in her cell, her head was shaved, she was dressed in women's clothes, and left to the mercy of the guards. Their rude handling convinced her to reassume men's clothing, which violated her recantation. At the same time she decided that she had been wrong to fear the fire. She told the court that her voices said: "Do not distress yourself about your martyrdom." Some historians have suggested that this change of mind played into Cauchon's hands. He might have been censured for burning an uneducated heretic, but no question would be raised about burning a relapsed heretic.

Cauchon summoned a new group of assessors, who condemned her to death. On May 30, 1431, she was led to the stake in Rouen marketplace, wearing a dunce's cap inscribed with the words *Heretica, Relapsa, Apostata, Idolater.* She was then burned to death. Usually, out of compassion, the executioner killed the victim before the flames could. But Joan's bonfire had been built so high that the executioner could not reach her, and she died a slow and painful death. To prove that she had been a mere woman, her charred body was left to public view. Her ashes were thrown into the Seine.

Nineteen years later, with Charles VII master of the whole of France and the English expelled, a series of inquiries was launched into Joan's trial, intended to validate the French king's coronation. In 1456 her trial was declared irregular and the verdict rescinded.

CHRONOLOGY

1420 Treaty of Troyes. The dauphin is disinherited, and Henry VI of England is named heir to France.

1422 Henry V dies; Charles VI dies. Charles VII is declared king of France at Mehun-sur-Yèvre; Henry VI is proclaimed king of England and France at London and Paris.

1425 Joan first hears voices.

1428 The siege of Orléans begins.

1429 Joan raises the siege of Orléans on May 8. The French "summer of victories" begins. July 17, with Joan's help, Charles VII is crowned king of France at Reims.

1430 Joan is captured at Compiègne on May 23. In July, Cauchon begins proceedings to bring her to trial.

1431 Joan faces the Inquisition in January. February 21, the trial begins. May 30, Joan is put to death. December 16, Henry VI is crowned king of France. The Hundred Years War continues until 1450.

1920 Joan is canonized as a saint.

Appeasing Divine Wrath

St. Julien Residents *v.* Local Weevils

May 16 – December 20, 1587

Above The vine weevil, *Otiorhynchus sulcatus*, eating its way through a leaf. When present in great numbers, as they were in 16th-century St. Julien, these pests can cause extensive damage to crops.

*I*n the summer of 1587 the vine growers of the village of St. Julien were at the point of desperation. Their valuable crop of grapes, nestled on the slopes of Mont Cenis in the Savoie region of France and prized for making wine, was under heavy attack, and the villagers faced economic disaster. The culprit—a kind of beetle known as the vine weevil—seemed unstoppable. The people of St. Julien decided to seek expert help, and in keeping with the beliefs and practices of their time, they instituted legal proceedings against the destructive pests.

This was not the first time that the villagers had brought a case against weevils. In May 1545 Pierre Falcon had represented the weevils and Claude Morel had represented the citizens of St. Julien in proceedings conducted before Judge François Bonnivard, who came to the conclusion that the weevils were a manifestation of the wrath of God. Bonnivard issued a proclamation in 1546 prescribing high masses and acts of repentance to be performed by the local farmers. These measures were duly followed, and a written report from the parish curate, Father Romanet, confirmed that the insects had disappeared. Over forty years later, in 1587, the weevils reappeared and a new generation of St. Julien vine growers insisted that the pests be brought to trial.

The proceedings were conducted by the vicaire-général, François de la Crose, and organized by two lawyers, François Amenet and Petremand Bertrand. In the name of the people of St. Julien, they made the following statement: "Formerly by virtue of divine services and earnest supplications, the scourge and inordinate fury of the aforesaid animals did cease; now they have resumed their depredations and are doing incalculable injury. If the sins of men are the cause of this evil, it behooveth the representatives of Christ on earth to prescribe such measures as may be appropriate to appease the divine wrath. Wherefore we, the aforementioned, François Amenet and Petremand Bertrand, appear anew and beseech the official, first, to appoint another procurator and advocate for the insects in place of the deceased Pierre Falcon and Claude Morel and, secondly, to visit the grounds and observe the damage and then to proceed with the excommunication."

What the prosecutor requested was anathematization, the excommunication of animals, which relied primarily on precedents in the Bible, first among them the serpent's expulsion from the

Animal Trials

Bringing animals to justice for "crimes" was standard procedure in Europe for many centuries. Animals accused of homicide were tried before secular tribunals and condemned to death, exactly as a human being would be. Guilty animals (often dressed in human clothes) were publicly hanged, burned at the stake, or whipped and tortured. Such punishment was evidently not intended as a deterrent, since nobody brought other animals to witness the fate of their fellows. Pigs most frequently came before secular courts, and records of 34 cases have been discovered in local archives in which pigs were executed for the murder of children.

Most of the animal trials heard in ecclesiastical courts involved hordes of rodents or insects (rats, mice, locusts, or weevils) accused of destroying property. The pests were necessarily tried in absentia, and the court would prescribe a religious means of dealing with them—normally a solemn curse that declared them an anathema.

The notion of animals as criminals survived until the end of the 19th century. The last known such trial was a Swiss case in 1906, in which two men and a dog were tried for robbing and killing a man. The men were given life sentences, but the dog was condemned to death.

ASSERTING CHURCH AUTHORITY

CXD. P.N.ROW

The most illuminating material on animal trials is found in a treatise written in 1531 by an eminent French jurist and criminal lawyer, Bartholomew Chassenée. In the eyes of the Catholic Church, Chassenée made clear, the greatest manifestation of evil was a breakdown of the natural order. The "unnatural" destructive actions of animals, whether pigs or weevils, showed that Satan was acting through them to subvert the natural order of God's world. In Chassenée's view,

swarms of pestilent vermin were simply choirs of demons in another form.

Ecclesiastical trials against these offending animals reinforced the notion of a natural order, guaranteed on earth by Holy Mother Church. The sentence of banishment or anathema pronounced on these animals affirmed the accepted order. At the same time, it upheld the church's position of authority in the community. The church claimed that it punished animals in accordance with the covenant set out with Noah in Genesis 9.

Above A 19th-century engraving by P. N. Row featured in *The Book of Days* showing a sow and her piglets being tried for murdering a child in Lavegny, France, in 1457.

This covenant stipulated that animals would be held responsible for their violent actions to the same extent that a human would be held accountable. Specifically, the Bible stated that "if an ox gore a man or woman that they may die, then the ox shall be surely stoned and his flesh shall not be eaten."

Garden of Eden. By the 16th century the Catholic Church had been practicing anathematization for centuries as a way of dealing with pests or plagues of insects. In cases in which the accused (such as insects or rodents) could not be seized and imprisoned, it was the most important sanction an ecclesiastical court could impose. As early as the year 824, representatives of the church anathematized moles in the Aosta Valley of northern Italy. In 880, when Rome suffered a plague of locusts and attempts to exterminate them failed, the church resorted to exorcism and sanctified the area with holy water, and the plague disappeared. In 1487 the bishop of Autun gave a

Above One of the prized vineyards of the Savoie region, where the weevils damaged the harvest in 1587. The area produces distinctive red wines, still valued by connoisseurs today.

public warning to an infestation of slugs, stipulating that they leave or be accursed. Sometimes when anathema was pronounced, a few "culprits" were brought into court and solemnly crushed as an example to others.

ANIMALS WERE GIVEN THE SAME RIGHTS AS PEOPLE for the purposes of a formal trial. In St. Julien in 1587, Pierre Rembaud was appointed defense counsel to the insects, and Antoine Filliol acted on behalf of the villagers as prosecutor. Both parties appeared before the vicaire-général on May 30 and again on June 6. The prosecution argued that the insects were the same ones that had been admonished 30 years earlier—although all the humans connected with that case had since died—and so deserved excommunication. Counsel for the defense argued in his opening statement that his "clients" should not be cursed, because the Bible expressly stated that the lower animals were created prior to people and given the right to "every green herb." The weevils, he declared, were simply exercising a God-given right when they overran and devoured St. Julien's vines. The prosecution responded that the lower animals were created to be subject to humankind. Furthermore, to hold them accountable before the law was eminently reasonable—animals lived in communities with laws of their own, ordained

for the common good, and among themselves they punished transgressors. Domestic animals showed consciousness of their own wrong-doing by trying to conceal what they had done. Similarly, people recognized the moral responsibility of any animals that caused a nuisance by punishing the transgressing animals in accordance with the legal code of the area.

Although the central issue in the St. Julien trial was characteristic of a former era, the proceedings were curiously modern. The defense counsel, like a 20th-century attorney, equivocated at every turn. After several adjournments and endless arguments over technical points of law, each side presented its arguments again on July 18: the prosecution asked for a quick decision; the defense for an annulment. The bishop granted the defense's request for more time, but in the meantime, the weevils continued feasting, and the vine growers became increasingly alarmed. After mass on June 29 they held a public meeting in St. Julien's main square presided over by the deputy mayor, Jean Depupet. They decided to allocate to the weevils a suitable piece of land where they could live without harming the vines. A spot was chosen and approved by the bishop and the local community.

Above Pierre de Lambert, Bishop of Maurienne 1567–91. He was closely involved in the court's final decision at the trial of the weevils in 1587.

Below The earliest surviving records of the trial of the weevils, preserved in turn-of-the-century volumes by the Historical and Archeological Society of Maurienne.

THE PROSECUTION ASKED THAT THE DEFENDANTS BE EXPELLED from the vineyards on July 24 and forbidden to return on pain of banishment. Rembaud, for the defense, demanded time to consider the offer of land from the vine growers and secured yet another adjournment, this time until August 20. Fate played into the hands of the defense when troop movements in the area postponed the trial until September 3. At that point, Rembaud formally declined the land offered by the vine growers to his clients; it was infertile, he claimed, and insufficiently supplied with food. Filliol countered that the chosen spot was perfect for the weevils and demanded an adjudication in his favor. In response, the judge collected all the documents and reserved his decision, pending the appointment of a panel of experts who could draw up a report on the suitability of the proffered land. The date December 20, 1587, annotated in the margin of the original copy of that report, suggests that the trial took some eight months to reach its conclusion. By an ironic turn of events, we do not know the final outcome—the last page in the St. Julien archives was destroyed (perhaps by hungry weevils?).

But It Still Moves

THE HOLY OFFICE *v.* GALILEO GALILEI

APRIL 12 – JUNE 22, 1633

Above The title page of Galileo's *Dialogue*, the publication for which he was brought to trial. It shows the figures of Aristotle, Ptolemy, and Copernicus discussing the merits of the Ptolemaic system (that the sun revolves around the earth) compared with the Copernican system (that the earth revolves around the sun).

"I think that in discussions of physical problems we ought to begin not from the authority of scriptural passages, but from sense-experiences and necessary demonstrations.... Nor is God any less excellently revealed in Nature's actions than in the sacred statements of the Bible."

GALILEO GALILEI
in his *Dialogue*,
1632

Galileo Galilei stood before the Inquisition on April 12, 1633, charged with questioning the authority of the Roman Catholic Church. His crime was disseminating a new idea. In his book, *A Dialogue Concerning the Two Chief World Systems*, published in 1632, he argued that the sun, and not the earth, is at the center of the universe. In adopting this theory he supported the Polish astronomer Nicolaus Copernicus (1473–1543) against the Catholic Church and its chief authority on science, the Greek philosopher Aristotle. In the eyes of the church, his publication was heresy, an accusation that, if proved, carried the death penalty. Only 33 years earlier another scientist, Giordano Bruno (1548–1600), had been burned at the stake for supporting the Copernican theory.

As early as 1616 the Holy Office had forbidden Galileo to hold or defend the teachings of Copernicus. Understanding his frustration, one friend had stood by him. His name was Maffeo Barberini, the future Pope Urban VIII. In 1620, while still a cardinal, Barberini wrote a long poem addressed to Galileo, called *Adulatio Perniciosa* ("Dangerous Adulation"). In it he assured the scientist that even in a crisis, he would defend scientific innovation. Trusting Barberini's promise, Galileo sought his advice before publishing the *Dialogue*. His friend, by then Pope Urban VIII, reassured him. Two years later the political climate had changed so radically that Urban warned Galileo through a third party that he "had better take care not to be summoned through the Holy Office."

WHEN 70-YEAR-OLD GALILEO WAS HAULED FROM HIS SICKBED in Florence to appear before the Inquisition, he declined sanctuary from the republic of Venice, confident that his friendship with the pope would see him through. He also believed that the Dominican friar Maculano, head of the Holy Office, would be sympathetic. What he did not know was that the Jesuit order had turned Pope Urban's mind against him and had planted new documents in the Vatican archives altering what had been stipulated during Galileo's appearance before the Inquisition in 1616. Instead of recording what had actually been said, that to "hold or defend" Copernicanism would lay him open to the charge of heresy, the altered documents read as if Galileo had been explicitly ordered by the Holy Office to make no mention of the Copernican theory. Were this true, the *Dialogue* would have been a clear-cut case of heresy in deliberate defiance of the church's orders.

There was a wider political context to the trial, too, of which Galileo was ignorant. The pope, locked in conflict with the grand duke of Tuscany, wanted to humiliate the Medici family by humbling Galileo, who was their protégé. Galileo's trial would also demonstrate to the Christian world the Catholic Church's newfound confidence in dealing with intellectual challenge, whether from the religious free thought of the Protestants or the scientific skepticism represented by new thinkers.

Above A representation of the Copernican universe, with the sun at the center.
This is the allegedly heretical theory that Galileo supported in his *Dialogue*.

THE FIRST HEARING TOOK PLACE ON APRIL 12, 1633, before Maculano
and his assistants. Galileo identified the *Dialogue* as his work and said that
he had come to Rome of his own accord to know what opinion it was
proper for him to hold about Copernicus's theories. He could then be sure
not to hold any opinions but those of the Holy Catholic Church.
Answering all the Inquisition's questions calmly and deferentially, Galileo
discredited on the first day the forged papers from the archives by producing unimpeachable papers of his own. The question of heresy in the
Dialogue was held over for further deliberation by the Inquisition, and a
new date of April 30 was set for the next hearing.

Galileo's apparent calm in court disguised his growing terror of being
tortured, one of the Inquisition's common practices. The pressure of the
trial was taking a heavy toll on his health. His signature on court documents dated April 12 is blotted and shaky, and during the 18-day interval
between hearings he was racked with sciatic pains and intestinal problems.
A friendly member of the Inquisition suggested to Galileo that he should
plead guilty to errors, rather than risk torture and imprisonment. At the
second hearing he accepted this advice, and pleaded guilty to "vainglorious

Trial by Inquisition

The Papal Inquisition, established in 1231
and dismantled in 1820, was set up to
challenge theories thought to be damaging
to the Catholic Church. More than one
hundred years before Galileo's trial, the
pope created the Holy Office as an
autonomous court, to strengthen the
Inquisition in the face of the Protestant
Reformation. It became active in 1542,
and was given great powers by canon
(church) law over Catholic doctrine, and
criminal jurisdiction over accusations of
heresy. It could pass sentence or make
public declarations on any matter, including superstition, magic, academic teaching, and the publication of forbidden
books. It recognized no limits to its powers
over people or territory; only the pope and
the cardinals were outside its jurisdiction.
Trials were conducted under "the secret of
the Holy Office"—a strict oath that bound
everyone to total silence on the case.
Maximum publicity was, however, given to
judgments, decrees, and sentences.

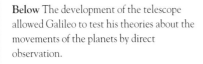

Below The development of the telescope allowed Galileo to test his theories about the movements of the planets by direct observation.

ambition and pure ignorance and inadvertence." He also offered to rewrite the *Dialogue*, excising the "errors" so that the book would not be banned. On May 10, Galileo read out a formal defense in which he drew attention to his "broken health." The court was adjourned for a month while the Inquisition considered its verdict. In the interim, anti-Florentine factions in Rome worked on the pope, linking the *Dialogue* to the teachings of Giordano Bruno and hinting that Galileo was an occult astrologer. Not even Maculano was able to curb the fury of Pope Urban, who felt betrayed and threatened by his onetime friend.

Below Galileo (in black) faces the Holy Office, by an unknown 18th-century artist.

> *"I did not ask permission to write the book, because I did not consider that in writing it I was acting contrary to, far less disobeying, the command not to hold, defend, or teach that opinion."*
>
> GALILEO GALILEI
> under cross-examination,
> 1633

WHEN THE HOLY OFFICE RECONVENED ON JUNE 16, it accepted Galileo's defense, but instead of the expected nominal sentence, the court ordered Galileo to be interrogated under threat of torture, on suspicion of heresy. In addition, they declared, "[the *Dialogue*] is to be prohibited. Furthermore, copies of the sentence shall be sent to all Apostolic Nuncios, to all Inquisitors against heretical depravity, and especially the Inquisitor in Florence, who shall read the sentence in full assembly and in the presence of those who profess the mathematical art." The tribunal stipulated that Galileo's rigorous interrogation was to be followed by a public recantation. The only mercies in the sentencing were that the *Dialogue* would not be burned publicly, and that Galileo would not be tried for heresy.

BIOGRAPHY

Galileo Galilei was born in Pisa, Italy, in 1564. His father, Vincenzo Galilei, was a musician, and Galileo grew up to become a talented painter, musician, and classicist, as well as an exceptionally gifted mathematician. In his 20s he explored the concept of motion, modeling his work on the writings of Archimedes. The research took 20 years to complete, but in 1604 he developed the principle of the motion of falling bodies that laid the foundation for Newton's laws of physics. While watching a lamp swinging in a cathedral he also discovered the principle on which a pendulum works, research that was applied to clockmaking in 1656 by a Dutch scientist, Christiaan Huygens.

Galileo was at the peak of his career when he became interested in the motion of the planets and the theories of Nicolaus Copernicus. He was convinced that the earth was in orbit round the sun, but could not prove it until, in 1610, he developed a telescope powerful enough to be used for astronomical observation. The new equipment allowed him to observe sunspots and how their position changed over time. His observations convinced him that Copernicus was correct, and he published his evidence in the *Dialogue* (1632), a treatise that argued against the teaching of the Roman Catholic Church and led to his trial for heresy. Following his trial, Galileo was placed under house arrest for the remaining eight years of his life. Oncoming blindness and health problems curtailed his research, and he died at his farm in Arcetri in 1642.

POPE URBAN VIII

When Cardinal Maffeo Barberini (1568–1644) became Pope Urban VIII in 1623, men of science all over the world rejoiced, expecting that the friction between progressive thinkers and the more orthodox church would come to an end. However, it became clear that the new pope would readily sacrifice his former interest in science and philosophy should any new idea threaten the traditional authority of the church. The trial before the Holy Office of his old friend Galileo Galilei caused considerable anger between the two men, each one feeling that he had been betrayed by the other. The rancor never died between them, and when Galileo died in 1642, Pope Urban vetoed a plan to build a memorial to Galileo's achievements on the grounds that it would be a slight to the church's authority.

On June 21, Galileo appeared before the Inquisition for the formal interrogation. Preferring humiliation to torture, he made a clear statement of recantation: "I do not hold and have not held this opinion of Copernicus since the command was intimated to me that I must abandon it. For the rest, I am in your hands—do with me what you please." Following the formal procedure, the judges spoke the words, "Truth or torture," and Galileo repeated dully, "I am here to submit, and I have not held this opinion since the decision was pronounced, as I have stated." Maculano, who was presiding, tipped the balance in Galileo's favor by choosing not to raise any of the points in the *Dialogue* that would have been difficult to explain away, and the ordeal ended within an hour. The court records state that, "As nothing further could be done in execution of the decree, his signature was obtained to his deposition, and he was sent back to his place." Galileo was still not released, but was kept at the headquarters of the Inquisition to receive the formal sentence.

THE SENTENCE WAS READ ON THE FOLLOWING DAY, JUNE 22, at the Dominican convent of Santa Maria sopra Minerva. Galileo knelt in a penitent's robe, shamed and broken, while members of the Holy Office listed the crimes in the *Dialogue*, declared it a banned publication, ordained penances for Galileo, and condemned him to "the formal prison of this Holy Office during our pleasure." Galileo accepted all this and replied: "I, Galileo Galilei, son of the late Vincenzo Galilei, Florentine, aged 70 years…have been pronounced by the Holy Office to be vehemently suspected of heresy, that is to say of having held and believed that the sun is the center of the world and immovable and that the earth is not the center.…With sincere heart and unfeigned faith I abjure, curse and detest the aforesaid errors and heresies." There is a legend, probably originating from a fanciful Spanish painting, that he made a last gesture of defiance by whispering under his breath: *"Eppur si muove"* ("But it still moves").

Two days after sentencing, Galileo was released into the custody of the Florentine ambassador, who wrote to a colleague: "He seems extremely downcast over the punishment, which came as a surprise; for as to the book, he showed little concern over the prohibition, which he had long forseen." Historians believe that, far from suffering a moral disgrace, Galileo knew exactly how far he could push his point. By the standards of the time his punishment was lenient. He had been sentenced to imprisonment, but this was commuted to house arrest for the rest of his life, and he retained his papal pension. Significantly, three of the ten judges protested that the formal sentence was too harsh and refused to sign it.

Left Galileo's formal recantation of the theory that the earth moves around the sun, which he signed before the judges of the Holy Office on June 21, 1633.

Above In spite poor health, blindness, and the restrictions of house arrest, Galileo continued to teach mathematics until the end of his life. Tito Lessi's 20th-century portrait shows him instructing his last pupil, the Italian scientist Vincenzo Viviani, circa 1641.

GALILEO RETURNED TO HIS HOME IN ARCETRI, NEAR FLORENCE, and despite encroaching blindness, wrote a book on engineering and mechanics implicitly critical of the Aristotelian view of the universe. Either this small act of defiance went unnoticed, or the Inquisition chose to ignore it, for no action was taken. Meanwhile the publicity surrounding the trial made the *Dialogue* a bestseller and spread the theory among foreign scholars.

When Galileo died in 1642, no memorial was erected to mark his achievements, since official recognition of his scientific work might have been interpreted as an insult to the church. It was almost one hundred years later that the first monument to Galileo was erected in the church of Santa Croce in Florence. Meanwhile the Catholic Church retained its stubborn faith in the earth-centered universe, against all scientific evidence, for another 200 years (the doctrine was officially abandoned in 1822, by which time proof of Galileo's theories had become irrefutable). It was not until 1992, more than 350 years after Galileo's ordeal, that Pope John Paul II formally rehabilitated him within the Catholic Church and acknowledged his contribution to the growth of scientific knowledge.

The last words on the subject should be left to the scientist himself, written in the margin of his personal copy of the *Dialogue* after his release from the terrors of the Holy Office: "When people of whatsoever competence are made judges over experts and are granted authority to treat them as they please…these are the novelties that are apt to bring about the ruin of commonwealths and the subversion of the state."

Above In spite poor health, blindness, and the restrictions of house arrest, Galileo continued to teach mathematics until the end of his life. Tito Lessi's 20th-century portrait shows him instructing his last pupil, the Italian scientist Vincenzo Viviani, circa 1641.

"Who can doubt that it will lead to the worst disorders when minds created by God are compelled to submit slavishly to an outside will? When we are told to deny our senses and subject them to the whim of others?"

GALILEO GALILEI
after his release,
June 1633

Salem Witch-Hunting

THE COMMUNITY *v.* ALLEGED WITCHES

MARCH 1 – 5, 1692

Above A painted woodcut reflects popular superstitions of the time. It shows three witches with animals' heads flying through the air on a forked stick.

Early American Law

In 1692 Massachusetts was a British colony operating under British law. However, local justices of the peace, far removed from their ruling legislative body, decided independently how trials should be conducted. Although trial by jury was part of the legal process, judges were not bound by the decisions of a jury. The preliminary hearings at Salem were guided by interpretations of the Old Testament, not the British Penal Code, and bore more resemblance to an inquisition than to a court of law. The usual assumption—that an accused person was innocent until proven guilty—was effectively ruled out by the three principles that Hathorne and Corwin used to conduct proceedings: people were deemed witches if they had an unusual mark on their body, if any mischief came to their neighbors following a dispute, or if anyone said their shape had been seen doing harm. This third condition, "spectral evidence," was dangerously unfair to the accused. Not one of the magistrates who conducted the preliminary hearings provided the accused with defense counsel, nor was it the custom of the time to let defendants speak on their own behalf.

In 1692 in the small town of Salem, Massachusetts, an extraordinary series of events took place that culminated in one of the most notorious witch-hunts in recent history. A number of theories have been advanced to explain the bizarre phenomenon; the most likely one suggests that the entire episode began with a game of make-believe among a group of adolescent girls. In this backwater community, already rife with conflict and resentments, the girls' secret play triggered an outbreak of mass hysteria. The courtroom dramas that followed resulted in a human tragedy that has been fixed in Western memory.

The townspeople first became alarmed when Betty, the nine-year-old daughter of Salem's minister, Samuel Parris, his niece Abigail Williams, and a number of their friends began barking, shouting, and twitching as if in a trance. They were examined by the local pastors after the physician, William Griggs, suggested that they were under the influence of witchcraft. "Who torments you?" the men asked. Receiving no answer, they ran through a list of local names. Under this guided inquiry the girls identified as witches Samuel Parris's West Indian slave, Tituba, and two residents of Salem, Sarah Good and Sarah Osborne. The men took further testimony from the girls, and warrants were issued for the arrest of the three women on February 29, 1692. The women were taken to Ipswich prison, while preparations were made for a preliminary examination to see if there was sufficient evidence for a trial. Meanwhile, the girls went on naming other "witches"—Martha Corey, a woman known for her great piety, Ann Pudeator, a widow and leading citizen of Salem, and Sarah Good's daughter Dorcas, among many others. There arose such a frenzy of accusation that eventually dozens of people were involved.

THE PRELIMINARY HEARINGS WERE HELD FROM MARCH 1 TO 5, 1692. Three principles were laid down that would determine how the formal witch trials, set to begin in June 1692, would proceed. The Massachusetts General Court sent two representatives, John Hathorne and Jonathan Corwin, to hear the case. Both had some legal experience, but typical of their time, they lacked formal training. Though officially justices of the peace, they were in effect prosecuting counsel, and they based their prosecution on the Bible—mainly the Old Testament—in which they found the statement, "Thou shalt not permit a witch to live." They read all the available books on witchcraft and agreed on what would constitute acceptable evidence: any accused person whose body bore a "devil's mark" or "teat" (any unnatural or unusual lump) would be found guilty; any accused person whose neighbors became victims of mischief following a dispute would be strongly suspect; and any person whose "shape" was seen doing harm would be deemed a witch, because it was believed that the devil could not assume the shape of any innocent person to hurt another.

Above A Victorian portrait called *The Examination of Sarah Good* shows the jury searching for a "devil's mark" on Good's body. According to popular belief, witches had an extra teat with which to feed the devil, and juries were entitled to search for it. They would stick pins in any abnormality.

> "You're a liar.
> I am no more a Witch
> than you are a Wizard,
> and if you take away my life,
> God will give you Blood
> to drink."
>
> SARAH GOOD
> at her execution,
> July 19, 1692

Above A warrant for the arrest of Ann Pudeator, who was charged with "sundry acts of witchcraft." The warrant was signed by Hathorne and Corwin on May 12, 1692; Ann was hanged on September 22.

Above Chief Justice Stoughton, who presided over the formal trials for witchcraft in Boston during 1692.

Below A verbatim record of the court's examination of Martha Corey in March 1692. She refused to confess. In September she was sentenced to death, excommunicated from the church and hanged.

These three tests were accepted in all the trials to come. Jury members searched the accused witches' bodies minutely for "devil's marks" and stuck pins in any abnormality. Using the "mischief following anger" principle, many Salem inhabitants revived old grievances against their neighbors to back up accusations of witchcraft. Because an accusation that a person's shape had done harm was accepted as proof of guilt, hysterical girls would scream out accusations against any member of the community concerning their shape ("spectral evidence") and "prove" that person guilty.

THE FIRST HEARING WAS HELD IN SALEM CHURCH to accommodate the crowds. Hathorne and Corwin sat behind a large table, while the girls, seated in the front benches, faced them. Onlookers packed the rest of the church. Sarah Good was questioned first. Although the daughter of a prosperous Massachusetts innkeeper, she had been reduced to poverty by the time of the trials. Onlookers described her as a "crone," but she was only about 38, pregnant, and mother of a four-year-old child. When accused of hurting the girls and employing spirits, she replied, "I scorn it." The magistrates accused her of not going to church, and villagers testified that she was guilty of "malefaction"—bringing harm on people who refused to give her alms. The magistrate asked: "What is it that you say when you go muttering away from a person's house?" Good answered: "If I must tell, I will tell. It is the commandments I say. I may say the commandments, I hope." When asked to recite them, she could only mumble phrases of a psalm. The magistrates dismissed her and asked for Sarah Osborne to be brought in. As Good was being marched out she cried, "It is Gammer Osborne that doth pinch and afflict the children."

Sarah Osborne had been taken to jail from her sickbed and was moved, with difficulty, to the courtroom. Her neighbors had two grievances with her, both based on hearsay: she was rumored to have lived with a younger man before taking him as her second husband; and she was said to have swindled her sons from her first marriage out of their inheritance. She denied dealing with the devil and pointed out, reasonably enough, that in her present state of health she was more likely bewitched than a witch. She did tell a garbled story of how she had dreamed of a thing "like an Indian which…pinched her on the neck and pulled her by the back part of her head to the door of the house." She was then led away.

WHEN TITUBA WAS BROUGHT IN TO GIVE EVIDENCE, the girls, who had been yelling and writhing whenever the accused women looked at them, seemed to go berserk. As soon as Tituba "confessed," they fell silent. She told the court a long tale of red cats and red rats, dogs and hogs, a creature with wings and Sarah Osborne's face, and a tall man who said that she must serve him. Hathorne probed every detail. Tituba claimed the tall man had shown her a book. How many names were in it? Hathorne asked. Nine, she replied; one was "the tall man of Boston," but she was vague about the others.

However, Tituba admitted that she had gone to witches' sabbats with the man, the winged creature, a hog, and two cats. When the girls writhed, Hathorne asked, "Who hurts the children now?" "I am blind now, I cannot see," Tituba replied, claiming to have lost her powers after confessing.

THE HEARINGS ENDED ON MARCH 5, and two days later the three women were sent to Boston to be held for trial. The formal proceedings later that year simply rubber-stamped both the decisions made by Hathorne and Corwin and the three principles. In effect, the examination had been the trial; its records were regarded as proven facts, and the accused were condemned without a defense. An avalanche of witch trials followed in Boston between June and September 1692. The girls continued to accuse respectable residents of Salem, including George Burroughs (a former pastor of Salem Church) and such leading Bostonians as Samuel Willard, president of Harvard College. Some of the accused "confessed" to save themselves, naming others. Of the more than 200 accused (most of whom were women), 100 were jailed and 19 were hanged. Of the three original defendants, Sarah Good was executed, Sarah Osborne died in prison on May 10 before she could be tried, and Tituba escaped hanging by confessing to crimes of witchcraft, admitting that she had experimented with voodoo and black magic and had involved the Parris children and their friends in her activities. It is believed that Parris sold Tituba to pay her jail fees.

> *"What I said was altogether false against my grandfather and Mr. Burroughs, which I did to save my life and liberty."*
>
> MARGARET JACOBS,
> whose testimony ensured that George Burroughs was hanged,
> August 1692

POSTSCRIPT

The witch-hunts came to an abrupt end in October 1692 after the girls named Lady Mary Phips, the wife of the governor, as a witch. On October 29, Phips canceled all scheduled trials, released the suspects, and proclaimed a pardon for the accused. Five years later, on January 15, 1697, the citizens of Massachusetts held a day of fasting and repentance to honor those who had suffered and died. In 1702 the Massachusetts General Court declared the witchcraft procedures unlawful, and singled out for censure the acceptance of "spectral evidence." In 1711 the same court annulled the convictions and granted compensation to all the surviving accused. The following year the First Church of Salem revoked the excommunications that had been pronounced on the "witches."

Of the many theories that attempt to explain what happened in Salem, four have gained significant support. One socio-economic interpretation stresses pent-up anger born of conflict between the subsistence farmers of Salem village and the more prosperous inhabitants of the port of Salem. Another theory points to rapid change in Massachusetts: as this isolated Puritan community became a commercial center, a climate of extreme insecurity developed. A third interpretation focuses on the psychology of the adolescent girls and compares the phenomenon with other manifestations such as poltergeist activity, that adolescent girls are thought to trigger.

Above The public repentance of Judge Samuel Sewall in 1697 for his part in condemning innocent citizens of Salem to death.

In his play *The Crucible*, Arthur Miller suggests a fourth possibility. By drawing an analogy between the trials and the McCarthy hearings of the 1950s, he suggests that outbreaks of collective paranoia occur periodically.

MILITARY

The armed forces of most nations are charged with preserving the integrity of the state and upholding its laws. But what happens when a member of the armed forces breaks that law or runs afoul of the military's own code of justice? Such cases fall under the jurisdiction of military courts, whose main function is to regulate the armed forces and punish its wrongdoers. The principal instrument of military justice is the court-martial, whose wide ranging powers can be used effectively to impose military discipline or abused to punish the wrongly-convicted beyond the limits set down in a civil court. The second major type of military court is the military tribunal, established to try individuals accused of war crimes and to formulate international laws of war to be applied in future conflicts. Because international warfare is necessarily conducted outside peacetime treaties and accords, the military tribunal often becomes a vital link to restoring peace.

While members of the armed forces are subject to both civil and military law, if a case involves a breach of military law, it will be tried by a court-martial. The judges in such cases are typically military personnel, as are counsel for the defense and prosecution. As in all systems of justice, those conducting courts-martial have at times used the system inappropriately, or even for unjust purposes. Two classic examples of courts-martial gone awry are the trials of Wolfe Tone in 18th-century Ireland and Alfred Dreyfus in 19th-century France. Although Wolfe Tone—a British citizen—admitted to actions that made him guilty of treason, he was never a member of the British armed forces and so should never have been tried by court-martial. Irish civil courts at the time shared that view but failed to prevent his execution. In the Dreyfus case, in which the defendant was accused of espionage, the military establishment refused to admit any wrongdoing, even after Dreyfus' innocence had been widely acknowledged. Military leaders sacrificed justice to their fears that discipline among the ranks would be undermined.

The Nuremberg and Tokyo trials of alleged war criminals posed a different problem because they involved international issues. Since each sovereign state maintains its own military law, no accepted standard existed across national boundaries. The special international military tribunals set up by the Allies were temporary courts designed specifically to try German and Japanese leaders, both military and

COURTS

civilian, accused of war crimes. The members of those tribunals were not required to be members of the armed forces; indeed, most of them were not. As shocking revelations accumulated in the aftermath of World War II, they were called on to distinguish between aggression and defense, acts of war and acts of inhumanity. The verdicts rendered by the Nuremberg and Tokyo tribunals established a law of war crimes for the future.

The trial of John Brown was a hybrid mixture of civil and military procedure that resulted in a summary military execution. The case grew out of Brown's admitted attack on a federal arsenal with intent to steal arms and ammunition. Although grave doubts remain as to whether Brown should have been tried in a Virginia court for an offense against the federal authority, a court-martial was never in question. Brown was not a member of the armed forces of the United States, yet he was hanged by military personnel barely six weeks after the alleged crime, with a total suspension of due process and no possibility of appeal.

80 THE BRITISH ARMY *v.* WOLFE TONE

86 THE STATE OF VIRGINIA *v.* JOHN BROWN

92 THE FRENCH ARMY *v.* ALFRED DREYFUS

98 THE ALLIED NATIONS *v.* NAZI LEADERS

106 THE ALLIED NATIONS *v.* HIDEKI TOJO

The Sacrifice of My Life

THE BRITISH ARMY v. WOLFE TONE

NOVEMBER 10, 1798

Above Wolfe Tone in French military uniform, wearing the "cropped" hairstyle fashionable among revolutionary soldiers.

On November 10, 1798, Theobald Wolfe Tone was tried for his life in front of a British court-martial in Dublin. He was not allowed to call witnesses in his defense, and his execution was a foregone conclusion. Tone was an Irish Protestant political activist who aimed to achieve a united and independent Ireland. In 1791 he co-founded the Society of United Irishmen to promote these aims by political campaigning. By 1795 the society had been banned and Tone was in exile. There he enlisted the help of the postrevolutionary government, which was at war with England, to help the United Irishmen overthrow the English in open conflict. To the French revolutionary general Lazare Hoche, Tone quoted an old adage: "England's difficulty is Ireland's opportunity." He won Hoche's support for his proposal that the French government send an expedition to Ireland. On June 19, 1796, Tone wrote to Hoche: "We intend, Citizen General, to restore to a people ripe for revolution the independence and liberty for which it clamors."

A GREAT INVASION FORCE SET SAIL FOR THE BRITISH ISLES in December of 1796. Altogether there were 14,750 French troops in 43 ships, including 17 warships. Tone knew the precariousness of his own position. With French forces at war with England, his comrades, if captured, would be treated as legitimate prisoners of war and returned to France. Tone, however, would still be regarded as a British citizen turned traitor, despite his post as a commissioned officer in Hoche's French army. On December 22, Tone's ship, the 80-gun flagship *Indomptable*, reached Bantry Bay off the southwest coast of Ireland, but the frigate carrying Hoche, *La Fraternité*, was delayed by heavy fog and bad weather. For three days, in ever worsening weather conditions, Tone and the French commanders waited for Hoche. In low spirits, Tone wrote in his journal: "If we are taken, my fate will not be a mild one; the best I can expect is to be shot as an *émigré rentré*, unless I have the good fortune to be killed in the action....Perhaps I may be reserved for a trial, for the sake of striking terror into others, in which case I shall be hanged as a traitor, and disembowelled...." On December 25 the winds increased to gale force, then storm force. The *Indomptable*, carrying Tone, was caught in the high winds and forced to cut her cables and run for safety. Tone returned to Paris to consider what to do next.

Through the following months, as political tension in Ireland continued

British Law in Ireland

British law, laid down as early as 1351, defined treason as a violation of the allegiance owed to the sovereign by all British citizens. Since Ireland was a British colony in the 18th century, Tone's action in organizing French forces to attack the British in Ireland was regarded as a treasonous attack on the king's realm. As an officer in the French Army when he was captured, Tone should have been treated as a prisoner of war, but this was long before the Hague and Geneva Conventions defined codes of conduct for times of war. The British authorities regarded him as a threat and ordered a court-martial to dispose of Tone as quickly as possible, before he could become a hero.

Tone questioned the legitimacy of a military court throughout the trial, since he was not and had never been a member of the British armed services. If he were to be regarded as a British citizen, he argued, he should at least have had a civil trial. If he were tried as an officer, then he had the right to be executed by firing squad. The British bent every rule to rid themselves of an embarrassment but achieved the one thing that they had tried to avoid: they created a high-profile martyr for the Irish cause.

THE SOCIETY OF UNITED IRISHMEN

In October 1791, three Irish Protestant political activists, Theobald Wolfe Tone, James Napper Tandy, and Thomas Russell, established the Society of United Irishmen in Belfast. They sought two main goals: to promote the cause of Catholic emancipation by campaigning against political and economic restrictions placed on most of the population by the British government; and to improve the representativeness and autonomy of the Dublin parliament, which exercised limited responsibility, and was controlled by London.

The British authorities responded by suppressing the society in 1794. It reorganized in secret with three declared aims: "First, resolved, that the weight of English influence in the government of this country is so great, as to require a cordial union among *all the peoples of Ireland* to maintain that balance which is essential to the preservation of our liberties, and the extension of our commerce. Second, that the sole constitutional mode by which this influence can be opposed, is by a complete and radical reform of the representation of the people in Parliament. Third, that no reform is practicable, efficacious or just, which shall not include Irishmen of every religious persuasion."

In April 1794 Tone appealed to France (then at war with England) for aid, pointing out the tactical advantages to France of making the English fight on the home front as well as abroad. When the United Irishmen staged a hasty rebellion in late May and early June 1798, poorly backed by the French navy, the English quickly overcame them. Tone was viewed as the ringleader, and the lord lieutenant made an example of him to deter others.

Above Bastille Day celebrations in Belfast, 1792. A nationalist faction in the north sympathized with French revolutionaries.

Above The United Irishmen's crest, with the cap of liberty and motto "Ireland Forever."

"I was willing to encounter danger, as a soldier, but…I had a violent objection to being hanged as a traitor."

WOLFE TONE
to General Henri Jacques Clarke,
requesting a commission,
March 1796

BIOGRAPHY

Theobald Wolfe Tone (1763–98) was born in Dublin on January 20, 1763, the son of a coachmaker. He entered Trinity College, Dublin, in 1781, where he studied law. Four years later, at the age of 21, he eloped with Maria Witherington, the 16-year-old sister of a fellow student, and they set up house together at Bodenstown outside Dublin. Tone was called to the bar in 1789 but concentrated on making his reputation in politics. Although a Protestant by birth, he became a hero among the Catholic population after the publication of his 1791 pamphlet, *An Argument on Behalf of the Catholics of Ireland.* In the pamphlet he campaigned for Catholic emancipation as the first step toward founding an independent and democratic Ireland that was free from any kind of religious oppression. To further this goal, he co-founded the Society of United Irishmen, whose aim was to reduce the power of English rule in Ireland.

After the English banned the United Irishmen, Tone fled first to Philadelphia in 1795 to seek support in the United States, then moved on to France in 1796, where he obtained a commission in the French Army. He petitioned the post-revolutionary French government—the Directory—for military aid and succeeded in organizing two invasions, one in 1796 and a second in 1798. Neither succeeded, and Tone was captured during the second. He was court-martialed and avoided public execution by cutting his own throat in prison on November 11, 1798. He died on November 19.

to rise dramatically, communication between Tone and the rebel forces in Ireland remained poor. In the spring of 1798, buoyed by the belief that the French would come to their aid, the United Irishmen broke into outright rebellion in County Wexford, in the southeast of Ireland. At the same time, the new commander of the French Army, Napoleon Bonaparte, made the fateful decision to concentrate military resources on the French campaign in Egypt, leaving little manpower to pursue the situation in Ireland.

NEWS OF INITIAL SUCCESSES BY THE IRISH REBELS IN LATE MAY took both Tone and the French by surprise. They prepared an expedition that would quickly prove itself too little, too late. The plan was that the French general, Jean Hardy, would sail from Brest with a force of three thousand veterans, including Tone aboard the *Hoche,* and would link up with three warships sailing from Rochefort under Gen. Jean Joseph Humbert. They were to make for County Donegal in the far northwest, or, failing that, for Killala Bay, slightly to the south. Hardy was to assume overall command of the combined forces. Humbert set sail on August 6 as planned, and arrived in Killala Bay on August 22, only to discover that the Irish rebels had been crushed two months earlier at the battle of Vinegar Hill, County Wexford. Meanwhile Hardy's force, delayed by a shortage of men and supplies, attempted to sail on August 14, but was forced to return to port by the British blockade. Without Hardy's reinforcements, Humbert was outnumbered by more than 10 to 1, and was forced to surrender to the British at Ballinamuck. Hardy and Tone finally set sail on September 6. They were intercepted by the Royal Navy near Lough Swilly in the northwest. In the ensuing four-hour battle, the *Hoche* was captured and Tone taken prisoner.

Tone was the first officer to step off the boat of French prisoners that arrived in Buncrana, County Donegal, on November 3. He was recognized

Above The British battle ships *Ethalion, Bellone,* and *Anson* fire on the French fleet on October 12, 1798, near Lough Swilly. Tone's ship, the *Hoche* was captured during this encounter.

by Sir George Hill, a former adversary at the bar who had since become a colonel in the British militia. Denying Tone all the customary rights of a prisoner of war, the British military took him to Dublin in fetters and lodged him in barracks while a court-martial was arranged.

Tone's commission in the French Army should have given the British pause. Tone accepted death as inevitable, but he was outraged to be denied due process in a court of law. Hardy wrote immediately to Lord Cornwallis, the lord lieutenant of Ireland: "I will not touch on the question of grievances you may have against this officer; but he is a French citizen, member of the French army, prisoner of war, and…should be treated with consideration and respect." Cornwallis's secretary replied: "Tone is known only to his Excellency as a traitor, who sought to return to Ireland in order to attempt by armed force what he failed to achieve by intrigue."

ATTEMPTS TO RUSH THROUGH A DEATH SENTENCE FOR TONE FAILED when some of the officers detailed to serve on Tone's court-martial received their marching orders. Not until November 10 could a full court be assembled in the Royal Barracks. It consisted of seven officers and a judge advocate. Would-be spectators crowded the streets

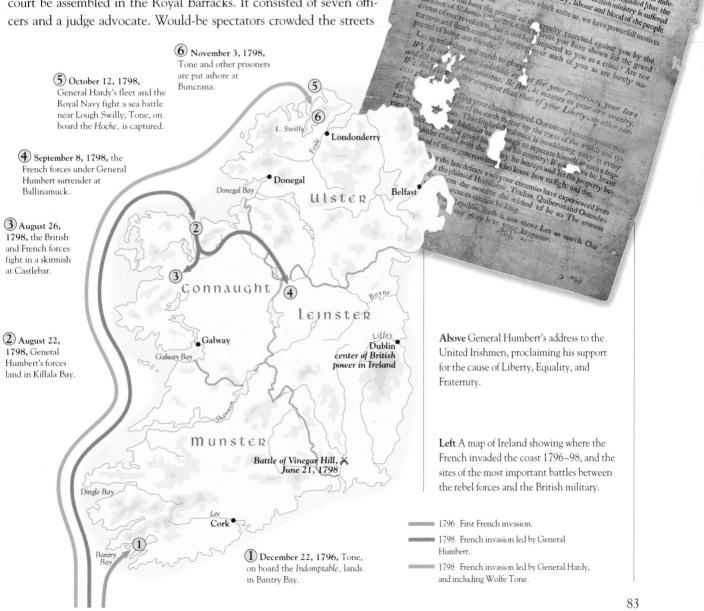

⑥ **November 3, 1798,** Tone and other prisoners are put ashore at Buncrana.

⑤ **October 12, 1798,** General Hardy's fleet and the Royal Navy fight a sea battle near Lough Swilly; Tone, on board the *Hoche*, is captured.

④ **September 8, 1798,** the French forces under General Humbert surrender at Ballinamuck.

③ **August 26, 1798,** the British and French forces fight in a skirmish at Castlebar.

② **August 22, 1798,** General Humbert's forces land in Killala Bay.

① **December 22, 1796,** Tone, on board the *Indomptable*, lands in Bantry Bay.

Battle of Vinegar Hill, June 21, 1798

Above General Humbert's address to the United Irishmen, proclaiming his support for the cause of Liberty, Equality, and Fraternity.

Left A map of Ireland showing where the French invaded the coast 1796–98, and the sites of the most important battles between the rebel forces and the British military.

—— 1796 First French invasion.

—— 1798 French invasion led by General Humbert.

—— 1798 French invasion led by General Hardy, and including Wolfe Tone.

Above Lord Cornwallis, the British viceroy and lord lieutenant of Ireland, and ultimate legal authority during Tone's trial.

"Detach Ireland from England, and she will be reduced to a second-rate power and deprived of most of her superiority over the seas. The advantages to France of an independent Ireland are so manifold that they need not be listed."

THE FRENCH DIRECTORY
to General Hoche,
June 19, 1796

in anticipation. As soon as the doors of the courtroom were opened, they thronged in and filled every corner of the hall. Tone was dressed in the uniform of a French *chef de brigade* (the equivalent of an adjutant general). The members of the court took the usual oath, and the judge advocate informed the prisoner that he was on trial before a court-martial instituted by the lord lieutenant of Ireland, Lord Cornwallis, to determine whether he had acted traitorously toward His Majesty, George III, king of Great Britain and Ireland. When asked how he pleaded, Tone admitted all the allegations against him and asked only for permission to read to the court an address he had prepared.

One of the officers of the court cautioned Tone that to admit to the facts in the indictment meant pleading guilty to treason. Tone replied that he had certainly been found in arms against King George in his native country but wished to explain his motives: "Mr. President, and gentlemen of the court-martial. It is not my intention to give the court any trouble; I admit the charge against me in the fullest extent; what I have done, I have done, and I am prepared to stand the consequences. The great object of my life has been the independence of my country; for that I have sacrificed everything that is most dear to man....I have submitted to exile and to bondage; I have exposed myself to the rage of the ocean and the fire of the enemy....I have been marched through the country in irons to the disgrace alone of whoever gave the order; I have devoted even my wife and children; after that last effort it is little to say that I am ready to lay down my life....Whatever I have said, written, or thought on the subject of Ireland I now reiterate: looking upon the connection with England to have been her bane I have endeavored by every means in my power to break that connection; I have labored in consequence to create a people in Ireland by raising three million of my countrymen to the rank of citizens."

Here the president of the court interrupted Tone, declaring that all this was irrelevant. Another member of the court called it political propaganda designed to appeal to United Irishmen in the audience. Tone offered to say no more about his motives but move on to his concluding remarks. He was warned to confine himself to whatever he could offer in his own defense. Tone was then allowed to continue.

He spoke of his disinterested motives in seeking the help of the Directory in France, where he had been adopted as a citizen and had risen to a superior rank in the army of the Republic. The serenity with which Tone expressed his sentiments held his courtroom audience spellbound as he concluded: "I will not detain you longer; in this world success is everything; I have attempted to follow the same line in which Washington succeeded and Kosciusko failed; I have attempted to establish the independence of my country; I have failed in the attempt; my life is in consequence forfeited and I submit; the court will do their duty and I shall endeavor to do mine."

There followed a long silence, finally broken by Tone himself, who asked whether it was not usual to assign an interval between sentence and execution. The judge advocate said that all this would be decided by the lord lieutenant but that if the prisoner had anything further to say, now was the moment. Tone requested a soldier's end—death by firing squad—which was the appropriate punishment for one who held a French commission. Loftus said that this request too would be submitted to the lord lieutenant.

LORD CORNWALLIS DELIVERED TONE'S SENTENCE on the spot. He was to suffer a traitor's death in 48 hours, on November 12. Tone's friends, including the orator John Philpot Curran, moved for a writ of *habeas corpus*. Since Tone had never been in the British armed services, they argued, he could not be tried by a British court-martial. The chief justice of the Court of King's Bench ordered a writ to be dispatched by the sheriff to the barracks to delay the execution. Those in charge of the barracks refused to take any notice of the writ; so the chief justice issued orders for their arrest for contempt of court. The sheriff returned again to say that he had been refused admittance to the barracks. It was clear that the military, with the connivance of the lord lieutenant, was prepared to defy the civil authorities in order to proceed with the execution.

Then came the news that Tone had apparently taken matters into his own hands. As soon as he learned that his request to be shot had been turned down, he wrote final letters to his wife and the Directory. Around midnight on November 11, he cut his throat with a smuggled penknife. He missed the carotid artery and severed his windpipe instead. At last, the execution was abandoned. Tone lingered in agony for a week before dying on November 19. The fact that Tone was held incommunicado during the last week fueled rumors that the military had murdered him rather than surrender him to the civil authorities, a belief that only added to Tone's reputation as a national hero among Protestants and Catholics alike.

Above A plaster cast of Tone's face, one of several made by his family as mementos after the body had been returned to them.

Left Tone's pocketbook, stained with blood from his suicide. The last pages of his journal, written in his prison cell, are recorded inside.

"To break the connection with England, …and to assert the independence of my country—these were my objects. To…substitute the common name of Irishman in place of the denominations of Protestant, Catholic, and Dissenter—these were my means."

WOLFE TONE'S
written declaration,
August 1796

Fighting For This Cause

THE STATE OF VIRGINIA *v.* JOHN BROWN

OCTOBER 27 – NOVEMBER 2, 1859

Above An antislavery image from an 1849 edition of *The Liberator*, the journal published by the civil rights campaigner William Lloyd Garrison (1805–79).

On Wednesday, October 19, 1859, John Brown was brought before a grand jury in the courthouse of Charles Town, the county seat of Jefferson county, Virginia. Three days earlier the 59-year-old defendant and 21 abolitionist followers had attempted to seize the federal arsenal at Harper's Ferry, a few miles from Charles Town. Brown's plan was to carry off all the arms and ammunition there, kidnap a number of leading citizens, and flee with them into the Blue Ridge Mountains. He intended to hold his prisoners hostage for an equal number of slaves, who would then be armed to further the antislavery cause. Brown also hoped to establish a stronghold in the Blue Ridge Mountains where he could offer sanctuary to escaped slaves from all over the region.

The plan miscarried. Col. Robert E. Lee led a detachment of 90 U.S. marines against the attackers, and after heavy losses Brown and his men retreated into the arsenal's engine house. Two of Brown's sons were among the 10 men killed, and the abolitionists surrendered. Nevertheless, Marine Lieutenant Israel Green struck Brown on the head with the hilt of his dress sword, knocked him down, and struck him again. Then one of Green's men ran a bayonet twice through Brown's prostrate body, badly injuring him. The prisoners were taken to Charles Town where the local court hastily arranged to try them.

BROWN AND HIS COMRADES WERE CHARGED with "feloniously conspiring with each other, and other persons unknown, to make an abolition, insurrection, and open war against the Commonwealth of Virginia," and with the additional crimes of murder and fomenting rebellion by slaves. At 10:30 A.M. on October 25, the proceedings began. A guard of 80 armed men escorted Brown and the other prisoners from jail. Another large military force surrounded the courthouse, in part to prevent sympathizers from attempting a rescue, in part as a precaution against a lynch mob in the strongly proslavery town. Brown, whose wounds were such that he could not stand without assistance, was manacled to another prisoner for support.

Charles Harding, the attorney for Jefferson county, and Andrew Hunter, counsel acting for the state of Virginia, appeared for the prosecution and requested that counsel be assigned for the defense. Brown intervened to say that a fair trial was impossible because of the extent of his wounds. Either the trial should be postponed, he argued, or his captors should simply take him out before a firing squad so that he

State and Federal Law

Since ratification of its Constitution in 1783, the United States has operated a dual system of federal and state courts. Each state has jurisdiction over crimes committed within its boundaries. Federal courts have priority in dealing with interstate issues and with violations of the U.S. Constitution.

Because John Brown seized the federal arsenal at Harper's Ferry, he should have been turned over to the federal authorities to stand trial for treason. Instead, Governor Henry A. Wise of Virginia argued that the trial had to be a quick one if Brown and his

men were not to be lynched first, and that a federal prosecution would take too long to set up. What he did not say was that his own prestige would be enhanced by trying Brown in front of the community in Virginia instead of handing him over to Washington officials. The Virginia court acted so quickly that the federal government did not have time to stop the proceedings. The semi-annual session of the Charles Town circuit had just begun, and a grand jury was already in place, ensuring that Brown stood trial within a week of capture. He was executed on the spot.

could be spared what he believed would be a mock trial. "I have now little further to ask, other than that I may not be foolishly insulted, as only cowardly barbarians insult those who fall into their power."

The court ignored Brown's objections and assigned two proslavery lawyers from Virginia, Charles J. Faulkner and Lawson Botts, to present the case for the defense. Meanwhile eight witnesses came forward to testify to the events that had taken place at Harper's Ferry. After hearing what the witnesses had to say, the presiding judge, Richard Parker, instructed the grand jury of local citizens to retire with the witnesses to hear the evidence and to decide if there was a case to answer. The grand jury returned with the decision to go ahead and prosecute.

THE PRISONERS WERE FORMALLY ACCUSED ON THE FOLLOWING DAY (Wednesday, October 26). The charges were threefold: conspiring with Negroes to cause insurrection, treason against the commonwealth of Virginia, and murder. The accused, many still suffering with injuries, were made to stand for the indictment. Brown asked for a short delay, claiming that the blows to his head had affected his hearing and that he had not heard anything that had been said at the earlier hearing. In addition, he was still waiting for his own defense counsel to arrive from the North, and in the interest of a fair trial, he requested that the court should wait as well. The judge, however, allowed the indictment to be read.

Each of the prisoners pleaded not guilty and requested separate trials. Botts, acting for the defense, asked for a delay of a few days, reiterating the

Above Harper's Ferry, shortly after Brown's raid on the federal armory. The antislavery group was finally captured in the engine house on the left of the photograph.

"I have only a short time to live—only one death to die, and I will die fighting for this cause. There will be no more peace in this land until slavery is done for."

JOHN BROWN,
after a clash with proslavery Missourians at Osawatomie, 1856

> *"Old Brown,
> Osawatomie Brown, may
> trouble you more than ever
> when you've nailed his
> coffin down."*
>
> E.C. STEDMAN'S song,
> *How Old Brown Took Harper's Ferry*,
> written during the trial,
> 1859

BIOGRAPHY

John Brown (1800–59) was born in Torrington, Connecticut. His parents, frugal and deeply religious, encouraged him to read the Bible, fear God, and keep the Commandments. He received little formal education and once said that he learned his best lessons in the "school of adversity." When the United States declared war on England in 1812, Brown worked with his father supplying beef to the American forces in Michigan. There he encountered slavery for the first time. The experience made him a determined abolitionist in later life.

At 16, Brown trained to become a minister but decided instead to follow his father into tanning and farming. He married Dianthe Lusk in 1820, and the couple had seven children before her death 12 years later. Within a year Brown married Mary Anne Day, who bore him 13 children. His failed business ventures kept the family constantly on the move, in debt, and often on the verge of starvation. In addition, he began to act on his antislavery beliefs.

When Brown attacked Harper's Ferry in 1859, he believed that he was an instrument of God's will, destined to die fighting for his cause. Many accused him of monomania, but his beliefs and actions won him a place in international history.

Above A photograph of John Brown in a posture of characteristic determination.

points that Brown had made. Judge Parker said that unless Brown's injuries were such as to render him *non compos mentis* there could be no delay, as the legal term of the court was about to run out. A physician declared that Brown's wounds did not affect his powers of reasoning or recollection, and the judge decided that Brown should be the first of the defendants to be tried. A preliminary jury of 24 men, all of them slave owners, was selected by the judge. Defense counsel had the right to object to eight of them; despite the openly stated bias of some of the prospective jurors, the defense remained silent. The final selection of 12 jury members was decided by lot.

THE TRIAL BEGAN ON THURSDAY, OCTOBER 27. Brown, still too weak to walk, was helped into court by two warders. He then lay down within the bar, a move considered by the prosecution to be an act of defiance. Some Northern sympathizers had petitioned the court for clemency on the grounds that Brown was insane, but he rejected their attempts because it would demean his commitment to the cause. He asked again for a delay to allow for his recuperation and for his Northern counsel to arrive. Once again the prosecution opposed this, claiming that Brown was playing for time until a rescue could be mounted.

THE ABOLITIONIST CAUSE

In the 20 years that followed the American Revolution, slavery was abolished throughout the northern part of the United States. When, in 1833, slavery was finally abolished throughout the British Empire, a mass of abolitionist propaganda flooded into the United States from Britain, reinforcing the campaign throughout the southern states. The work of antislavery societies—of which there were 2,000 by 1840 with a membership of some 200,000 campaigners—did much to disseminate information about the evils of slavery. By the 1840s the abolitionist cause had gained militant activists in the U.S. Congress, and the issue dominated national politics.

The culmination of so much hard-hitting propaganda was the publication of Harriet Beecher Stowe's novel *Uncle Tom's Cabin*, which sold an astonishing 1.5 million copies in 1852 alone. Its influence on public opinion was enormous. Soon a network of dedicated people began to help escaped slaves to reach Canada or any of the abolitionist "free-soil" states, mostly in the North.

In 1854 the Democrats sponsored the Kansas-Nebraska Act, which allowed the residents of those territories to outlaw slavery within their own borders. Enforcement of the act was met with bitter opposition, since most of the neighboring southern states were fiercely proslavery. Numerous brawls

ensued when proslavery settlers from Missouri (popularly known as border ruffians) began crossing into the territories and raiding the settlements of free-soil abolitionists. Five of John Brown's sons moved to Kansas in 1854 to join the free-soil cause. The following year they appealed to their father for help against a steady stream of attack from slave owners. Brown and other members of his family formed a vigilante militia in Kansas to release as many slaves as possible.

On May 24–25, 1856, John Brown organized an assault on Pottawatomie Creek in retaliation for an attack by border ruffians on the town of Lawrence on May 21. After several of these incidents, the state was dubbed "Bleeding Kansas" by the Republicans.

Below Violence breaks out at what was intended to be a peace conference held at Fort Scott, Kansas, between representatives of the local free-soilers and slave owners from the neighboring state of Missouri.

The jury was sworn in and the indictment read; Brown pleaded not guilty. Because Charles Faulkner refused to continue representing Brown, a new defense counsel, Thomas C. Green, was assigned. Green began by making three vital points. First, treason could be proven only if it could be demonstrated that Brown intended to set up a separate government in the state of Virginia, and no evidence had been provided of this. Second, a charge of conspiracy with slaves could be tried by a Virginia court only if the conspiracy took place wholly within Virginia's state limits. If part of the conspiracy was hatched, say, in the state of Maryland, this made the offense an interstate, or federal, matter, especially if the alleged conspiracy took place on federal territory at the Harper's Ferry arsenal. Third, the charge of murder incontestably did relate to the events that took place at Harper's Ferry, which was under federal jurisdiction, so Brown and his fellows could not legally be tried by the state of Virginia.

The prosecution could make no effective answer to these points. Instead it bombarded the court with details of the Harper's Ferry attack,

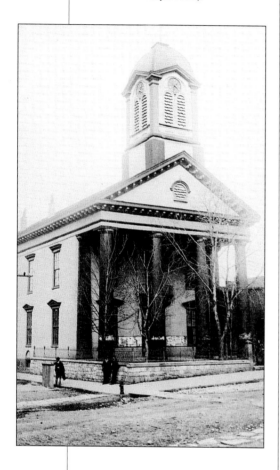

Below The courthouse in Charles Town where John Brown was tried, located about 10 miles from Harper's Ferry.

"This court acknowledges, as I suppose, the validity of the law of God.... That teaches me that 'whatsoever I would that men should do unto me I should do even so to them.'"

JOHN BROWN
in his final words to the court,
November 2, 1859

summoning witness after witness to make essentially the same point. When Green tried to call witnesses for the defense, none appeared, and Brown struggled to his feet protesting that it was nonsense to call the proceedings a fair trial. The defense witnesses had either not been subpoenaed or had ignored the summons through fear of reprisal; his pleas for a delay had been ignored; and the $260 in cash that he had on his person when arrested had been taken away to prevent him from hiring people to run errands and round up his witnesses. Brown then lay down, drew the blanket over him, and appeared to go to sleep. Upon hearing that Brown's Northern advocates were arriving that night, the court adjourned until the following day.

The court reconvened on Saturday, October 29, at 10 A.M. Brown was brought in and laid on his pallet. His new lawyers were introduced—Samuel Chilton of Washington and Hiram Griswold of Ohio. They requested a delay to acquaint themselves with information that should have been passed on to them by the decamped Faulkner, but Judge Parker refused. They called a few defense witnesses, but the judge insisted that the trial move swiftly to the summations. When Brown's attorneys asked for time to prepare the defense speech in light of national interest in the case, the judge refused on the ground that the jury wanted to go home early. Under extreme pressure, Judge Parker adjourned the court until the following Monday morning, on the condition that the final speech for the defense would not be longer than 2½ hours.

THE COURT RECONVENED ON MONDAY, OCTOBER 31, early in the morning. Both sides summed up, and the jury, after retiring for three-quarters of an hour, found Brown guilty on all three charges. Two days later, Brown limped into court and sat by his counsel. When asked by the clerk of the court if he had anything to say as to why sentence should not be passed, Brown was taken by surprise, for the trials of the others were still in progress, and he had expected that all the sentences would be passed at the same time. Nevertheless, he took the opportunity to outline his motives to the court.

Brown's only defense was that he saw himself as an instrument in the hands of Divine Providence a claim many saw as evidence of insanity. His sole intention, he said, was not to start a revolution, but to free slaves. The winter before, he had guided slaves from Missouri to freedom in Canada without a shot being fired in anger. "I feel no consciousness of guilt," he declared. "I never had any design against the life of any person, nor any disposition to commit treason, or excite slaves to rebel, or make any general insurrection. I never encouraged any man to do so." Had he done for whites what he did for the slaves, he continued, he would be a national hero and would be rewarded rather than punished.

Brown then appealed to a higher, divine court: "I believe that to have interfered as I have done...in behalf of His despised poor, was not wrong, but right. Now, if it

is deemed necessary that I should forfeit my life for the furtherance of the ends of justice, and mingle my blood…with the blood of millions in this slave country whose rights are disregarded by wicked, cruel, and unjust enactments—I submit: so let it be done."

THE JUDGE CONDEMNED BROWN TO HANG on Friday, December 2, 1859. After the sentence was pronounced, the garrison of Virginia received 17 separate affidavits by neighbors and friends attesting to Brown's insanity and requesting a reprieve on the grounds that he had not known what he was doing. All these were ignored, but Brown's power to inspire sympathy for his cause was so great that the court took steps to discourage any last minute attempts to rescue him. As many soldiers as the state of Virginia could muster were ordered to surround the gallows in Charles Town and to prevent any civilians from witnessing the execution.

Brown's cause survived him. Sixteen months after the events at Harper's Ferry, the North was at war with the South in a conflict that eventually ended legal slavery in the United States. On January 1, 1863, President Abraham Lincoln signed a proclamation emancipating the slaves.

"I, John Brown, am now quite certain that the crimes of this guilty land will never be purged away but with blood. I had as I now think, mainly flattered myself that without very much bloodshed it might be done."

JOHN BROWN
on the day of his execution,
December 2, 1859

Below A note in Brown's own hand, found by his guards at Charles Town jail. In it (see above) he predicts the civil war.

Below A contemporary etching of John Brown's execution. The entire area was cleared of civilians because the authorities feared a rescue mission or a riot.

J'Accuse

The French Army v. Alfred Dreyfus

August 7 – September 9, 1899

Above The memorandum, or *bordereau*, intercepted by the French Intelligence Service in September 1894, containing evidence of spying. Handwriting experts wrongly attributed authorship to Dreyfus.

In the 20-year period following France's humiliating defeat in the Franco-Prussian war of 1870–71, the French government dedicated itself to keeping official secrets out of Prussian hands. In 1894 Commandant Hubert-Joseph Henry of the Section of Statistics, a division of the War Office devoted to espionage, received from a French spy the contents of a wastebasket used by the German attaché in Paris. As Henry pieced together the torn scraps of a memorandum, he realized that someone in the French Army must be feeding military information to the Germans. The only clues to the spy's identity were the signature D and the handwriting. Henry pointed the finger at a young captain named Alfred Dreyfus. Not only was Dreyfus from Alsace, a former French territory that had been annexed by Germany in 1871, but he was a Jewish officer in a largely Roman Catholic army at a time when anti-Semitism was rife. Three out of five handwriting specialists verified his handwriting as that on the memorandum (or *bordereau*, as it was called).

Dreyfus was court-martialed in 1894, found guilty, publicly stripped of his rank, and transported to Devil's Island, a penal colony off French Guiana. More than a year later, French intelligence agents brought to Colonel Georges Picquart, head of the Intelligence Service, fragments of a telegram that were discovered in the same wastebasket in which the *bordereau* had been found. This communiqué, addressed to a Major Esterhazy, thanked him for information received. Esterhazy's handwriting, it turned out, matched that on the *bordereau*. When Picquart took the matter to his superior, General Gonse, he was reprimanded and asked: "What difference does it make to you if that Jew remains on Devil's Island?"

Picquart, convinced that a gross injustice had been done, refused to drop his investigation of Esterhazy. Commandant Henry—who wanted both to please his superiors and to protect his friend Esterhazy—decided to forge a document containing definitive proof of Dreyfus's guilt. Picquart was then

Appeal to the Higher Court

Normally in the 19th century all appeals, whether from civil or military courts, went to the French Supreme Court, which was composed of various chambers. In 1898 the Criminal Appeal Division scheduled to hear Dreyfus's appeal included a number of Jewish judges. Because the appeals court had to be above suspicion, and the presence of the Jewish judges aroused the suspicion of favoritism for Captain Dreyfus, the Chamber of Deputies (France's political assembly) felt that the case should be heard by another body. A special appeals court was created especially to review the 1894 case. The time it took to agree on its composition accounted for the long delay between Major Esterhazy's confession and the second Dreyfus trial. This second court set aside the original court-martial's verdict, opening the way for the later Rennes trial.

Le Petit Journal

SUPPLÉMENT ILLUSTRÉ

Le Petit Journal
CHAQUE JOUR 5 CENTIMES

Le Supplément illustré
CHAQUE SEMAINE 5 CENTIMES

Huit pages : CINQ centimes

ABONNEMENTS

	TROIS MOIS	SIX MOIS	UN AN
PARIS	1 fr.	2 fr.	3 fr. 50
DÉPARTEMENTS	1 fr.	2 fr.	4 fr.
ÉTRANGER	150	350	5 fr.

Sixième année — DIMANCHE 13 JANVIER 1895 — Numéro 217

LE TRAITRE
Dégradation d'Alfred Dreyfus

Above An artist's impression of the degradation of Dreyfus, on the cover of a Paris journal, 1895.

BIOGRAPHY

Alfred Dreyfus (1859–1935) was born at Mulhausen in Alsace, the son of a rich Jewish manufacturer. In 1871, when Alsace was annexed to Germany, Dreyfus's family opted to take French citizenship. Dreyfus was sent to Paris, where at the age of 15 he began a military career. He had advanced through 19 years of service to the rank of captain by the time the scandal of 1894 broke and he was falsely accused of leaking secrets to the Germans. Later that year he was court-martialed and transported to the penal colony of Devil's Island, off the coast of French Guiana. The controversy over the injustice of his trial polarized public opinion: the Catholic Church, the French Army, and right-wing politicians applauded his sentence; the Freemasons, social liberals, and the political left deplored it. Anti-Semitism lay barely beneath the surface, and passions ran so high that serious commentators thought that France verged on civil war. After five years of exile, Dreyfus was pardoned in 1899 and restored to his rank in 1906.

"My honor belongs to me; it is the patrimony of my children. I have demanded that honor from my country."

ALFRED DREYFUS,
in a letter to his wife
from Devil's Island,
1898

dismissed. Meanwhile, Mathieu Dreyfus, the convicted man's brother, discovered that Esterhazy's handwriting exactly matched that on the *bordereau*. He was given the information by a stockbroker who, by chance, had bought a facsimile of the *bordereau* and recognized the handwriting of one of his clients. Mathieu initiated a vigorous attack in the press against the army and accused Esterhazy of the original offense. The groundswell of pro-Dreyfus feeling that followed reached such proportions that the French Army was forced to court-martial Esterhazy. Nonetheless, the military refused to acknowledge any mistake and acquitted Esterhazy in January 1898.

On January 13, 1898, the French novelist Émile Zola joined the fray. He published in a special edition of the newspaper *L'Aurore* an open letter to the president, beginning with the words *"J'accuse."* In this very public challenge, Zola took up the cause of Dreyfus. He summarized the affair for the public and accused the army's high command and all the investigators, military judges, and handwriting experts of lies, treachery, and "monstrous partiality." In just a few hours, more than 200,000 copies of the paper sold.

The army sued Zola and *L'Aurore* for libel. To Dreyfus supporters, Zola's trial seemed an ideal opportunity to press for the Dreyfus case to be reopened. But once again officialdom protected its own; the judges suppressed evidence and secured a quick conviction for Zola, who fled to London to avoid imprisonment. Mathieu Dreyfus continued the fight, and months later his patience was rewarded. On August 31, 1898, the minister of war, Godefroy Cavaignac, discovered that the document containing the definitive proof against Dreyfus had in fact been forged by Commandant Henry. Cavaignac and the army chief of staff resigned, Henry cut his own throat, and a month later Major Esterhazy confessed and fled to London.

IN SEPTEMBER 1898 DREYFUS'S WIFE, LUCIE, petitioned the army to reopen the case, but the government delayed. Tension mounted in Paris: anti-Semites conducted newspaper campaigns, while nationalists demonstrated to voice their confidence in the army. By February 1899, President

Below A postcard showing a view of Devil's Island. Dreyfus's hut is marked with an "X."

Émile Loubet pushed for the affair to be resolved quickly. The 1900 Universal Exhibition was due to be held in Paris, and an ongoing scandal surrounding Dreyfus's wrongful conviction could only embarrass France. In spring 1899 the United Courts of Appeals set aside the 1894 sentence and pinned the guilt for writing the *bordereau* on Esterhazy. That was enough to free Dreyfus, but without another court-martial, it left the story of anti-Semitism untold. Dreyfus wanted a new trial.

He arrived at the military prison at Rennes in Brittany on July 1, 1899. Five years on Devil's Island had exacted a heavy toll: although he was only 39, Dreyfus was emaciated, his hair was thin and white, and his voice was badly damaged. For a month, his brother and the defense team briefed him on what had happened during his exile and prepared for the new court-martial. The authorities, meanwhile, faced the hundreds of journalists and lawyers who descended on Rennes; at the same time, they dealt with the more troubling large number of death threats against Dreyfus. By the time the trial began on August 7, 1899, so many troops and police had been brought into the town that Rennes looked like a fortress under siege. The local *lycée* (school) was prepared as the courtroom.

DURING THE FIVE-WEEK TRIAL the prosecution called 70 witnesses, the defense 20. The same people who had given evidence in 1894 returned to accuse Dreyfus of treason, gambling, and womanizing. The judges ignored the prosecution's digressions and interruptions but cut the defense short whenever possible. The military establishment was not about to let justice take its course at the expense of the army.

Reporting for *La Petite République*, the French Socialist leader Jean Jaurès wrote of Dreyfus: "How deep

Right A photograph of Émile Zola, inscribed "To Captain Alfred Dreyfus admiration and affection." The famous author threw his full influence behind the Dreyfus cause.

Below Zola's open letter to the president of France, published in *L'Aurore* on January 13, 1898—the day after Esterhazy's acquittal—denouncing the dishonesty of the French authorities.

> *"I accuse the first court-martial of having violated the law in convicting a defendant on the basis of a document kept secret. I accuse the second court-martial [Esterhazy's]...of knowingly acquitting a guilty man."*
>
> ÉMILE ZOLA'S
> open letter in *L'Aurore*,
> January 13, 1898

was my feeling of pity when I first saw him.…His whole presence reveals depths of unspeakable suffering." Dreyfus addressed the chief judge with courage: "For five years…I have suffered everything, but once again for the honor of my name and that of my children I repeat, I am innocent."

Gen. Auguste Mercier, chief prosecutor and former minister of war, insisted that even if no proof existed that Dreyfus was a spy, circumstantial evidence together with his own "moral conviction" should tip the scales of the law. Mercier claimed that if he had the slightest doubt of Dreyfus's guilt he would say so. Dreyfus was on his feet instantly, and croaked, "Then say it, say it, because you are lying." The general replied: "I have just said—" but Dreyfus interrupted him. "It is your duty," he cried. To mixed applause and hisses from the crowd, a guard pulled Dreyfus back into his chair.

One week into the trial, on August 14, Dreyfus's lawyer, Fernand Labori, failed to appear for the day's proceedings. News soon arrived that he had been shot in the back, almost certainly in an assassination attempt. Labori recovered from his wounds and eight days later was back in court. The trial dragged on into September. The judges' dilemma was summed up by an officer at the time: "I am convinced of Dreyfus's innocence, but if it were for me to judge I would condemn him again for the honor of the army." The high command could not allow justice for a captain to prevail over the reputation of the army and, as they saw it, the security of France itself.

Below A colored lithograph from 1898 telling the Dreyfus story in pictures and captions.

> *"What sustained me was the unshakable faith that France would one day proclaim my innocence to the world."*
>
> ALFRED DREYFUS
> writing to Picquart on hearing the news of his vindication, July 12, 1906

CHRONOLOGY

1894 Captain Henry discovers the *bordereau*, evidence of a spy in the French army.

1894 Dreyfus is court-martialed and sent to Devil's Island.

January 1898 Esterhazy is court-martialed and found innocent.

August 1898 Minister of war discovers Henry's forged document incriminating Dreyfus.

September 1898 Esterhazy confesses and flees to London.

Spring 1899 United Courts of Appeals sets aside the guilty verdict of the 1894 court-martial.

June 1899 Dreyfus is brought back from Devil's Island.

August 1899 Trial to clear Dreyfus's name begins.

September 1899 Dreyfus, found guilty of high treason, appeals to the president, and sentence is annulled.

July 1906 High Court of Appeal annuls verdict of 1899 court-martial. Dreyfus is restored to his rank and awarded the Legion of Honor.

HISTOIRE D'UN INNOCENT

Un beau matin, un colonel d'État-Major, le brave et magnifique colonel Picquart, découvrit le vrai traître. Il s'écria alors: « Il faut sauver l'innocent et punir le coupable! »

Il y eut aussi des civils comme Zola, Bernard Lazare, Jaurès, Duclaux (celui qui guérit la rage), qui réclamèrent la justice pour l'innocent, car eux aussi avaient découvert le vrai traître.

C'était un autre officier, le pire des mauvais sujets, appelé Esterhazy, à la solde de Prusse et qui voulait se faire uhlan pour massacrer des Français.

Pour mieux tromper la France, ils firent emprisonner le colonel Picquart et voulurent faire condamner Zola, sous prétexte d'insultes à l'armée, mais ils n'y réussirent pas.

Les mensonges ont les jambes courtes. Henry, pris la main dans le sac, avoue avoir fabriqué les faux papiers. On l'arrête, mais ses remords sont si terribles qu'il se coupe la gorge.

L'autre faussaire, Du Paty, fut chassé l'armée. Quant au vrai traître, Esterhazy s'enfuit en Allemagne. Bon voyage! monsieur le uhlan!

THE SEVEN JUDGES FOUND DREYFUS GUILTY OF HIGH TREASON by a 5 to 2 majority, recording their verdict on September 9, after one hour's deliberation. However, they also pronounced that "extenuating circumstances prevailed in the case" and sentenced him to 10 years' detention, 5 of which he had already served. Across France, Dreyfus opponents erupted with joy, Dreyfus supporters with anger. Mathieu Dreyfus, who had worked tirelessly on his brother's behalf, left at once for Paris to begin lobbying for a pardon. Mathieu knew his brother could not survive another term of imprisonment. He asked Prime Minister René Waldeck-Rousseau to secure an immediate presidential pardon, which he believed would indicate a clear rejection of the army's judgment. World opinion was behind him. Demonstrations were held in Antwerp, Milan, Naples, London, and New York. The prime minister wanted above all to end the affair and to restore public tranquillity. A compromise on both sides was required. If Dreyfus would accept the verdict of guilty and withdraw his petition against it, the prime minister would agree to a pardon. Mathieu, concerned now only with saving his brother's life, persuaded Dreyfus that this was the best course of action.

A decree signed on September 19 annulled Dreyfus's sentence and canceled his military degradation. The army could take some satisfaction from the knowledge that the military judges' verdict of guilty had been accepted, but many Dreyfus supporters remained furious that his name had still not been cleared. Dreyfus himself felt that his case at least attempted to expose and discredit institutionalized anti-Semitism. In his memoirs he described the affair as, "…an accomplishment that will resound into the most distant future, because it will have marked a turning point in the history of humanity, a grandiose stage on the road to an era of immense progress for the ideas of freedom, justice, and social solidarity."

POSTSCRIPT

On September 29, 1902, Émile Zola died in Paris. Dreyfus kept a vigil over Zola's body through the night before his funeral and stood at the graveside, listening to an oration devoted to Zola's lifetime struggle on behalf of justice and truth. Although Zola did not live to see it, Dreyfus eventually achieved the victory with honor for which Zola had expatriated himself. On July 11, 1906, France's High Court of Appeal voted by 31 votes to 18 to annul the verdict of the Rennes court-martial in its entirety and *sans renvoi* (without review). Dreyfus had waited 12 years, almost to the day, to be vindicated of guilt.

On July 13, a vote in the French Senate restored Dreyfus to his rank as a captain, gave him the additional rank of squadron chief, and awarded him the Cross of the Legion of Honor. A few months later Dreyfus retired from the army and retreated into family life.

Paris. — Imp. Pochy

Du Paty et Henry, qui ne voulaient r revenir Dreyfus, se mirent à fabri- faux papiers qu'ils mirent sur son et protégèrent Esterhazy, le traître.

our prochain, on rendra ses galons à s et la France glorieuse réparera noble- njustice faite à un de ses soldats les voués.

Below The 1896 telegram sent to Esterhazy thanking him for information received. At the 1899 appeals court hearing, it confirmed Esterhazy's guilt and cleared Dreyfus.

The Nuremberg Trials

THE ALLIED NATIONS v. NAZI LEADERS

NOVEMBER 20, 1945 – OCTOBER 1, 1946

Above The Iron Cross, a German military decoration instituted in 1813 for exceptional bravery or leadership. Hitler revived the medal in 1939, imprinting it with the swastika, the Nazi symbol.

Outlawing War

The Nuremberg Trials became a landmark in legal history. They were test cases for a new international law of war, superseding laws in existence, many of which had never been formally codified. The legal framework was formulated by a team of New York lawyers, who during the winter of 1944–45 created an international military tribunal to try Nazi leaders, rather than use the court-martial system of individual victor nations. This avoided the need for several national trials, where the defendants would have been tried for crimes committed against each individual country. At the insistence of the United States, which had a more comprehensive vision of a neutral trial and particularly wanted to avoid the accusation of exercising victors' justice, the legal proceedings were thorough and the verdict carefully considered. Since the United States took a leading role, Anglo-American adversarial procedures took precedence at the tribunal over the European inquisitorial system, in which witnesses are not cross-examined and the defendants do not testify under oath. Despite controversy over the validity of some of the charges, the proceedings at Nuremberg have generally been accepted as a guide to drawing up subsequent charges under international law.

As the outcome of World War II became inevitable, the victorious Allied leaders began to consider how to deal with high-ranking Nazis after peace was restored. International law provided no grounds for prosecuting war criminals (one of the reasons why a similar attempt to hang the Kaiser after World War I had failed). But as the full extent of the horrors enacted under Adolf Hitler came to light, the evidence cried out for justice. The British prime minister, Winston Churchill, suggested that Nazi leaders be shot without trial, but Henry L. Stimson, the U.S. secretary of war, opposed him. In the summer of 1944 Stimson persuaded President Franklin D. Roosevelt that the Nazi leaders should be tried before an international court. He argued that if the Nazi leaders were executed by firing squad, the world would say that the Allies had been afraid to bring them to trial. Moreover, he suggested, a war-crimes trial would inaugurate a new era in which war was outlawed. The Allies embraced this plan and, under the influence of the newly formed United Nations, signed the London Agreement on August 8, 1945, establishing an international military tribunal to bring major war criminals to trial.

THE CHARGES WERE DRAWN UP ON FOUR COUNTS. Count one was conspiracy to wage wars of aggression in violation of international agreements. Count two was crimes against peace. Count three was war crimes—particularly breaching international agreements about the treatment of prisoners of war. And count four, probably the most important in the Nuremberg

Above American armed guards check observers' security passes outside the Nuremberg courtroom.

THE FINAL SOLUTION

In the 1930s and 40s the watching world was horrified by Adolf Hitler's treatment of the Jews in Europe. According to *Mein Kampf*, Hitler's account of his vision published in 1925, the goals that he set himself as an international leader were to destroy communism and to break the financial power of the Jewish people. The Nazi party had begun to persecute Jewish citizens in the 1920s, even before Hitler became influential. When Hitler came to power in 1933, he intensified anti-Semitic activity with a series of decrees. Two years later, in September 1935, he signed the Nuremberg laws, which deprived German Jews of citizenship on redefined racial grounds and forbade marriage and sexual relations with Germans of "pure blood."

In the prewar years, anti-Semitism continued to grow, despite opposition through the League of Nations. Jewish passports were stamped with a red "J," and Jews were barred from the professions. During 1933–38 approximately half of the Jewish population (about 500,000 people) fled from Germany. Meanwhile the Nazi Party set up concentration camps to contain "undesirables," political and religious dissidents, Gypsies, trade unionists, homosexuals, and Jews. Buchenwald was established in 1937, and the Nazi Party began to deport Jews there as well. Following *Kristallnacht* in 1938, when Nazi sympathizers destroyed hundreds of Jewish properties, more than 35,000 Jews were arrested, bringing the numbers in the camps to about 60,000.

Above A group of survivors from Mauthausen, a slave-labor camp in Nazi-occupied Austria. Forty percent of prisoners died there every year.

Following Germany's invasion of the Soviet Union in June 1941, the camps overflowed and almost 1.5 million Jews were executed by firing squad. But Himmler needed a more efficient method, and he ordered his deputy, Reinhard Heydrich, to organize a "final solution." By then emigration from occupied Europe had been forbidden and the Jewish population confined to ghettos. At the Wannsee Conference (January 20, 1942) Heydrich authorized the use of death camps, where gas chambers were disguised as communal showers. Fully operational death camps at Chelmno, Belzec, Sobibor, Treblinka, and Auschwitz were set up by the middle of 1942, and between then and 1945 the Nazis murdered another 4.2 million Jews with Zyklon-B gas. In all nearly 6 million Jews were killed in the course of the notorious Final Solution.

trials, was crimes against humanity—murder, extermination, enslavement, deportation, and other inhumane acts against civilian populations.

The London Agreement had little basis in international law. Conventions at Geneva and the Hague and the Kellogg–Briand pact of 1928 (which condemned war) provided precedents. But in effect the International Military Tribunal created new laws and then applied them retroactively. The accused were put on trial for acts that were not recognized as crimes when they committed them. Yet the sense of outrage in 1945 over Nazi atrocities compelled the Allies to seek public retribution.

International feeling ran particularly high over the treatment of the Jews. Nazi records produced at the trial showed that approximately six million Jews had perished, along with Communists, homosexuals, and

"I herewith commission you to carry out all preparations with regard to…a total solution of the Jewish question in those territories of Europe that are under German influence."

HERMANN GOERING'S
order to Heydrich,
July 31, 1941

Above A can that originally contained Zyklon-B gas, retrieved from a death camp after liberation by the Allies. The Nazis used the gas to kill Jews, Gypsies, and people from other minority groups.

Below Robert H. Jackson (left), the chief prosecutor for the United States, and Uri Pokrovski, assistant prosecutor for the Soviet Union listen to the summing up speeches for the defense on April 10, 1946.

blacks. Establishing guilt for this slaughter was problematic. Hitler had committed suicide on April 30, 1945, to avoid being taken captive. Goebbels, his minister for propaganda, killed himself and his family in Hitler's bunker on May 1. Himmler and Heydrich, the principal architects of the Nazi agenda against the Jews, were also dead, Himmler by his own hand and Heydrich from wounds received in an assassination attempt. Of the party leaders, only Reichsmarshall Hermann Goering was in Allied hands, and although it was established that he had been a Nazi decision maker, documentary evidence linking him conclusively to what would later be known as the Holocaust could not be produced.

THE INTERNATIONAL MILITARY TRIBUNAL OPENED IN NUREMBERG, Germany, on November 20, 1945, and continued for almost a year. The tribunal consisted of eight judges, two each from the United States, Britain, the Soviet Union, and France. For the prosecution there was a team of 23 U.S. attorneys headed by Judge Robert H. Jackson, 7 British barristers headed by Sir David Maxwell-Fyfe and the British attorney general Sir Hartley Shawcross, 5 French advocates, and 11 Soviet lawyers. The first two days were taken up with reading aloud a 30,000-word indictment. It was a tedious beginning to lengthy proceedings that would eventually require 400 open sessions of court, during which everything said was translated into English, German, French, and Russian. The indictment categorized Nazi crimes under the four counts named in the London Agreement. Count one, conspiracy to wage aggressive (undeclared) war, recapitulated the history of the Nazi movement, since the charges centered on the activities of the Nazi Party as a warmongering organization and its aggression against Austria, Czechoslovakia, and Poland. Count two, crimes against peace, dealt with Germany's undeclared hostilities against Denmark, Norway, Belgium, the Netherlands, Yugoslavia, Greece, and the Soviet Union. It also included the war against Britain and France, though the Allies, not the Germans, initiated hostilities. Counts three and four distinguished war crimes—the execution of British airmen and escaped prisoners of war, the starvation of Russian prisoners of war, the shelling of torpedoed merchant seamen—from crimes against humanity, including the massacre of Jews, deporting civilians for slave labor, killing hostages, plundering property, and conscripting civilian labor.

While the indictment was read, most of the defendants stared blankly ahead, apparently not listening to the charges. Rudolf Hess read a novel in the dock and acted as though absorbed in it throughout the opening days. Only Goering reacted to events around him. When the charges listed the theft of 87 million bottles of French champagne, he smiled at the prosecution. Extracts from a huge mass of evidence were quoted to support the indictment. Major Airey Neave, a British observer, described an atmosphere of "shocked stillness" as the court listened to Hitler's

Above Correspondents in the pressroom sort through the paperwork from just one day in court.

confidential orders. His brief to staff officers dated November 29, 1941, began: "The Führer has decided to erase from the face of the earth the city of St. Petersburg...." Even the legal professionals were visibly emotional as they presented the indictment. A French prosecutor, reading aloud from documents on the occupation of France, broke down when he came to the words, "Out of a convoy of 230 French women deported from Compiègne to Auschwitz in January 1943, 180 died of exhaustion within four months." By the end of the two-day opening session, Goering sat with his head in his hands. The other defendants continued to stare ahead or to read.

On the third day the defendants entered their pleas. On being asked if he pleaded guilty or not guilty, Goering began to make a fully prepared rebuttal of the charges but was cut short by the presiding judge. He entered a plea of "not guilty in the sense of the indictment." The other defendants responded in various ways, from Jodl's declaration, "I have a clear conscience before God and my people," to Hess's enigmatic answer, "Nein," which was entered, like the other pleas, as "not guilty."

Right Cartoons of Hess and Goering by the Russian artist Boris Yefimov, drawn for *Red Star*, December 6, 1945.

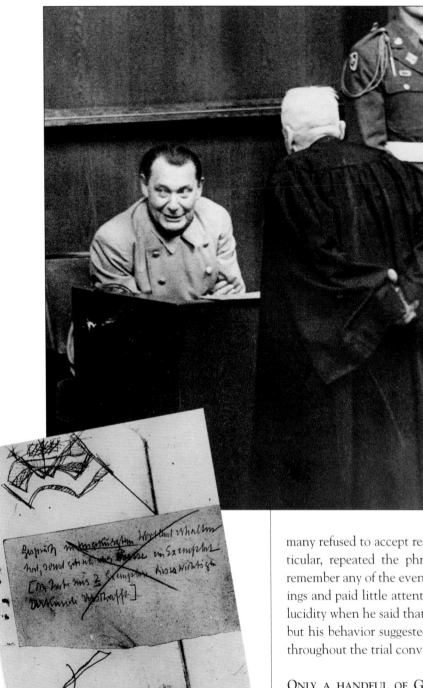

Above Some of Goering's doodles and notes to himself, all made in idle moments during the proceedings.

THE PROSECUTION OPENED ITS CASE against the defendants a few days later and presented its most dramatic piece of evidence on November 29, 1945—a film shot by Allied troops in the spring of that year when they liberated a series of German concentration camps. Each one of the defendants shared in the responsibility, the prosecution declared, for what the court was about to see. As the camera focused on piles of corpses at Belsen, and the voice of the commentator described the horror around him, members of the court sobbed in the darkened room. Many of the spectators were themselves survivors of the death camps, and several had to be taken out of the courtroom. Only the dock was illuminated (for security reasons), and the defendants' reactions were on full view. Few of them could bear to watch. Walther Funk and Hans Fritzsche had tears streaming down their cheeks, and Hjalmar Schacht, who had personal experience of the camps, sat with his back to the screen.

During the questioning that followed, many refused to accept responsibility for what had happened. Hess, in particular, repeated the phrase, "I don't understand," and claimed not to remember any of the events. He often slept in the dock during the proceedings and paid little attention to anything that was said. He had periods of lucidity when he said that he was only pretending to have lost his memory, but his behavior suggested mental instability, and his non sequitur replies throughout the trial convinced the court that he was insane.

ONLY A HANDFUL OF GERMAN LAWYERS APPEARED FOR THE DEFENSE. They labored under disadvantages that ranged from receiving inferior food to lacking adequate backup staff. More to the point, certain lines of argument had been ruled out by the terms of the charter. The defense could not raise the issue of the legitimacy of the tribunal by, for example, pointing out that the crimes listed in the indictment were specified as illegal acts only after the war was over. Nor could they use the expression "victors' justice" or resort to the *tu quoque* ("you did it too") argument by mentioning the deliberate Allied bombing of civilians in the raids on Hamburg, Berlin, and Dresden. The net effect of the London Agreement was to limit the defense to rebuttal of evidence put forward by the prosecution. Answering charges on count one—waging aggressive war—they dared not antagonize Soviet members of the tribunal by mentioning that Hitler could wage such war only because of the Russo-German pact of 1939. Before the Soviet Union joined the Allies, it had a nonaggression treaty with the Nazis in which each side promised not to interfere with the other's strategy. The defense was also barred from pointing out that the Nazis were on trial for aggressive war, yet another nation guilty of such action (the Soviet Union against Finland in 1939 and against Japan in 1945) was represented on the bench.

The most effective counterarguments to the prosecution were put forward by the defendants themselves, and especially by Goering. He took the stand on March 13, 1946, armed with a huge sheaf of notes. Major Airey Neave wrote that his manner in the dock was "menacing and confi- dent....He might have been addressing the Nuremberg rally, not the Nuremberg tribunal." Goering began: "Though I received orders from the Führer, I assume full responsibility for them. They bear my signature. I issued them. Consequently I do not propose to hide behind the Führer's order." Over the following four days he projected a heroic vision of Hitler and the Nazi party, while the other prisoners nodded in agreement. His ability as an advocate shocked members of the prosecution, and a few admitted off the record that he had impressed them by his courage. Sir Norman Birkett, on the British team, wondered if it had been a mistake to let Goering testify. The purpose of the trial, he wrote, was to discredit the Nazis. "If for any reason that design should fail, then the fears of those who thought the holding of any trial to be a mistake would be in some measure justified." The U.S. prosecutor, Robert H. Jackson, was ill-prepared to cross-examine such an able witness and was outmaneuvered in his opening questions. When he began to fumble with his papers, Goering offered in a loud voice to help him continue. At one point Jackson flung down his ear- phones in rage at one of Goering's long replies.

The presentation of the prosecution's evidence, and cross-examination of the 22 accused men (all of whom appeared in court except one, Bormann, who was tried in absentia), lasted until July 1946. Beginning on July 26, the prosecution presented its final arguments, and the court adjourned for a month while the judges considered the evidence.

ON OCTOBER 1 THE JUDGES DELIVERED THEIR VERDICT. Only three of the 22 defendants were acquitted—Papen, Schacht, and Fritzsche. Nine men found guilty of the less heinous crimes received lengthy terms of imprison- ment. Eleven defendants were found guilty on all four counts and sen- tenced to death. Goering had concealed a cyanide capsule since his capture and he swallowed it a few hours before the execution. In the middle of the night on October 17, 1946, the 10 remaining condemned men, dressed in civilian clothes, were taken to the gymnasium in the complex that includ- ed the jail and courtroom, and were hanged. Von Ribbentrop led the way to the scaffold, followed by Jodl, Keitel, Seyss-Inquart, Rosenberg, Streicher, Frick, Kaltenbrunner, Frank, and Sauckel. Later the bodies were taken to the former concentration camp at Dachau to be cremated. Their ashes were never released, lest they become relics for Nazi sympathizers.

Although the Nuremberg trials satisfied the immediate need to call the Nazi establishment to account, the idealistic aims of the tribunal—to outlaw war and to provide an international forum where those waging war could be tried—only gave rise to arguments that continue today.

"I hope that this execution is the last act of the tragedy of the Second World War and I hope that out of this disaster, wisdom will inspire the people."

ARTUR SEYSS-INQUART, as he was led to the scaffold, October 17, 1946

Above The executioner, U.S. serviceman John C. Woods, with the rope used to execute 10 of the defendants in the gymnasium attached to Nuremberg jail.

DEFENDANTS AT THE TRIAL

THE CHARGES
Count 1. Waging a war of aggression
Count 2. Crimes against peace
Count 3. War crimes
Count 4. Crimes against humanity

HERMANN GOERING (1893–1946), number two in the Nazi hierarchy and Hitler's only Reichsmarshall. He founded the Gestapo, the Nazi secret police, and created the first concentration camps. At Nuremberg he was found guilty on all four counts and sentenced to death, but committed suicide a few hours before he was due to be hanged.

RUDOLF HESS (1894–1987), deputy party leader and number three in the Nazi hierarchy. Hess aroused the most interest at the trial because of his unexplained flight to Scotland in 1941, apparently to discuss Anglo-German peace terms. He was imprisoned by the British until the end of the war, and many thought him mad and harmless rather than a dangerous criminal. The issue of his sanity was central to his defense. He was found guilty on counts one and two and imprisoned for life. He spent the last 11 years of his life as the solitary inmate of Spandau prison.

JOACHIM VON RIBBENTROP (1893–1946), a former champagne salesman and linguist who acted as German ambassador to Britain in 1936–38 and German foreign minister in 1939–45. He was found guilty on four counts, sentenced to death, and hanged.

WILHELM KEITEL (1882–1946), field-marshal and chief of the supreme command of the armed forces from 1938. He was believed to be Hitler's "yes-man" and was nicknamed *Nickesel*, after a German children's toy donkey that continuously nodded its head. He was found guilty on all four counts, sentenced to death, and hanged.

ERNST KALTENBRUNNER (1903–46), deputy to Himmler in the SS and head of the security police from 1943. He was a supporter of Himmler's policy to establish gas chambers for mass executions from 1942. He was found guilty on counts three and four, sentenced to death, and hanged.

ALFRED ROSENBERG (1893–1946), the leading Nazi theoretician of anti-Semitism, who was famous for his belief that "anti-Semitism is the unifying element of the reconstruction of Germany." His writings on the rise of the Third Reich impressed Hitler greatly and he was appointed Reich minister for the occupied Eastern Territories in 1941. He was found guilty on all four counts, sentenced to death, and hanged.

HANS FRANK (1900–46), governor-general of Poland from 1939, where he established Jewish ghettos and deported slave labor to Germany. Later Frank became Hitler's personal lawyer. He was found guilty on counts three and four, sentenced to death, and hanged.

WILHELM FRICK (1877–1946), minister of the interior in 1933–43 and Reich protector of Bohemia and Moravia in 1943. A lawyer by training, Frick was responsible for securing Hitler's German citizenship (the Führer was born in Austria). With Hitler and Hess he co-signed the Nuremberg laws of 1935, which, among other things, stipulated that anyone who had three Jewish grandparents, or two if they practiced their religion, was considered to be a Jew by the Third Reich and subject to numerous restrictions. Frick was found guilty on counts two, three, and four, sentenced to death, and hanged.

JULIUS STREICHER (1885–1946), the editor of the anti-Semitic weekly *Der Sturmer* and known as the "Beast of Nuremberg" because of his insatiable appetite for sadism. He was responsible for instigating the exclusion of Jews from all professions and places of learning (the Nuremberg laws). He was found guilty on count four, sentenced to death, and hanged.

Left The defendants, photographed in the dock on the opening day of the trial. They are (*front row from left to right*): Hermann Goering, Rudolf Hess, Joachim von Ribbentrop, Wilhelm Keitel, Ernst Kaltenbrunner, Alfred Rosenberg, Hans Frank, Wilhelm Frick, Julius Streicher, Walther Funk, Hjalmar Schacht; (*back row*): Karl Doenitz, Erich Raeder, Baldur von Schirach, Fritz Sauckel, Alfred Jodl, Franz von Papen, Artur Seyss-Inquart, Albert Speer, Konstantin von Neurath, and Hans Fritzsche.

WALTHER FUNK (1890–1960), minister of economics and president of the Reichsbank after Hjalmar Schacht. He coined the term *"Kristallnacht"* (the night of broken glass) to describe the massive destruction of Jewish property by the Nazis on the night of November 9, 1938. He was also responsible for having Jewish prisoners murdered to recover the gold in their teeth. He was found guilty on counts two, three, and four and sentenced to life imprisonment. He was released in 1957 due to illness.

HJALMAR SCHACHT (1877–1970), minister of economics in 1934–37 and president of the Reichsbank until 1939. He was arrested by the Gestapo in 1944 on suspicion of being involved in the July plot on Hitler's life and held in three different concentration camps until the end of the war. At Nuremberg, Schacht was acquitted and released from internment after appeal in 1949. He returned to his career in banking.

KARL DOENITZ (1891–1980), commander-in-chief of the German navy from 1943 and Hitler's successor as head of state. He was convicted on counts two and three and sentenced to 10 years' imprisonment.

ERICH RAEDER (1876–1960), commander of the German navy until 1943. He was acquitted of charges that he made no effort to rescue survivors of torpedoed ships (a crime against humanity) and found guilty on counts one, two, and three. Though sentenced to life in prison, he was released in 1955.

BALDUR VON SCHIRACH (1907–1974), head of the Hitler Youth Movement and Gauleiter of Vienna from 1940. In this capacity he was responsible for mass deportation of Jews to extermination camps. He wrote admiring poetry and song lyrics about Hitler that became extremely popular before and during the war. Von Schirach was found guilty on count four and sentenced to 20 years' imprisonment.

FRITZ SAUCKEL (1894–1946), Hitler's chief recruiter of slave labor for Nazi purposes in 1942–45, Sauckel was named chief commissioner for the utilization of manpower. The verdict described how he masterminded the deportation of five million people. He was found guilty on counts three and four, sentenced to death, and hanged.

ALFRED JODL (1890–1946), chief of operations staff of Hitler's armed forces. Highly intelligent and a powerful personality, he was a great admirer of Hitler. He was found guilty on all four counts, sentenced to death, and hanged.

FRANZ VON PAPEN (1879–1969), chancellor under Hindenburg in 1932 and Hitler's vice-chancellor in 1933–34. He was found not guilty and acquitted.

ARTUR SEYSS-INQUART (1892–1946), chancellor of Austria from 1938 and Reich commissioner for the Netherlands from 1940. He was responsible for deporting slave labor from the Netherlands to Germany. He was found guilty on counts two, three, and four, sentenced to death, and hanged.

ALBERT SPEER (1905–81), minister of armaments in 1942–45. He was found guilty on counts three and four and sentenced to 20 years' imprisonment. He was the only defendant to admit responsibility for his actions.

KONSTANTIN VON NEURATH (1873–1956), Hitler's foreign minister in 1933–38 and Reich protector of Bohemia and Moravia in 1939–43. He was found guilty on all four counts and imprisoned for 15 years, until 1954.

HANS FRITZSCHE (1899–1953), head of the press in Goebbels's propaganda ministry from 1938 and chief of the propaganda ministry's radio division from 1942. He was found not guilty and acquitted, but was imprisoned by a German denazification court until 1950.

I Accept Full Responsibility

THE ALLIED POWERS *v.* HIDEKI TOJO

MAY 1946 – JUNE 1948

Above Tojo listening to his death sentence being pronounced, November 12, 1948. Headphones were used for Japanese translation of the court proceedings.

"I believe that Japan's war was a just one, although I know your country would not accept that. History will decide who is right."

HIDEKI TOJO
after his arrest by Allied personnel,
September 10, 1945

On September 2, 1945, the Japanese signed a formal surrender on the American flagship *Missouri* in Tokyo Bay, bringing World War II in the Pacific to an end. Their capitulation was forced—much against the will of Japanese military leaders—by atomic bomb attacks on Hiroshima and Nagasaki that caused tens of thousands of civilian deaths. In the weeks that followed, the Far Eastern Commission, consisting of representatives from the 11 Allied nations, delegated virtually dictatorial powers to Gen. Douglas MacArthur, then Supreme Commander of the Allied forces in Japan. MacArthur responded by setting up the International Military Tribunal for the Far East (IMTFE), intent on trying certain Japanese leaders as war criminals.

TWENTY-EIGHT "CLASS A" PRISONERS WERE INDICTED on 36 counts of crimes against peace, 16 counts of murder, and 3 counts of crimes against humanity, or conventional war crimes. The prisoners were military men in their sixties, the most important of whom was the wartime prime minister Hideki Tojo. Twenty-one of the accused faced charges of planning aggressive war against China: this was defined as attacking a foreign power without an official declaration of war, as Japan had done when it invaded

Manchuria in 1931. The indictment stated that those planning the war in the Pacific had foreseen and expressly approved the use of atrocities as a means of social control: the attack on Nanking, when Japanese troops subjected the Chinese city to four days of looting, killing, and rape; the evacuation of Korean and Chinese prisoners to labor camps in Japan; and the use of prisoners of war (POWs) to build the Burma–Siam "death railway," so named because so many people died in its making from lack of food and brutal treatment. In his opening address the chief prosecutor, Joseph Keenan, called the accused "plain, ordinary murderers."

THE TRIAL BEGAN IN THE FORMER WAR MINISTRY BUILDINGS at Ichigaya, a suburb of Tokyo, on May 3, 1946, and lasted more than two years. The defense counsel was headed by Japanese attorneys and assisted—at the request of the Japanese government—by American lawyers. From the start the proceedings were controversial, the defense counsel repeatedly contesting both the legitimacy of the charges and the legality of the court itself. General MacArthur, as a U.S. citizen bound by the U.S. Constitution, had not been authorized by Congress to establish an international tribunal and had thereby exceeded his authority. The defense counsel objected as well to the charter establishing the tribunal, which stated explicitly that it would not be bound by the rules of technical evidence. This meant, for example, that the prosecution could use affidavits sworn by absentee witnesses who could not be cross-examined in court. The defense was allowed only three translators against the prosecution's 102. Extra translation help at the defense's own expense was ruled out because the court had frozen all the assets of the defendants.

The Tribunal

Gen. Douglas MacArthur established the International Military Tribunal for the Far East (IMTFE) in Tokyo in 1946, the second (after Nuremberg) of two tribunals investigating World War II crimes. A 17-article charter set out the tribunal's powers, including Article 5, defining a category of crimes against peace, and Article 6 ruling out the defense offered at Nuremberg, that the accused were merely obeying orders. Working within the charter, the IMTFE established three categories of war criminals. Class A consisted of those who had "planned, initiated, or waged war in violation of international treaties." Class B were those who had violated the laws and customs of war. Class C had carried out orders to torture and murder.

The Australian judge Sir William Webb presided, but the full panel was to consist of not less than 6 and not more than 11 judges drawn from the Allied nations. Justice Pal from India made it clear that he opposed the notion of singling out individuals like Tojo to be responsible for the crimes of a nation, and the U.S. chief prosecutor, Joseph Keenan, emphasized that the proceedings were "always intended to be more than a mere trial of individuals." The doctrine of individual responsibility, which was made law at Nuremberg in 1945, has remained in existence ever since. However, the matter of laying down standards of international morality relating to war is an issue that continues to vex legal experts, and the concept of "waging a war of aggression" has never been satisfactorily defined.

Left The bombing raid on Pearl Harbor, December 7, 1941, a surprise attack that almost destroyed the U.S. fleet and brought the United States into World War II. Pearl Harbor was cited by the prosecution as an act of "aggressive" war, for which, they alleged, Prime Minister Tojo was entirely responsible.

Above Tojo (third row back, third from left) and the other defendants at the start of the tribunal.

Hideki Tojo (1885–1948) was born in Tokyo. He attended military college, and served with the notorious Kwantung army after the invasion of Manchuria in 1931, which led to setting up the puppet Manchukuo regime. He became chief of the secret police in Manchuria in 1935. From 1937 to 1938 he was chief of staff of the Kwantung army in Manchuria, became Japanese vice-minister for war in 1938, and was promoted to minister for war in 1940. In November 1941, just before the attack on Pearl Harbor, Tojo became prime minister. In 1944, at a low point in the war, Japanese military leaders requested his resignation. He was arrested by the Allies soon after the Japanese surrender in 1945. He attempted suicide rather than be taken captive, but failed, and stood trial for war crimes. His execution was virtually a foregone conclusion. General MacArthur declined Tojo's widow's request to receive his ashes.

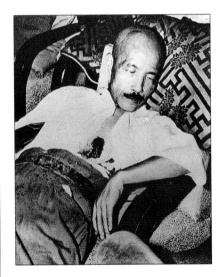

Above Tojo after attempting suicide to avoid being taken captive after the Japanese surrender.

Judge Webb dealt summarily with these objections. In contrast to the usual rule that any court should be answerable to a higher authority, Judge Webb announced that there was no right of appeal from the tribunal. The only authority in this case was General MacArthur. Webb answered the point about MacArthur's status simply by stating that the military tribunal had taken no judicial notice of the ideals set out in the U.S. Constitution.

Tojo's American defense lawyer, George F. Blewett, and the other defense lawyers for the accused also contested the charges. In the first place, they argued, there was no such thing in international law as "crimes against peace" or "aggressive war"; these were new offenses invented for the purpose of trying the defeated leaders. The prosecution had based its case on the fact that Japan had signed the Kellogg–Briand pact of 1928, which outlawed wars of aggression. But in fact this pact outlawed all war and provided for no criminal sanctions if the treaty were breached. Secondly, any war crime analogy between Germany and Japan would not hold, since in Asia there was no equivalent of the Holocaust. Unlike the Nazi regime, wartime Japan could boast of no continuing government or set of officials making policy. For a fair trial in Tokyo, the tribunal should rightfully put the leaders of Japan's corporations—the *zaibatsu*—in the dock, for it was their economic interests that had fueled Japanese expansionism. It followed that the clash between Japan and the allied western nations was an old-fashioned economic conflict over territory and resources.

THE PROSECUTION COULD NOT REPLY ADEQUATELY to Blewett's arguments. Prosecutor Keenan concentrated almost exclusively on piling up the details of atrocities committed by Japanese troops. No one disputed that atrocities had taken place, but the defense pointed out that no documentary evidence existed of the leadership's having ordered or condoned such behavior. Keenan focused on the injustices of Japanese policy in

China since 1931; the defense maintained that Japan had accepted the Potsdam agreement as a settlement to the war of 1941–45 only, and asked why events before that were being considered. Furthermore, why were the accused not being tried before representatives from neutral nations, or before those Japanese who had suffered for their opposition to the war? The proceedings, the defense argued, were "victor's justice" with a vengeance.

Keenan's talk of killing combatants in war as "murder," said the defense, was ludicrous. If the attack on Pearl Harbor in war had resulted in the murder of 4,000 persons, what about the 80,000 people who had perished with the destruction of Hiroshima and the 50,000 at Nagasaki? Keenan accused the Japanese leaders of seeking to destroy democracy, the defense continued, yet on the bench and at the prosecutor's table sat representatives of the colonial powers of Britain, France, and Holland, who had denied democracy to the citizens of the countries they had conquered. And who, the defense asked, could object to a lack of democracy in a court where the Soviet Union was represented as a plaintiff?

ON ONE ISSUE ALONE DID PROSECUTION AND DEFENSE AGREE, a conspiracy of silence over Emperor Hirohito. Logically, if the Japanese leadership was on trial for war crimes, the supreme leader, to whom they all owed unquestioning obedience, should be in the dock too. The absence of all reference to Hirohito was a political decision agreed upon by both sides. Washington had decided to make the emperor the centerpiece of its policy of postwar reconstruction. Beyond that, MacArthur warned, if Hirohito were brought to trial, MacArthur would need another million troops in Japan to contain the popular uprising that would inevitably result.

"I want nothing said or presented that will bring the emperor into this; I know they are going to hang me."

HIDEKI TOJO
to his defense lawyer,
Spring 1946

Right Chief prosecutor Joseph Keenan addressing the Military Tribunal for the Far East during court proceedings.

*"Never at any time...
did I conceive that the
waging of this war would
or could be challenged by
the victors as an
international crime."*

HIDEKI TOJO
under cross-examination
by Joseph Keenan,
December 31, 1947

FROM START TO FINISH TOJO SHIELDED THE EMPEROR AT ALL COSTS. In accordance with ancient Japanese custom, he had attempted to commit suicide rather than be taken captive in September 1945. His attempt failed, but Tojo came to believe that his life could—even yet—be used to protect his emperor. Following his arrest in 1945, Tojo made a statement to his captors: "Looking toward the imperial palace from afar, I pray for the health and long life of His Imperial Majesty....I am determined to devote the life of my spirit to the protection of the welfare and prosperity of the nation." He agreed to be represented by American defense counsel on the express understanding that Hirohito would not be held responsible for the war.

Both sides came close to implicating Hirohito without intending it. Webb had to silence Keenan when the prosecutor virtually admitted that the absence of Hirohito made the proceedings meaningless. Tojo himself slipped during his testimony when he implied the emperor's ultimate responsibility by saying: "None of us Japanese would dare act against the emperor's will." After this incident Keenan took the unprecedented step of asking the Japanese imperial court to persuade Tojo to change his testimony. Knowing that his execution was certain, the former prime minister bore not only this embarrassment but a two-and-a-half year trial as well.

Unlike most of the other prisoners, who entered pleas of mitigation, Tojo prepared a lengthy defense to refute Keenan. When he came to the stand on December 26, 1947, Tojo paused and blew his nose. Japanese

Below Tojo being sworn in by Capt. D. S. Van Meter, December 26, 1947.

observers understood this action as an expression of contempt for the IMTFE. Many of them had paid ticket touts five times the price of a seat in Tokyo's most expensive theater for a seat in the court. From the moment Tojo began to read his 250-page deposition, he swayed public opinion in his favor. Because he had failed in his suicide attempt and had been taken captive, the Japanese press had viewed him with contempt; but as he began to give his testimony, the newspapers rallied to his side with banner headlines such as "War of Defense Forced on Us," "Japan's Tragedy," and "Emperor Not Responsible."

Japan, Tojo argued, had pursued legitimate objectives of self-interest. It had never plotted aggressive war; rather, President Franklin Roosevelt had provoked the attack on Pearl Harbor. Moreover, he knew of Japan's intentions just before December 7, 1941, since the Allies had broken the Japanese code. Japan's policy in the Pacific had not been to enslave other nations, but to reclaim Asia from European colonialism. As for himself, Tojo declared, he had never ordered atrocities. He admitted giving permission for the use of prisoners of war on the Burma–Siam railway but denied that their treatment was inhumane. He ended by absolving Emperor Hirohito from all blame. Judge Webb, under strict instructions to keep Hirohito out of the proceedings, allowed this statement to be made in open court and it was widely reported in the press. However, Webb admitted later that privately he thought that the emperor should have been tried with the others. As it was Tojo willingly took on his own shoulders absolute responsibility for Japanese foreign policy from 1941 to 1945 and for his country's defeat in the war. Far from showing remorse, he declared openly to the court: "I feel that I did no wrong. I feel I did what was right and true."

Below Gen. Douglas MacArthur with Emperor Hirohito, meeting while the trial is in progress to discuss Japan's rehabilitation and reconstruction. General MacArthur ensured that Emperor Hirohito was excluded from the tribunal to safeguard the future of Japanese–American relations.

THE TRIBUNAL DELIVERED ITS VERDICT on November 12, 1948, several months after the hearings had finished. Tojo, along with six other defendants, was sentenced to death by hanging; the other accused received life sentences, though most were paroled between 1954 and 1956. After receiving his death sentence, Tojo bowed low to the court. On November 20 the defense prepared an appeal to MacArthur to review the court's sentences, claiming that the defendants had not received a fair trial. Four days later MacArthur made public his decision to uphold the sentences given by the tribunal. Tojo was executed by hanging at one-thirty in the morning on December 23, 1948, with a Buddhist priest in attendance. Just before he died, the 63-year-old general reaffirmed his loyalty to Emperor Hirohito by crying out, "May His Glorious Majesty live for ten thousand years."

"I can conceive of no juridical process where greater safeguard was made to evolve justice."

GENERAL MACARTHUR, speaking of the IMTFE in his statement upholding the court's final verdict, November 24, 1948

JURY

At the heart of the jury system lies the dynamic network of relationships among judge, jury, counsel, and accused. Of all those relationships, none holds greater significance than the link between counsel for the defense and the jury. Defense counsel needs to argue the case sympathetically enough to capture the attention of the jury. Paradoxically, members of a defense team are bound by professional duty to defend even a prisoner whom they themselves believe to be guilty.

Though separated by almost 3,000 years, both the oldest and the most recent of the cases that follow (Socrates and Byron de la Beckwith) were tried by jury. Jury trial is one of the most important elements of the accusatorial system of justice employed today in the United States and the present and former British Commonwealth. In essence, one party brings a case against another, with each side presenting evidence to an impartial body, the court, which then proceeds to make a decision. It is not the purpose of the judge presiding over such a trial to seek out the truth by questioning the witnesses. He or she awaits the work of the two parties arguing the case. The jury examines the evidence produced in court and must reach its decision on the basis of that evidence alone.

The notion of trial by one's peers rather than by legal experts is one that captures the essence of democracy. The ordinary citizen comes, with no ax to grind, from everyday life to decide a case, then returns to wherever they came from. Experts agree that while jury reaction at a criminal trial is extremely hard to predict, the defendant's interests seem to be well served in a jury trial.

Whether or not the judge is permitted to indicate his or her own opinion as to guilt or innocence varies from legal system to legal system; a judge may comment more freely in some than in others. However, throughout the systems based on the common law tradition, the jurors must be told that they are sovereign over facts, the judge's sole power being over points of law. Some jurors respond to this information by taking no account of the judge's opinion. Others, anxious for guidance, willingly take their lead from the judge. In particularly emotional cases, a jury is more likely to produce an unexpected decision. In the Chamberlain dingo trial, in which only circumstantial evidence existed against a couple accused of killing their baby, the jury convicted both parents despite the judge's clearly expressed opinion that they should acquit.

TRIALS

The persuasive ability of the advocate can be the deciding factor in a jury trial. Clarence Darrow's legendary oratory in front of a jury defined the outcome in the Leopold and Loeb case and in the anti-evolutionist Scopes monkey trial. It is doubtful that Darrow could have spoken so movingly to the jury had he not believed passionately in what he was saying. The defense lawyer in the Madeleine Smith trial, however, seems to have believed his client guilty. How, then, could he properly defend her?

The argument for taking a case even when defense counsel is not convinced of his or her client's innocence is eloquently expressed by the lawyer Thomas Erskine in defense of his client Thomas Paine, author of the *Rights of Man*. During Paine's prosecution for seditious libel against Britain in 1792, Erskine said: "If the advocate refuses to defend, from what he may think of the charge or of the defense, he assumes the character of the judge; nay, he assumes it before the hour of judgment; and in proportion to his rank and reputation, puts the heavy influence of perhaps a mistaken opinion into the scale against the accused, in whose favor the benevolent principle of English law makes all presumptions, and which commands the very judge to be his counsel."

114 MELETUS *v.* SOCRATES

118 THE CROWN *v.* THE "TOLPUDDLE MARTYRS"

122 THE CROWN *v.* MADELEINE SMITH

126 JAMES MCNEILL WHISTLER *v.* JOHN RUSKIN

132 THE CROWN *v.* FLORENCE MAYBRICK

136 OSCAR WILDE *v.* THE MARQUESS OF QUEENSBERRY

142 THE STATE OF ILLINOIS *v.* LEOPOLD AND LOEB

148 THE STATE OF TENNESSEE *v.* JOHN T. SCOPES

152 THE PEOPLE *v.* JULIUS AND ETHEL ROSENBERG

156 THE CROWN *v.* WILBERT COFFIN

160 THE CROWN *v.* PENGUIN BOOKS LTD.

166 THE STATE OF SOUTH AFRICA *v.* NELSON MANDELA

172 THE U.S. GOVERNMENT *v.* DANIEL ELLSBERG

176 THE CROWN *v.* LINDY AND MICHAEL CHAMBERLAIN

180 THE ATTORNEY GENERAL *v.* HEINEMANN PUBLISHERS AND PETER WRIGHT

184 THE STATE OF MISSISSIPPI *v.* BYRON DE LA BECKWITH

Corrupting Athenian Youth

MELETUS v. SOCRATES

399 B.C.

Above A Greek bust of Socrates, one of Athens's most famous philosophers. He developed the "Socratic method" of education, in which a teacher asks pupils leading questions and encourages them to work out their answers aloud.

*I*n 399 B.C., the most renowned philosopher in Athens, 70-year-old Socrates, was brought to trial. The indictment, "made under oath by Meletus, son of Meletus from Pitthos, against Socrates, son of Sophroniscus from Alopece," read as follows: "Socrates is guilty of refusing to recognize the gods the city recognizes, and of introducing other new divinities; he is also guilty of corrupting the youth. The penalty demanded is death." In reality the charge of "corrupting the youth" of Athens should have been "encouraging the political ambitions of young men with new ideas." One of the principal reasons Socrates was on trial was so that he could not gather around him any more disciples.

THE PROSECUTION'S MOTIVATION for bringing the case against Socrates was probably based on religious and moral grounds. Socrates's attempts to understand moral concepts led him rigorously to question people's beliefs and expose their inconsistencies and contradictions. This was regarded by the prosecution as a skeptical subversion of common ethical values, and hence, as potentially corrupting. The case was lent further credence by Socrates's politically suspect associations during Athens's disastrous conflict—which lasted nearly three decades—with its rival city-state, Sparta.

By the end of the fifth century B.C. Sparta had brought Athens—the leading city-state of ancient Greece—to its knees. The city that had produced the statesman Pericles, the sculptor Phidias, and such dramatists as Aeschylus, Sophocles, Euripides, and Aristophanes was transformed into a garrison city ruled by traitors. Athens's defeat in what became known as the Peloponnesian War (431–404 B.C.) had been aided from within by subversive Spartan sympathizers, who then became members of the victors' ruling body, the so-called Thirty Tyrants. Among these were two extremists, Critias and Charmides, both former students of Socrates. Socrates had also associated with the politician Alcibiades, who until his assassination in 404 B.C.—most likely instigated by the Thirty Tyrants—was an obvious candidate to lead a counterrevolution.

Less than a year later, civil war broke out against the Thirty Tyrants in Athens. The revolt was led by Thrasybulus and Anytus, of the rival democratic faction. After the brief battle in which Critias and Charmides were killed, the remaining tyrants were expelled, a political amnesty was called, and by the end of 403 B.C. democracy was restored in Athens. Four years later Socrates was brought to trial.

Trial by Jury

The first codes of law to be recorded in Ancient Greece evolved with the growth of city-states in the eighth century B.C. Although each city devised its own laws, only the Athenian system has been well documented.

Every year, 6,000 male citizens over the age of 30 were chosen by lot to serve as jurymen. Each juror was paid a small allowance—enough to let him support his family. Courts heard cases on about 300 days of the year. Each day that the courts sat, the jurors were chosen by lot and sent to different courts. The use of the lottery was a safeguard against bribery. The size of juries varied probably in proportion to the importance of the case. The principles on which decisions were made are not known. (Athenian law did not distinguish between civil and criminal cases in the modern sense, so the kind of trial was probably irrelevant.) The jury at Socrates's trial is estimated by scholars to have been about 500. In all cases, the jury decided the verdict by majority vote.

Although women, slaves, and resident aliens were excluded from serving on juries, these courts were some of the first to implement the democratic principle that the citizens of a state should administer the laws.

Above In this mosaic from Pompeii, Socrates (rubbing his chin) is deep in philosophical debate with his pupil Plato (seated under tree). It was for potentially corrupting his students through moral debate that Socrates was brought to trial.

Three prosecutors—Lycon, Anytus, and Meletus—appeared at the main Athenian jury-court where the trial of Socrates was held. Nothing is known of Lycon, except that he was a rhetorician. Meletus, the person named in the indictment, delivered the main speech. Anytus, the general who had been instrumental in opposing Socrates's former students and restoring democracy to Athens, probably attended to lend support. It was common practice in a trial of public importance to obtain the backing of an influential politician. It was also customary, however, for that politician to act through his junior associates. Anytus may actually have been the force behind the prosecution, delegating the case to Meletus.

In the open-air court, a low barrier separated the public from the participants, which included a jury of about 500 male citizens. Although no transcripts of the speeches made at Socrates's trial exist, over the centuries scholars have pieced together what probably occurred by examining later accounts, such as the one made by Plato in his *Apologia* after his attendance at the trial. The prosecution presented its case first, then the defense had its turn. Both were allowed to speak for an equal amount of time, which was measured by a water clock. There was no formal cross-examination of witnesses, as in a modern court. The prosecution's case was simple: it was well

> *"Nothing can harm a good man, either in life or after death."*
>
> SOCRATES
> at his trial,
> 399 B.C.

115

BIOGRAPHY

Socrates (c.470–399 B.C.), son of the sculptor Sophroniscus, performed distinguished military service during Athens's war with Sparta (431–404 B.C.). He became the greatest of the early Greek philosophers and Plato's teacher. We know him not by his own written works—he left none—but by the writings of Plato, Xenophon, and Aristophanes. Nowhere is he more vividly portrayed than in Plato's *Dialogues*, in which he emerges as a man of wit, vitality, shrewdness, and irony as he examines moral concepts—such as, "What is justice?"—through the relentless question-and-answer method known as dialectic. Some scholars have argued that the Socrates of Plato's *Apologia* is merely a mouthpiece for Plato's own views. Xenophon's Socrates is less penetrating in his questioning and more apt to affirm a conventional platitude. Aristophanes's portrait of Socrates in his comedy *The Clouds* is in fact a composite caricature of various contemporary intellectuals. Only Plato portrays a convincing and remarkable philosopher.

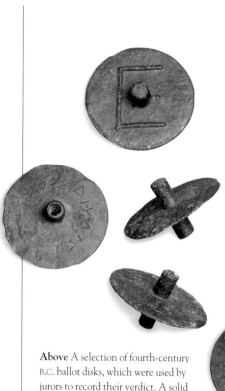

Above A selection of fourth-century B.C. ballot disks, which were used by jurors to record their verdict. A solid hub was a vote for acquittal; a hollow hub, for condemnation.

known that Critias and Charmides, two of the leaders of the insurrection, had been pupils of Socrates. Furthermore, everybody knew that Socrates scoffed at the idea of Zeus and the pantheon of gods; Aristophanes had satirized the philosopher in his comedy *The Clouds*—originally produced in 423 B.C.—as someone who had no respect for conventional religion, who had taught his pupils (for a fee) to question conventional ethical norms, and who had invented a whole new set of gods.

SOCRATES CONDUCTED HIS OWN DEFENSE. He began by apologizing for his ignorance of legal niceties: he was 70 years old and had never been in a court of law before. He explained that he found his position difficult: in addition to the three formal prosecutors, there existed a vast body of hidden accusers in Athens, who had influenced the climate of opinion against him for the previous 20 years. These detractors, nameless except for Aristophanes, created a steady drip of prejudicial opinion against Socrates. Let the record state straightaway, he urged, that he was not a man of science, did not speculate about the physical universe, was not a teacher (since he did not take money for tuition), and was not a "professional" philosopher or a Sophist—in fact he despised the Sophists.

Socrates then proceeded to deal with the formal indictment. He first questioned Meletus: if he (Socrates) had corrupted the young, who, then, were the people who had improved them? In his reply, Meletus first mentioned the jurors. Socrates led him, step by step, to mention everyone in the entire citizen body. This resulted in the ludicrous conclusion that every Athenian except Socrates had improved the young.

The philosopher continued his spirited defense by describing his role in society as that of a gadfly, "to sting people and whip them into a fury, all in the service of truth." He explained that "if you kill a man like me, you will injure yourselves more than you will injure me. Nothing will injure me, not Meletus nor even Anytus—they cannot, for a bad man is not permitted to injure one better than himself."

He then rounded on the court with his strongest point: that there were hundreds of his former pupils present, yet the prosecution had not produced a single one to testify that he had corrupted them. He concluded by saying that he would not play the usual trick of producing weeping children in court to soften the hearts of the jurors, if only because such scenes would bring Athenian democracy only ridicule and contempt. It was his business to convince his judges, not to ask them a favor.

THE JURY FOUND SOCRATES GUILTY AS CHARGED by an estimated 280 to 220 votes. His long defense speech, by turns spirited, witty, haughty, and defiant, had merely annoyed them. Their next task was to decide on the penalty. Except where a charge carried a fixed sentence, the condemned had the right to propose an alternative sentence to that demanded by the prosecution, which in this case was the death penalty. It was left to the jury to choose between the two sentences. If Socrates had proposed banishment, it would certainly have been accepted, for Athens would gain nothing in the estimation of ancient Greece by executing its leading philosopher. Socrates's friends urged him to take

this way out, but he was adamantly opposed. If he went into exile, he would betray his life's work and prove the truth of his detractors' accusation that he hated democracy. There could be no better proof of his loyalty to the state, he believed, than his willingness to die for it.

Socrates further alienated the jury by saying that what he really deserved was a state pension for his life as a public benefactor. In a contemptuous refusal to compromise, he proposed as his sentence a fine of 30 minae (about 3,000 times the daily wage of a skilled laborer). The jury responded by voting for the death penalty by a larger majority than had originally found him guilty. In his address to the jury, Socrates denounced those who had condemned him: "I prophesy to you, my murderers, that immediately after my departure punishment far heavier than you have inflicted on me will surely await you....The easiest and the noblest way [of escape] is not to be disabling others, but to be improving yourselves."

NORMALLY THE EXECUTION WOULD HAVE BEEN CARRIED OUT AT ONCE. But Socrates's trial coincided with an annual religious ceremony, during which the death penalty could not be pursued. Because the ceremony involved sending envoys to the temple of Apollo on Delos, its duration depended on sailing conditions. These proved unfavorable, and the execution was postponed for a month. During this time Socrates could easily have escaped from prison. But he refused to, on the grounds that he owed obedience to the law. A month after the trial Socrates was administered a fatal dose of hemlock. His last words were to his friend Crito: "We owe a cock to Aesculapius; please pay it and don't forget it."

"If you think that by killing me you can prevent someone from censuring your evil lives, you are mistaken; that is not a way of escape which is either possible or honorable."

SOCRATES
in his address to the jury,
399 B.C.

Below "The Death of Socrates," painted by the French artist Jacques-Louis David in 1787. Socrates is just about to take the dish containing a fatal dose of poison, which was the prescribed method of his execution.

An Example to Others

THE CROWN v. "TOLPUDDLE MARTYRS"

MARCH 17 – 19, 1834

Above The Tolpuddle Martyrs, drawn for *Cleave's Penny Gazette,* May 12, 1838. From right to left George Loveless (41), James Loveless (29), John Standfield (25), Thomas Standfield (48), and James Brine (25). James Hammett is not pictured here.

The British Assizes

The British assize system dates from the 13th century, when itinerant justices traveled from town to town. This arrangement settled into a seasonal cycle; judges traveled to each county town four times a year to hear cases in the Quarterly Sessions. The summer and winter assizes dealt with civil and criminal proceedings; those at Easter and in the fall heard only criminal cases. The assize system was abolished in Britain in 1971 when the current Crown Court system was established.

The initial charges in any case were heard by a grand jury. This consisted of between 12 and 23 laymen, chosen by ballot, who scrutinized the indictment. If necessary they heard the evidence, and then decided whether there was a "true bill"—sufficient cause to send the case to trial. This did not indicate guilt; it merely authorized a trial by petty jury (from the French *petit*), made up of 12 property-owning men. The use of the grand jury as a standard part of the English legal system persisted until 1933, though it declined in importance long before that date.

*I*n 1834 England's Whig government longed to find some way to curb the growth of trade unions. Such groups posed a serious threat to the government's power, and at the turn of the 19th century, they had been outlawed as criminal conspiracies under the Combination Acts. A quarter of a century later, in 1824, unions were made lawful again by an act of Parliament passed by Lord Liverpool's Tory administration. However, unrest soon surfaced among agricultural laborers who wanted a guaranteed minimum wage. When, in 1834, the Whig home secretary, Lord Melbourne, saw a chance to suppress labor protest, he grabbed it.

IN JANUARY 1834 A MAGISTRATE NAMED JAMES FRAMPTON wrote to Melbourne about laborers in Dorset who were organizing themselves into a union. Although belonging to a trade union in itself was not illegal, Frampton told Melbourne that he believed that sworn oaths had been taken by the laborers. A Sedition Act passed in 1817 classified the taking of any oath not required or authorized by law as a misdemeanor. By taking such an oath, the laborers established themselves as members of an unlawful combination or confederacy.

But actually to bring the unions down, Melbourne had to identify some aspect of the organizations that could be considered a felony, clearly difficult in the light of the 1824 act, which had made collective bargaining lawful. After trawling through the statute book, he eventually found what he was looking for. The 1797 Mutiny Act made it a felony to administer any oath in which a person swore not to reveal an unlawful confederacy. Although aimed especially at the armed services, the statute did not exclude other applications of the law.

Frampton meanwhile had found the evidence he wanted, not from his spies but from a weak character among the Dorset laborers named Edward Legg, whom Frampton's men had browbeaten into informing against his fellow workers. In February 1834 Legg testified that a secret oath had been administered by six men who had established the Friendly Society of

THE LAST LABORERS' REVOLT

Between 1770 and 1830 the British Parliament passed a series of Enclosure Acts that placed 6 million acres of previously common land into private ownership, as part of a process of profit maximization. The measures entitled the new owners to plant hedges and erect gates to keep the local villagers out. These villagers and their ancestors had long possessed collective rights on the common land, including grazing for their animals, the right to collect wood, the use of a small strip for individual farming, and the right to gather the harvest from that strip. Such fringe benefits contributed about a quarter of the average rural family's income (added to wages from the landlords for whom they worked) and for most of them made the difference between subsistence and starvation. In August of 1830, a movement began among the agricultural laborers in Kent, a "revolt" that spread across the whole of southern England by the end of the year. The laborers demanded a legally imposed minimum wage in return for the loss of their ancient land rights. When their demands were ignored, they began an increasingly violent wave of protest that included the burning of haystacks and the destruction of threshing machines.

STATE OF THE COUNTRY.

The government's reaction to unrest was extremely harsh. Death sentences were passed on 252 laborers (19 were executed), 481 were sentenced to transportation (banishment) to Australia, and 644 imprisoned. The agricultural disturbances of 1830 so worried the home secretary, Lord Melbourne, and his government that they knowingly sanctioned a miscarriage of justice at Tolpuddle.

Above An 1831 cartoon showing rural workers protesting against machine labor and campaigning for higher wages.

However, in prosecuting the Tolpuddle Martyrs, the British government created a group of popular working-class heroes. The struggle to establish their innocence became an important landmark in the history of trade unionism.

Agricultural Laborers in Tolpuddle. They were local Methodist preacher George Loveless and his brother James, Thomas and John Standfield (father and son), James Brine, and James Hammett. Legg claimed that the oath had been taken in the Standfields' cottage in December 1833.

ON FEBRUARY 22, 1834, FRAMPTON AND HIS FELLOW MAGISTRATES posted a "Caution" notice in Tolpuddle and nearby districts, declaring that anyone involved in taking unlawful oaths to enter into "Illegal Societies or Unions" would be deemed felonious and thus liable to seven years' transportation (banishment) to Australia. In theory, this gave the men of Tolpuddle due warning. But the posting took place on Saturday, February 22, and at dawn on Monday, February 24, the six men were arrested.

After walking the seven miles from Tolpuddle to Dorchester with the arresting constable, the men were interrogated by Frampton and Charles Wollaston, Recorder of Dorchester. Legg was brought in to identify the men and repeat his testimony, after which the six were removed to Dorchester jail and subjected to the treatment normally meted out to felons (shaven heads, body searches, and other indignities). On Saturday, March 1, they appeared before magistrates, and Legg repeated his evidence. They were

"It was something concerning wages— something about striking for wages; that we were to strike when others did, or something to that effect."

EDWARD LEGG, laborer, giving evidence to the court, March 1834

CAUTION.

WHEREAS it has been represented to us from several quarters, that mischievous and designing Persons have been for some time past, endeavouring to induce, and have induced, many Labourers in various Parishes in this County, to attend Meetings, and to enter into Illegal Societies or Unions, to which they bind themselves by unlawful oaths, administered secretly by Persons concealed, who artfully deceive the ignorant and unwary.—WE, the undersigned Justices think it our duty to give this PUBLIC NOTICE and CAUTION, that all Persons may know the danger they incur by entering into such Societies.

ANY PERSON who shall become a Member of such a Society, or take any Oath, or assent to any Test or Declaration not authorized by Law—

Any Person who shall administer, or be present at, or consenting to the administering or taking any Unlawful Oath, or who shall cause such Oath to be administered, although not actually present at the time—

Any Person who shall not reveal or discover any Illegal Oath which may have been administered, or any Illegal Act done or to be done—

WILL BECOME

Guilty of Felony,

AND BE LIABLE TO BE

Transported for Seven Years.

ANY PERSON who shall be compelled to take such an Oath, unless he shall declare the same within four days, together with the whole of what he shall know touching the same, will be liable to the same Penalty.

Any Person who shall directly or indirectly maintain correspondence or intercourse with such Society, will be deemed Guilty of an Unlawful Combination and Confederacy, and on Conviction before one Justice, on the Oath of one Witness, be liable to a Penalty of TWENTY POUNDS, or be committed to the Common Gaol or House of Correction, for THREE CALENDAR MONTHS; or if proceeded against by Indictment, may be CONVICTED OF FELONY, and be TRANSPORTED FOR SEVEN YEARS.

Any Person who shall knowingly permit any Meeting of any such Society to be held in any House, Building, or other Place, shall for the first offence be liable to the Penalty of FIVE POUNDS, and for every other offence committed after Conviction, be deemed Guilty of such Unlawful Combination and Confederacy, and on Conviction before one Justice, on the Oath of one Witness, be liable to a Penalty of TWENTY POUNDS, or if proceeded against by Indictment may be

CONVICTED OF FELONY,

And Transported for SEVEN YEARS.

COUNTY OF DORSET,
Dorchester Division.

C. B. WOLLASTON,
JAMES FRAMPTON,
WILLIAM ENGLAND,
THOS. DADE,
JNO. MORTON COLSON.

HENRY FRAMPTON,
RICHD. TUCKER STEWARD,
WILLIAM R. CHURCHILL,
AUGUSTUS FOSTER.

February 22d, 1834.

G. CLARK, PRINTER, CORNHILL, DORCHESTER.

Above The Crown Court in Dorchester, West Dorset, preserved to look the same as it did in 1834 when the Tolpuddle Martyrs were tried there. It was first used for local assizes and quarter sessions in 1796 and was Dorset's main courthouse until a new building was opened in 1955.

committed for trial at the next assizes, but not before George Loveless had been offered immunity if he would turn king's evidence and betray his companions. He refused. Melbourne, whose task it was to prepare the indictment, assured Frampton that the 1824 repeal of the Combination Acts was not relevant to this case. But he was sufficiently worried to consult the law lords (senior judges), for unions now seemed to be at once legal, according to the 1824 Union Act, and illegal, according to the 1817 Sedition Act.

The spring assizes opened in Dorchester on March 14, 1834. The next day, after nearly suffocating in the boxlike cells beneath the Crown Court, the six accused were brought before the grand jury, which had to decide whether the indictment was valid. Since the grand jury included James Frampton, his son Henry, his stepbrother Charles Wollaston, and the other magistrates who had signed the warrant, and was headed by Melbourne's brother-in-law, it is hardly surprising that the men were committed for trial. The judge, Mr. Baron Williams, was presiding over his first assizes. His opening comments to the jury virtually directed them to find the accused guilty before the trial had even begun.

ON MONDAY, MARCH 17, THE ACTUAL TRIAL COMMENCED, before a petty jury of 12 men. The prisoners were brought in and the charges read. In addition to 11 minor counts, the primary charge stated that the accused "feloniously and unlawfully did administer unto one Edward Legg a certain oath." The prosecutor, Sir John Gambier, cited the 1797 Mutiny Act and the precedents for applying this act to trade unions. The prosecution mixed parts of various acts to build its case: that the prisoners were members of an unlawful combination through having taken a secret oath (according to the terms of the 1799 and 1817 acts); and that this action in turn was felonious (according to the 1797 act). Legg and John Lock (one of Frampton's gardeners) testified about the meeting in the Standfields' cottage in December 1833, but their terror at betraying their friends made their accounts in the witness box far less detailed and polished than their original depositions. Although an oath had been administered, the prosecution failed to prove this in court and resorted to bombast on the perils to society from the "anarchy" of trade unions. Even worse, as George Loveless said: "The greater part of the evidence against us, on our trial, was put into the mouths of the witnesses by the Judge."

THE DEFENSE, PRESENTED BY BUTT AND DERBISHIRE, made a decisive rebuttal. The accused men were not allowed to give evidence in their own defense (this right was not granted in England until the Criminal Evidence Act of 1898). When asked if they had anything to say, the prisoners appointed George Loveless as their spokesman. He handed the judge a note, which stated: "…if we have violated any law, it was not done intentionally; we have injured no man's reputation, character, person, or property;

were uniting together to preserve ourselves, our wives, and our children, from utter degradation and starvation." In a final travesty of justice, Judge Williams allowed this statement to be read out to the court in such a mumbled manner that its impact was lost.

It took only minutes for the jury to return with a verdict of guilty. On March 19, after a 36-hour delay, during which the defense made pleas in mitigation, Judge Williams pronounced a sentence of seven years' transportation to Australia. He showed the government's intention clearly by concluding: "The object of all legal punishment is not altogether with the view of operating on the offenders themselves, it is also for the sake of offering an example and a warning."

Below A gold watch presented to James Hammett in 1873 by the Laborers' Union, Dorset, "as a mark of great respect for his patience and courage."

POSTSCRIPT

The convicts reached Botany Bay on September 4, 1834. Back in England, condemnation of the trial gathered force, with the first mention of "martyrs" appearing in the press on March 26, 1834. On March 30 a deputation presented a petition to Lord Melbourne, while a crowd of 12,000 waited outside the Home Office. The Grand National Consolidated Trades Union mounted a major campaign, calling the men symbols of the struggle for workers' rights. On April 21 a huge crowd demonstrated peacefully in London; even the conservative *Times* newspaper reported that 30,000 people turned out to support the laborers. It was two years before the government admitted its error by pardoning the men. On their return from Australia in 1838 (1839 for James Hammett), the union set them up on farms in Essex. By the mid-1840s all but Hammett had emigrated to Ontario, Canada.

Below The Grand National Consolidated Trades Union demonstrates against the Tolpuddle Martyrs' sentence of transportation to Australia and petitions King William IV for a pardon, April 21, 1834.

Not Proven

THE CROWN *v.* MADELEINE SMITH

JUNE 30 – JULY 9, 1857

Above Madeleine Smith's letter, dated March 21, 1857, asking her lover, L'Angelier, to meet her in secret.

"I cannot think why I was so unwell after getting that coffee and chocolate from her…. It is a perfect fascination, my attachment to that girl. If she were to poison me, I would forgive her."

L'ANGELIER
to his friend Mary Perry,
March 9, 1857

On June 30, 1857, Madeleine Smith entered the dock of the High Court of Justiciary in Edinburgh, Scotland, and pleaded not guilty to three charges: intent to murder (Pierre) Emile L'Angelier on February 19 or 20 of that year; intent to murder him on February 22 or 23; and his murder on March 22 or 23. Madeleine Smith had been L'Angelier's mistress for almost a year. But in the fall of 1856 she met a more eligible suitor, a prosperous merchant named William Minnoch. In January 1857, while still involved with L'Angelier, she accepted Minnoch's proposal of marriage. Her rejected lover refused to go away quietly, and Smith feared that he would ruin her reputation and disrupt her planned marriage by revealing the passionate and compromising letters she had written to him. On March 21 she wrote to L'Angelier, urgently requesting a meeting on the 22nd. She later claimed that he did not come to the rendezvous. He was found dead, poisoned by arsenic, on the morning of March 23.

THE TRIAL OPENED THREE MONTHS LATER ON JUNE 30. The courthouse was packed with reporters, who turned the case into a national sensation. After all, Madeleine Smith was not some serving girl or a streetwalker; she was the daughter of James Smith, a prosperous architect and one of Glasgow's eminent citizens. She stood accused of murdering a man who was a member of a lower social class and a foreigner (L'Angelier was of French extraction and a native of Jersey, one of the Channel Islands). Most horrifying of all to the sensibilities of Victorian Scots, Smith had made him her secret lover. It was not surprising, then, that the case drew the luminaries of the Scottish judiciary to the courtroom. The lord advocate of Scotland, James Moncreiff, led the prosecution, while John Inglis, dean of the faculty of advocates, led the defense. The case was heard by Lord Justice-Clerk John Hope, assisted by two other law lords, James Ivory and Robert Handyside.

The Scottish Legal System

Madeleine Smith was tried under Scottish law, which is significantly different from its English counterpart. In 19th-century English practice, a suspicious death prompted an inquest followed by a hearing before a grand jury, where it was decided whether there was enough evidence for an indictment against the accused. In Scotland the accused was removed from public view from the time of arrest until the trial. At the beginning of a murder case, the procurator-fiscal, or public prosecutor, would order the examination of witnesses. Each witness had to make a declaration, the equivalent of a statement.

In the Scottish trial system, neither the prosecution nor the defense made an opening address indicating the lines of inquiry that would follow; the story unfolded slowly as each presented the testimony of witnesses. The jury consisted of 15 men (in contrast with 12 in England and the United States), and the court accepted a majority verdict rather than demanding a unanimous vote. Unique to the Scottish system, "not proven" was a verdict that established neither innocence nor guilt, but consigned the accused to limbo. Cynics have described it as amounting to "not guilty, but don't do it again."

Above inset (Pierre) Emile L'Angelier, allegedly poisoned by Madeleine Smith at her home.

Above The Smith family house in Blythswood Square. Madeleine's bedroom windows are to the left of the side door, partly below ground level.

MONCREIFF, OPENING FOR THE PROSECUTION, called several witnesses to give details of L'Angelier's life in Glasgow—how he persuaded a mutual friend to introduce him to Madeleine Smith in 1855, their subsequent correspondence, the Smith family's opposition, and the bouts of sickness he suffered before his death. Smith's final letter to L'Angelier, requesting a meeting, was offered as evidence along with L'Angelier's journal, which demonstrated his extreme jealousy. Tom Kennedy, who worked with L'Angelier, testified that the deceased had said that he intended to keep Smith's letters and that he would never allow her to marry another man. Medical evidence showed that 82 to 83 grams of arsenic had been found in the deceased's stomach, and the prosecution established that this could have been ingested unnoticed in a cup of cocoa or chocolate.

The prosecution alleged that on the fatal night, Smith gave L'Angelier a drink containing the poison. Smith's maid, however, insisted that no one could reach her mistress's room without opening a creaking door next to the room that she (the maid) shared with the cook. Smith's case was helped by the testimony of the constable who patrolled Blythswood Square on the night of March 23. He told the court that he had often seen L'Angelier hanging around the house but had not seen him on the night in question.

Smith had made a statement after her arrest on March 31, and this was read to the court. She admitted that she had written to L'Angelier on March 20, asking for a meeting the next day, but she testified that he had not kept the appointment or contacted her. She admitted that she had been engaged to L'Angelier and that she had subsequently accepted Minnoch's

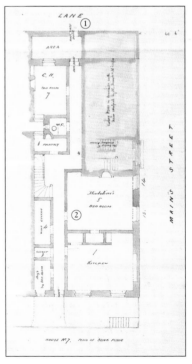

Above The floor plan of the Smith house, submitted in evidence. The shaded area shows the part of the building owned by another family and accessed by the side door. The Smith's maid claimed that L'Angelier would have had to enter by the noisy back door (1) and could not have reached Smith's room (2) without being heard.

Above A miniature bottle of arsenic found in Madeleine Smith's possession, and shown in court as evidence. Smith claimed that she used it for cosmetic purposes.

BIOGRAPHY

Madeleine Hamilton Smith (1835–1928) was the daughter of a distinguished Glasgow architect. Until the age of 20, she lived the life of a lady of genteel family. But in April 1855 she began a passionate correspondence with (Pierre) Emile L'Angelier, a packing clerk, and they became lovers. On March 23, 1857, L'Angelier died of arsenic poisoning, and Smith was accused of his murder. After she was acquitted, Smith moved to London, and in 1861 she married the artist George Young Wardle. She emigrated to the United States after his death, and there married an American named Sheehy. As Lena Wardle Sheehy she lived in New York until her death at the age of 93.

proposal. She confessed to buying arsenic on three occasions for cosmetic purposes but emphatically denied poisoning her former lover with it. This evidence was questioned when the prosecution called a close friend of L'Angelier, Mary Arthur Perry, a respectable spinster who made a good impression on the jury. Perry testified that L'Angelier had told her that Smith might try to get rid of him, and that he felt unwell after he had drunk a cup of chocolate prepared for him by Smith on February 23.

Public excitement reached a climax on the fifth day of the trial, when Smith's letters were read aloud. The defense knew how badly the contents would reflect on Smith and made a desperate attempt to prevent a public reading, claiming that no one could prove their authenticity. The court overruled this objection, and an elderly clerk read the letters in an expressionless drone. The public, titillated by the thought of what it would hear, was disappointed. Although the letters were full of intimate detail, the prosecution tempered its quest for truth with Victorian prudery and suppressed anything that an 1850s audience would have found indelicate or improper, in particular certain comments Smith wrote the day after she became L'Angelier's mistress. Nonetheless, staid Edinburgh society heard enough to be deeply shocked at this candid expression of passion.

Opinion was running against Smith at this point. But the balance tipped when the three judges, who evidently sympathized with her, decided by a two to one majority not to admit as evidence L'Angelier's diary, which chronicled his meetings with Smith and his gastric upsets. Lords Hope and Handyside stated that it would be "highly dangerous to receive as evidence a writing which may have been idle and purposeless." Only Lord Ivory dissented from this judgment, seeing the diary as the key piece of evidence.

THE WITNESSES FOR THE DEFENSE were less impressive. Several pharmacists claimed to have sold laudanum (a form of opium) to someone who looked like L'Angelier at the time of his last journey to Glasgow. One described the purchaser as a "military gentleman"—an unlikely description of L'Angelier, whose style was more that of a dandy. The defense read carefully selected extracts from Smith's letters that showed her in a better light. One physician spoke in general terms about the possibility that L'Angelier committed suicide by arsenic poisoning; another gave his opinion that washing in diluted arsenic—which Smith claimed to have done—was not harmful. Smith's 11-year-old sister, Janet, also gave evidence, describing in an emotional choking voice how she and Madeleine had gone to sleep in their shared bedroom as usual on March 22.

The lord advocate closed for the prosecution on the seventh day of the trial, in a precise and detailed summation. As he addressed the jury, he carefully associated sexual licentiousness with the capacity for murder. He spoke scornfully of Smith's explanation of the arsenic she had bought: "She says she poured it all in a basin and washed her face with it. Gentlemen, do you believe that?" He went on to discount the possibility that someone else had poisoned L'Angelier or that he had died by accident. It was unlikely, he pointed out, that having received Smith's last summons, L'Angelier would have poisoned himself before going to see her. In spite of the lack of evidence that L'Angelier and Smith were together on the fatal night or the night before, the lord advocate seemed to have built an unassailable case.

THE NEXT DAY INGLIS SUMMED UP FOR THE DEFENSE. He reiterated that Smith had tried to break off the relationship and that L'Angelier had resisted. He conceded that the letters contained examples of "low passion" but said that an innocent girl had obviously been corrupted by a worldly older man. He attacked the prosecution's attempt to link sexual immorality and murder. Then he reminded the jury that the charge was a capital offense; he cited a recent case in which a servant had been executed for allegedly putting arsenic in a pudding, after which the actual murderer made a deathbed confession. Stressing the real flaw in the prosecution's case—that no one had traced L'Angelier's movements on the night in question—he asked the jurors to consider what their moral position would be if the murderer were apprehended after they had consigned Smith to the gallows.

Inglis's rhetoric was greeted with loud applause. Lord Justice-Clerk Hope, in his instructions to the jury, pointed out that both prosecution and defense had dealt with hypothetical guilt and innocence; but the only thing the jury should consider was the evidence. He made it plain that he thought it unlikely that an alternative "murderer" would be found. At 1:00 P.M. on July 9 the 15-man jury retired. Half an hour later they returned, all in tears. The foreman read the verdict. On count one, not guilty by a majority; on count two, not proven by a majority; and on count three, the murder charge, not proven by a majority. Madeleine Smith was free. But onlookers thought it significant that Inglis neither spoke to nor looked at her. Later, at a private dinner, he was asked whether he thought Smith was guilty. He reportedly replied: "I would sooner have danced than supped with her."

Above John Inglis, dean of the faculty of advocates and Smith's defense counsel. He was one of the most prominent legal figures in Scotland at the time.

Below A sketch of the proceedings made by a courtroom artist while the trial was in progress.

Flinging a Pot of Paint

JAMES McNEILL WHISTLER *v.* JOHN RUSKIN

NOVEMBER 25 – 26, 1878

Above "On the Brain—Mr. Whistler," a cartoon from the illustrated London journal *Pick-Me-Up*, January 9, 1892. The caricatured figure of Ruskin, sitting on Whistler's head, is being tormented by a stinging butterfly, recognizable in the art world as Whistler's stylized signature.

*D*ifferences of opinion over the value of fine art are a perennial part of the art world. But when the painter James McNeill Whistler sued the distinguished art critic John Ruskin for libel, he pushed the debate further. Before the trial was over, a jury would have to decide the merit not only of Whistler's art but of his lawsuit.

In May 1877 John Ruskin had visited the luxurious new Grosvenor Gallery in New Bond Street, London. The gallery's inaugural exhibition contained examples of the different schools of contemporary painting and contrasted the Pre-Raphaelite school, which Ruskin had supported and praised for years, with the Impressionist school, which he disliked. Whistler, one of the more avant-garde Impressionists, was represented by seven of his paintings, including two abstract works from his series of nocturnes.

Ruskin attacked Whistler's work in the 79th issue of his periodical *Fors Clavigera*, aiming his heaviest criticism at a painting of fireworks over the Thames entitled "Nocturne in Black and Gold: The Falling Rocket," priced at 200 guineas (just over $1,000). Ruskin wrote: "For Mr. Whistler's own sake, no less than the protection of the purchaser, Sir Coutts Lindsay [the gallery owner] ought not to have admitted works into the gallery in which the ill-educated conceit of the artist so nearly approached the aspect of willful imposture. I have seen, and heard, much of Cockney impudence before now: but never expected to hear a coxcomb ask two hundred guineas for flinging a pot of paint in the public's face."

WHAT RUSKIN MOST DISLIKED ABOUT WHISTLER'S PAINTING was the apparent lack of finish and disciplined workmanship. His criticisms were echoed in other London newspapers, whose reviews of Whistler were generally unfavorable. The popular journal *Punch* described the same painting as "a tract of mud...above, all fog; below, all inky flood; for subject—it had none." But Ruskin's critique was by far the most vituperative. And it was to Ruskin that Whistler responded on July 28, 1877, by initiating a libel suit against him for 1,000 guineas in damages, the price of five such paintings. While Ruskin's attack spurred the young artist to retaliate, it puzzled the art world. Some thought that Ruskin was reacting to the high price tag; others, that he disliked Whistler's exhibitionism. Ruskin himself said that Whistler's work contained "no human expression and no moral intention," that there was nothing but an impartial comment on the shape and color of the visible world.

Jury Selection

Until the middle of the 19th century, all actions for damages in the British courts were decided by a jury, which also set the sum awarded to a successful plaintiff. Even after the law was changed and most actions for damages were heard by a judge alone, cases involving defamation of character continued to be decided by a jury. At the time of the Whistler v. Ruskin trial, the English legal system operated a two-tier jury system. Usually, a "common jury"—one chosen at random from male citizens on the electoral role, who were not paid a fee for jury service— would hear the case. However, either party could request a "special jury," chosen from men of property, from men with degrees from Oxford or Cambridge, or from men of "high degree," such as city merchants or bankers. Each special juror was paid one guinea per case. Both Ruskin and Whistler insisted on having a special jury to hear their case, which added to the costs they each had to pay later. With the exception of a few unusual cases, the special jury system was rescinded in 1949 and was abolished from British law in 1971.

Above "Nocturne in Black and Gold: The Falling Rocket," Whistler's controversial oil on panel completed in 1875.

"Gentlemen, you have seen the pictures. If they had been exhibited to you before Mr. Whistler's eloquent disquisition, would you not have thought them strange and extravagant? If you had gone to the Grosvenor Gallery and had seen one of them valued at 200 guineas, would you not have said 'That price is absurd'?"

SIR JOHN HOLKER
addressing the jury,
November 25, 1878

Above Sir John Walter Huddleston, the presiding judge in Whistler *v.* Ruskin. *Vanity Fair*, a popular journal of the day, described him as "...not over educated yet with a great store of general knowledge."

Whistler, for his part, was delighted at the prospect of the trial. He wrote to the Pre-Raphaelite painter Edward Burne-Jones: "It's mere nuts and nectar to me, the notion of having to answer for myself in court, and the whole thing will enable me to assert some principles of art economy which I've never got into the public's head by writing, but may get sent all over the world vividly in a newspaper report or two." Ruskin's poor health caused a 16-month delay before the trial could begin, and it was not until November 25, 1878, that the two-day hearing commenced in the London Court of the Exchequer, in a small room in Old Westminster Hall. The 60-year-old Sir John Huddleston presided, and the gallery was crowded with spectators whose interest had been stirred up by publicity in the papers.

SERJEANT JOHN PARRY OPENED FOR WHISTLER. He stressed that because Ruskin was recognized as a leading art critic, his comments had caused significant damage to Whistler's reputation. Then Whistler entered the witness-box. Ruskin's senior defense counsel, Attorney General Sir John Holker, questioned him about the price of "Nocturne in Black and Gold."

HOLKER: It was for sale at 200 guineas?
WHISTLER: Yes.
HOLKER: You thought this a fair price?
WHISTLER: Yes.
HOLKER: Is 200 guineas what we, who are not artists, would call a stiffish price?

Above The Courts of Justice (where the trial took place) and Palace of Westminster, circa 1878.

WHISTLER: Very likely.

HOLKER: As for the "Nocturne in Black and Gold," how long did it take you to knock it off?

WHISTLER: I beg your pardon?

HOLKER: I was using an expression which is rather more applicable to my profession.

WHISTLER: Thank you for the compliment. I knocked it off in a couple of days.

HOLKER: And for the labor of two days you asked 200 guineas?

WHISTLER: No. It was for the knowledge gained through a lifetime.

At this, the spectators in the public gallery applauded loudly, and the judge threatened to clear the courtroom.

Next, Holker asked the judge's permission to bring the disputed painting into the courtroom to show to the jury. Whistler's counsel objected because it would not show well in the poor light of Old Westminster Hall, which had no electricity. The prosecution agreed that another painting from the exhibition could be brought in on condition that the jury be allowed to view a group of Whistler's paintings hanging in the nearby Westminster Palace Hotel. Whistler's painting "Battersea Bridge" was displayed for the court, and the judge himself questioned Whistler about it. Members of the jury were then escorted to the Westminster Palace Hotel.

When the court reconvened, the prosecution allowed "Nocturne in Black and Gold" to be exhibited. The jurors passed it among themselves. Then Holker continued questioning an unperturbed Whistler. The first witness for the prosecution, called to speak for the merit of Whistler's work, was the art critic William Rossetti, brother of the painter Dante Gabriel Rossetti. Holker challenged Rossetti's credentials by establishing that he was not a painter, then dismissed his opinions. The *Whitehall Review* reported that during Rossetti's cross-examination Whistler's face was "an arrangement of blank dismay." The next witness, Albert Moore, a contemporary painter, fared better; Holker could not shake him. Holker succeeded, however, in portraying the third and last witness, William Gorman Wills, as a second-rate dramatist and dilettante painter who revered Whistler and identified with his plight because his own work had been savagely criticized. Holker left the jury with the impression that if Wills was the best person Whistler could muster in his support, then Whistler's status must be questionable indeed.

BIOGRAPHY

John Ruskin, born in 1819, began to acquire a detailed knowledge of modern art while a student at Oxford. By the 1840s he was championing the Victorian Gothic revival, the work of J.M.W. Turner, and the Pre-Raphaelite school of painters. Through his books and other writings—including *Modern Painters* (1842–60), *The Stones of Venice* (1851–53), *Sesame and Lilies* (1865), *Munera Pulvis* (1872), and his final work *Praeterita* (1885–89), he became the most respected art critic of his day. In 1869 he achieved national recognition with his appointment to the Slade Chair of Fine Art at Oxford, which he resigned nine years later following the Whistler trial. In later life Ruskin suffered bouts of mental illness, and after 1879 periods of insanity left him unable to work for months at a time. He died in 1900 after a long and incapacitating illness.

Above A portrait of John Ruskin by Sir Hubert von Herkomer, completed in 1879 when the distinguished critic was already suffering from the illness that would kill him in 1900.

Below The brief for the plaintiff, prepared by Whistler's solicitors in 1877–78. It has been preserved, along with the brief for the defendant, in the Library of Congress in Washington, D.C.

> *"A nocturne
> is an arrangement
> of line, form, and color
> first….I make use of
> any means, any incident or
> object in nature that will
> bring about this
> symmetrical result."*
>
> WHISTLER
> in the witness-box,
> November 25, 1878

THE ATTORNEY GENERAL THEN MADE THE CASE FOR THE DEFENDANT. He introduced Ruskin as professor of fine arts at Oxford University. As a critic of world renown, asserted Holker, Ruskin had every right to use strong language and even to ridicule an artist whose poor performance warranted it. The jury must judge whether Whistler's paintings were "strange and extravagant" and whether the price of 200 guineas was absurd. By the following day, Holker was drawing laughter from his audience with his own ridicule of "Battersea Bridge," concluding: "Gentlemen, I ask you not to paralyze the hand of one who has given himself wholly to the art he loves. If you decide against Mr. Ruskin, he will cease writing. It will be an evil day for art if he is prevented from…legitimate criticism, and if critics are forced to indulge in fulsome admiration."

Holker called as witnesses the painters Edward Burne-Jones and William Frith. According to Frith, the best that could be said for "Battersea Bridge" was that "…it has beautiful colors but no more than in a piece of wallpaper." Charles Bowen, the junior defense counsel, asked permission to bring in a painting by Titian to demonstrate true workmanship. The judge allowed this, once he was assured that the painting was a genuine Titian. Bowen then displayed a portrait of Andrea Gritti, a doge of Venice; he pointed out the high finish of the painting—a sure sign, he claimed, of a work of art. (Ironically, the painting was later shown not to be by Titian.)

BIOGRAPHY

James Abbott McNeill Whistler was born in Massachusetts in 1834 but left the United States when he was in his twenties. He moved to Paris to study European painting, adopted a dandified style, began to use an elaborate butterfly as his signature, and joined the aesthetic movement. His work achieved more popularity in England than in France, so he moved to London in 1859. He became a close friend of Oscar Wilde, and the two men duelled each other regularly in outrageous witticisms. In the years that followed, Whistler became the leading representative of Impressionism in England. The "nocturnes" of the 1870s represent the culmination of this style, a deliberate challenge to the Victorian establishment. Following his famous libel trial against Ruskin, Whistler fled to Venice to escape bankruptcy but returned a few years later. In 1884 he was elected a fellow of the Royal Society. Whistler continued to teach and lecture in London and Paris until his death in 1903.

Above Whistler, caricatured by the cartoonist "Spy" in the popular British periodical *Vanity Fair* of January 12, 1878.

IN HIS SUMMATION FOR RUSKIN, Bowen reminded the jury that the issue was not whether "Nocturne in Black and Gold" was worth 200 guineas but whether Ruskin's comments were fair and honest criticism. Serjeant Parry, putting forward the case on Whistler's behalf, claimed that Ruskin had not leveled warranted criticism but rather a personal attack. The judge advised the members of the jury that if they found for the plaintiff, they must then decide "whether the insult was so gross as to call for substantial damages, or whether it is a case for slight damages, indicating that the case ought not to have come to court."

The jury retired for an hour and 20 minutes. They returned with a verdict for the plaintiff, and awarded damages of one farthing to Whistler. Judge Huddleston pronounced a judgment for no costs, leaving each of the two men to foot his own bill for the litigation. It was, in the final analysis, a ruling against both painter and critic for taking up the court's valuable time with a matter of small consequence.

WHISTLER VERSUS RUSKIN

THE LAW ALLOWS IT
THE COURT AWARDS IT

NO SYMPHONY WITH THE DEFENDANT

FARTHING 1878

DAMAGES

COSTS

COSTS

OLD PELICAN IN THE ART WILDERNESS

DUN BROWN

POSTSCRIPT

Both parties suffered as a result of the Whistler *v.* Ruskin verdict. Humiliated, Ruskin resigned from his position at Oxford University. "I cannot hold a Chair from which I have no power of expressing judgment without being taxed for it by British law," he wrote on November 28, 1878. His legal costs amounted to just over £386, but a group of 120 wellwishers raised the sum through public subscription as "an expression of our opinion that your lifelong honest endeavors to further the cause of art should not be crowned by your being cast in the costs arising from that action." Nevertheless, the case left Ruskin's reputation tarnished.

The moral victory was Whistler's, but the legal costs of nearly £500 added to his already mountainous debts and pushed him further toward bankruptcy, which he formally declared on May 8, 1879. He lost his house and many of his personal possessions and eventually left the country. In spite of this setback, he achieved considerable fame in later life and lived to see his portraits command 1,000 guineas each (over $5,000) by 1891.

Above "An Appeal to the Law," Edward Linley Sambourne's cartoon for *Punch*, December 7, 1878. Pots of paint look on from the side as the judge awards a farthing to Whistler, drawn as a small black bird with tin-whistle legs.

"A victory which bears a very striking resemblance to a defeat."

THE EXAMINER,
reporting on the verdict,
November 1878

Poisoned Lives

THE CROWN v. FLORENCE MAYBRICK

JULY 31 – AUGUST 6, 1889

Above The two bottles of Valentine's meat juice that were presented as evidence in Florence Maybrick's trial. It was alleged that she added arsenic and water to the juice and administered it to her husband.

On July 31, 1889, 26-year-old Florence Maybrick entered the dock at St. George's Hall in Liverpool. She stood accused of the murder of James Maybrick, her husband, a 50-year-old wealthy cotton broker. He had died of apparent poisoning, and his brother Michael pointed the finger at Florence. The previous fall Florence had discovered that her husband was conducting an affair of 20 years with a woman who had borne him five children. By March 1889 relations between the Maybricks had deteriorated dramatically. Lonely and disillusioned, Florence started an affair with her husband's friend Alfred Brierley. On March 21 the couple checked into a London hotel for a weekend that would cost Florence dearly.

When Florence returned to Liverpool, Maybrick discovered what she had done, and violent arguments ensued. On April 13, Florence visited a Liverpool pharmacy and bought a dozen fly-papers coated with arsenic. By April 27 Maybrick was very ill, and on April 30 Florence bought another two dozen flypapers. She claimed that she soaked these in water to obtain a solution to use as a facewash, a common practice at the time. However, as Maybrick's health deteriorated, the family nursemaid, Alice Yapp, became convinced that Florence was poisoning him and voiced her suspicions to two visiting friends of Maybrick, the sisters Mrs. Matilda Briggs and Mrs. Martha Hughes. About that time, Florence wrote a letter to Brierley and asked Yapp to mail it for her; instead, Yapp gave it to Edwin Maybrick, another of the brothers. The letter described Maybrick as "sick unto death." Edwin showed it to Michael, who also believed Florence was trying to poison her husband so that she could be with her lover. When Maybrick died on May 11, Michael locked Florence in her room and called the police.

BIOGRAPHY

Florence Elizabeth Maybrick, née Chandler (1862–1941), was born in Mobile, Alabama, the daughter of a rich cotton dealer who died when she was an infant. Her mother, Caroline, met and married a Prussian cavalry officer, Baron von Roques, while on a trip to Europe. In 1880, 18-year-old Florence met a cotton broker 23 years her senior named James Maybrick on the ocean liner *Baltic*, which was sailing from New York to Liverpool. They were married on July 27, 1881; a year later a son was born to them, then a daughter. The Maybricks then settled in Aigburth, Liverpool. In 1889, Florence Maybrick was tried for the murder of her husband, found guilty, and sentenced to death. Her sentence was commuted under tremendous public pressure only days before she was to hang. Florence served 15 years of a life sentence before being paroled in 1904. She returned to the United States, where she wrote a book about her years in jail and lectured on prison reform. Defrauded of her family inheritance while in prison and completely cut off from her children, she became a recluse, living in lonely squalor and poverty. She died in Connecticut at the age of 79.

Above James Maybrick was married to Florence for eight years before he died, allegedly from poisoning, in their home (**right**), Battlecrease House, in Aigburth, Liverpool.

A CORONER'S INQUEST WAS CONDUCTED IMMEDIATELY, given the suspicious circumstances of Maybrick's death. The coroner and a jury of 14 members heard the evidence of the nurses, servants, and doctors. At the outset of the inquest the foreman of the coroner's jury had to be discharged when it was discovered that he was an acquaintance of James Maybrick. Much to Florence's disadvantage, this man's private testimony was also set aside, in which he had informed the coroner that Maybrick habitually took drugs; the foreman said that he had actually seen Maybrick taking strychnine recently. The postmortem examination revealed much less than a fatal dose of arsenic in Maybrick's body. Had the foreman's testimony been admissible, it would have suggested that the man took the arsenic himself for medicinal purposes, since no one intending murder would have used such a small dose. However, the coroner's jury found unanimously that Maybrick had died from an irritant poison, and 12 of them believed it had been administered with the intention of taking away life. On the basis of these findings, the coroner concluded that "Florence Elizabeth Maybrick did willfully, feloniously and of her malice aforethought kill and murder the said James Maybrick." Florence was remanded pending committal proceedings in the Magistrates' Court, where a panel of magistrates decided that the case should be heard by a jury.

On July 26 the grand jury of the Liverpool Assizes found a "true bill"—sufficient reason to bring a case to trial—against Florence. The hearing was scheduled for July 31, and a highly regarded judge, Sir James Fitzjames Stephen, was appointed to try the case. Florence's mother, Baroness von Roques, hired the successful and well-known Irish barrister Sir Charles Russell to defend her daughter. Appearing for the Crown was another

The Right to Appeal

In the 20 years after Florence Maybrick's trial, two acts of Parliament were passed that radically altered the English criminal justice system. The first was the Criminal Evidence Act of 1898, which allowed a person accused of murder to give evidence in their own behalf. In making a statement protesting her innocence, Florence Maybrick had gained no benefit. No corroboration of her statement from other witnesses had been admissible.

The second act of Parliament, passed in 1907, established a Court of Criminal Appeal. Any modern court of appeals would certainly rule that the verdict in the Maybrick case could not be justified. However, until the Court of Criminal Appeal was established, a convicted person could not ask to have his or her case reviewed. Beginning in 1848, judges could refer any question of law to the High Court (the equivalent of the U.S. Supreme Court) or postpone judgment. High Court judges, in turn, had the power to alter a verdict or to overturn a decision on a point of law. But this system did not help those prisoners who had been unfairly treated by the judge. The only safeguard in such a case was the home secretary's power to review a criminal trial on both conviction and sentence.

Irishman, John Addison. The case had attracted too much publicity for it to be tried by a Liverpool jury; so 12 men from Lancashire were appointed. The people of Liverpool nevertheless made their presence felt as they gathered outside St. George's Hall, ready to hiss and spit at the murderous adulteress about whom they had read and heard so much.

THE TRIAL OPENED WITH MEDICAL EVIDENCE that proved too inconclusive to secure a murder conviction. Because Maybrick regularly took arsenic himself, it was impossible to say whether the half grain found in his body was the residue of habitual use or the remains of one fatal dose. One astonishing piece of evidence was the no fewer than 117 poison medicines the police had collected from Maybrick's house, all prescribed by different pharmacists. The combined toxic dose, it was determined, was enough to kill 150 adults. As to the cause of Maybrick's death, the medical evidence established nothing more than severe gastroenteritis. Impatient with forensic medicine, Sir James Stephen focused the court on Florence's private life.

Giving evidence for the prosecution, nurse Alice Yapp reported opening Florence's letter to Brierley, claiming that she had seen it only because she had dropped it in a puddle and needed to put it in a clean envelope. While doing so, she explained, she could not help noticing that Brierley was addressed as "dearest," and that Florence spoke of Maybrick as being "sick unto death," and of the two lovers as "free of all discovery now and in the future." When Michael read the letter, he had exclaimed, "The woman is an adulteress!" Yapp also said that three days before James died she had seen Florence by the sick man's bed, pouring medicine from one bottle into another.

The judge allowed Florence to read a long statement to the court. Regarding the purchase of the flypapers, she explained that for many years she had used a prescribed facewash containing arsenic. Having lost the prescription, she had decided to make up a solution herself, using arsenic soaked from flypapers, a method she claimed was used by friends in Germany. She also stated that while giving her husband a powder he had requested, she had spilled some of his meat juice (a tonic recommended for convalescents) and had added water to make up the quantity; this, she insisted, must have been the incident witnessed by Alice Yapp. Florence's defense was her undoing. Admitting that she had given the powder to Maybrick, even though she swore it was at his express request, allowed the prosecuting attorney to dismiss the medical evidence as irrelevant.

The case became a newspaper sensation, and the public, aware that the doctors had been unable to agree on the cause of death, rallied in support

> *"The tittle-tattle of servants, the public, friends, and enemies,…must leave their traces and prejudice their minds, no matter what the defense is."*
>
> FLORENCE MAYBRICK
> in a letter to her mother, referring to a possible jury selected in Liverpool, June 28, 1889

Above The interior of Wokes, the Liverpool pharmacy, where Florence bought flypapers treated with arsenic. The shop assistants gave evidence at the trial.

Above A Victorian artist's impression of Florence reading her statement in the dock.

Above Mr. Justice James Fitzjames Stephen, whose competence in handling the Maybrick case was later questioned.

of Florence. By August 3, when Russell summed up the defense, a large crowd was cheering him and hissing Yapp. Yet Russell's closing statements made no reference to James Maybrick's adultery, which gave Florence grounds for divorce and removed the motive for murder; neither did he call Florence's mother to testify that Florence used arsenic for cosmetic reasons.

On August 6 the judge launched a twelve-and-a-half-hour summing up, a confused, rambling survey of the case, heavily weighted toward the prosecution. Though he muddled dates, he became quite lucid when he told the jury: "You must remember the intrigue which she carried on with this man Brierley and the incredible thought that a woman should be plotting the death of her husband in order that she might be left at liberty to follow her own degrading vices....It is easy enough to conceive how a horrible woman in so terrible a position might be assailed by some terrible temptation."

THE JURY NEEDED ONLY **45** MINUTES TO DECIDE that the adulteress was also a poisoner and a murderer, and she was sentenced to death by hanging. An angry mob, appalled at the verdict, booed outside the great hall, and the first of many mass meetings soon took place in St. George's Plaza. Barristers and others criticized the proceedings on the grounds that Florence had been sentenced not for the alleged murder but rather for her "immoral behavior."

In the days that followed, tens of thousands of supporters signed petitions demanding a reprieve. On August 22, 1889, four days before she was due to hang, the Home Office stepped in on Florence's behalf, stating that there was some doubt about how James Maybrick had actually died. Florence's death sentence was commuted to life imprisonment.

POSTSCRIPT

In February 1891, less than two years after Florence Maybrick's conviction, Judge Stephen's ability was questioned in the House of Commons. In April that year he was admitted to an asylum for the insane, where he died in 1894. After his death, books appeared on both sides of the Atlantic, criticizing the verdict. American women campaigned for Florence's release, and in 1897 U.S. president William McKinley asked for a pardon, without success. Sir Charles Russell lobbied on her behalf until his death in 1900, even visiting her in prison after he became England's Lord Chief Justice.

Florence's case did not end with her eleventh-hour rescue from the hangman's rope nor with her eventual release on parole in 1904. Justice could not excuse commuting her sentence to life imprisonment. If she murdered her husband, by law she should hang. If there was doubt about her guilt or the fairness of her trial, her case should be dismissed or retried. During the 1907 debate in the House of Commons on the creation of the Court of Criminal Appeal, supporters referred to the case extensively. Why, they asked, had Mrs. Maybrick ever been imprisoned?

Florence eventually returned to the United States, where her son, James, died in 1911 at age 29, after accidentally taking poison while working in a laboratory.

I Am the Prosecutor

OSCAR WILDE v. THE MARQUESS OF QUEENSBERRY

APRIL 3 – 5, 1895

Above Oscar Wilde, painted against the London skyline in 1895 by the French artist Henri de Toulouse-Lautrec.

"You are sure to lose it, you haven't a dog's chance, and the English despise the beaten—vae victis! (everyone hates a loser). Don't commit suicide."

FRANK HARRIS,
Wilde's editor and close friend,
March 1895

On March 1, 1895, the playwright Oscar Wilde swore out a warrant for the arrest of John Sholto Douglas, 9th marquess of Queensberry, on the charge of criminal libel. Ten days earlier the marquess had called at the author's club in London (the Albemarle) and left a card with the scrawled and misspelled message: "To Oscar Wilde, posing Somdomite." When he was apprehended and brought before the Marlborough Street police court magistrate, Queensberry told the official: "I have simply, your worship, to say this. I wrote that card with the intention of bringing matters to a head, having been unable to meet Mr. Wilde otherwise, and to save my son, and I abide by what I wrote." A trial date was set, and the case was adjourned for eight days.

AT THE TIME OF QUEENSBERRY'S ARREST, his younger son, Lord Alfred Douglas, had been the constant companion of the playwright Oscar Wilde for four years. After repeated requests, orders, and exhortations to his son to stop seeing Wilde, Queensberry threatened to make a public scandal. He called on Wilde at his Chelsea home on June 30, 1894, and accused him of sodomy. He prowled London, checking various gathering places to see if Lord Alfred and Wilde were there together. Alarmed, Wilde tried to engage a solicitor, Sir George Lewis, only to discover that Lewis had already been engaged by Queensberry. Instead Wilde hired Mr. C. O. Humphreys, a much less experienced solicitor.

Queensberry came to the point of desperation when his elder son and heir, Lord Drumlanrig, died in what was officially declared a shooting accident. Beside himself with grief, and convinced that his elder son had committed suicide to avoid a homosexual scandal, Queensberry intensified his pursuit of Wilde in hopes of separating him from his younger son. Rumors reached Wilde that Queensberry intended to demonstrate publicly against him at the premiere of his new play *The Importance of Being Earnest*. When

Private Acts and the Law

Sexual activity between men was punishable by death under British law until 1828, and by a lengthy prison sentence until the middle of the 20th century. (Sexual activity between women was so taboo, it was not even legislated against.) Although psychologists published studies on sexual behavior during the second half of the 19th century, the word "homosexual" was not defined until 1869, the result of the work of a Hungarian physician named Benkert. At the time of Wilde's libel suit against Queensberry, many practicing homosexuals with sufficient means were leaving England for the more permissive moral climate of mainland Europe, while others lived secret lives, often in fear of blackmail or social ruin.

The Wolfenden Report, published in Britain in 1957, recommended that private homosexual acts between consenting adults should no longer be considered a criminal offense, but there was considerable public opposition to changing the law. With the Gay Rights movement of the 1960s and its campaign for legal reform came passage of the Sexual Offenses Act of 1967, which decriminalized homosexual activity between people over the age of 21.

Above Oscar Wilde and Lord Alfred Douglas, photographed in Oxford circa 1893.

BIOGRAPHY

Oscar Fingal O'Flahertie Wills Wilde was born in Dublin, Ireland, in 1854, the son of a prominent surgeon, Sir William Wilde, and an eminent poet and Irish nationalist, Lady Jane Wilde, who wrote under the pseudonym "Speranza." As a student of Trinity College, Dublin, and later Magdalen College, Oxford, Wilde showed early signs of remarkable literary gifts. He embraced the ideal "art for art's sake" and while still a student made the first of many celebrated remarks: "Oh would that I could live up to my blue china." In 1884 he married Constance Lloyd, and they had two sons: Cyril, born in 1885, and Vyvian, born in 1886. Wilde's most enduring work was written during the next decade, beginning with his only novel, *The Picture of Dorian Gray* (1890). This was followed by a string of successful plays: *Lady Windermere's Fan* (1892), *A Woman of No Importance* (1893), *An Ideal Husband* (1895), and *The Importance of Being Earnest* (1895). Wilde's career came to an abrupt halt when he was found guilty of criminal indecency and sentenced to two years in prison. Released in 1897, he was bankrupt and disgraced. He moved to Paris, where he died from an inflammation of the brain three years later. In his dying moments Wilde was received into the Roman Catholic Church. His final work, *De Profundis*, a shortened version of his writings to Lord Alfred Douglas from his prison cell in Reading jail, was published posthumously in 1905.

Wilde had him banned from the performance, Queensberry appeared at the stage door to deliver a mocking bouquet of carrots and turnips.

Wilde wanted to take immediate legal action, but Humphreys advised against it, for no one at the theater was willing to testify on his behalf. Wilde's opponent was an immensely wealthy aristocrat, with powerful friends and far-reaching influence, while Wilde himself, indisputably a homosexual, was clearly on the wrong side of the law.

When Wilde called at his club on February 28 and was handed Queensberry's insulting message, he could contain himself no longer. Among other things, he had been insulted in front of his fellow club members. His friends advised him to tear up the card and forget it, but Lord Alfred Douglas ("Bosie") convinced him that to do so would be cowardly and disloyal. Wilde decided to take legal action. Douglas went with Wilde to Humphreys, where Wilde dictated an affidavit—most of which was untrue—about the relationship between Bosie and himself. Humphreys, ignorant of the real state of affairs and unaware that Queensberry had already obtained a number of love letters from Wilde to Bosie, assured his client that a case

> *"It would have been impossible for me to have proved my case without putting Lord Alfred Douglas in the witness box against his father.…Rather than put him in so painful a position I determined to retire from the case, and to bear on my own shoulders whatever ignominy and shame might result from my prosecuting Lord Queensberry."*

OSCAR WILDE'S
letter to the Editor
of the *Evening News*,
April 5, 1895

Below and right Shortly after the trial, the press reported that Bosie and his father had been arrested for fighting in the street. Witnesses reported that the crowds had cheered the marquess and booed his son.

against Queensberry for libel would succeed. When Wilde voiced his concerns about the expense of going to court, Bosie promised that his mother would be happy to pay the costs.

Wilde and Douglas, believing themselves on the verge of a great triumph, left to vacation in Monte Carlo. They returned to find the course of events turning against them. Sir George Lewis had withdrawn from the case out of friendship for Wilde, but he had been replaced as Queensberry's counsel by the Irish barrister Edward Carson, a hard-driving contemporary of Wilde's from Trinity College, Dublin. At first Carson was also unwilling to take the case, in part out of regard for Wilde, and in part because the defense was intrinsically weak. But Queensberry was prepared to spend large sums of money, and his team of private detectives had collected some damning evidence. Wilde's friend, the editor of *Fortnightly Review*, Frank Harris, learned through his contacts that Carson intended to present letters from Wilde to Douglas as evidence and advised Wilde to drop the case. Once again Bosie intervened. As Wilde wavered, Douglas turned on Harris, declaring: "Such advice shows you are no friend of Oscar's."

UNDER ENGLISH LAW THE DEFENDANT IN A LIBEL ACTION has to enter a plea of justification before the start of the trial, stating why he felt entitled to say what has since been charged libelous. Queensberry completed this on March 30, 1895, and when Humphreys showed the plea to his client, Wilde got the shock of his life. Of the 15 points in the plea, 13 concerned alleged acts of sodomy and gross indecency by Wilde, 10 of them with named persons whom the defense proposed to call. The other two attacked

THE QUEENSBERRY FRACAS.
POLICE COURT PROCEEDINGS.

There were several accounts given yesterday morning at the Marlborough Street Police-court of the encounter with which the Marquess of Queensberry and his son, Lord Douglas of Hawick, added to the animation of Piccadilly on Tuesday. There were also several attempts on the part of the Marquess of Queensberry to go into the causes and reasons of the quarrel and to explain to the magistrate (Mr. Hannay) that he had throughout been actuated by blameless motives. These explanations Mr. Hannay very properly cut short, and with equal propriety endeavoured to dissuade the Marquess from making any statement which would cast a reflection on family affairs such as had better remain private. The several accounts of the disturbance differed very little in detail, the witnesses believing that Lord Douglas struck his father first, and another that the Marquess was the aggressor.

A police-constable said that he noticed a crowd in Piccadilly and found the defendants fighting. He got together again. Again ... crossed Bond Street ... Marquess ...

138

the morality of his novel, *The Picture of Dorian Gray*—which portrayed a fashionable, arguably homosexual young man who never aged—and some of Wilde's more outrageous published sayings. Harris urged Wilde to drop the case, since it could only lead to ruin. But Wilde was already trapped. "I can't, I can't," he replied. "You only distress me by predicting disaster."

THE TRIAL OPENED ON APRIL 3 AT THE OLD BAILEY IN LONDON before Judge R. Henn Collins. Sir Edward Clarke for the prosecution made the opening speech on Wilde's behalf but unfortunately had prepared it before seeing the plea of justification. He defended *Dorian Gray* and claimed that the letters from Wilde to Douglas were mere literary conceits. He was not aware that the prosecution had a list of Wilde's homosexual partners.

Wilde took the stand. Although he was beginning to look more like the defendant than the wounded party, he reminded the court that "I am the prosecutor in this case." He started badly by stating under oath that his age was 39; Carson, his exact contemporary, knew it to be 41. However, Wilde recovered his composure and soon had the public laughing at his quips. When asked if it were true that blackmailers had approached him about some incriminating letters, Wilde responded: "He [the blackmailer] said, 'A man has offered me £60 for it.' I said to him, 'If you take my advice you will go to that man and sell my letter to him for £60. I myself have never received so large a sum for any prose work of that length. But I am glad to find there is someone in England who considers a letter of mine worth £60.'" Laughter filled the courtroom until Judge Collins threatened to clear the public galleries if there was any further disruption.

EDWARD CARSON BEGAN HIS CROSS-EXAMINATION FOR THE DEFENSE. His performance was highly praised in the press, but in fact his task was easy, given the mountain of evidence turned up by Queensberry's detectives. He made one ill-judged attempt to trap Wilde through a discussion on the content of *The Picture of Dorian Gray*. Wilde robbed the question of its effectiveness by turning it into a joke, delighting the onlookers.

CARSON: The affection and love of the artist of Dorian Gray might lead an ordinary individual to believe that it might have a certain tendency?
WILDE: I have no knowledge of the views of ordinary mortals.
CARSON: Have you ever adored a young man madly?
WILDE: No, not madly. I prefer love—that is a higher form.
CARSON: Never mind about that. Let us keep down to the level we are at now.
WILDE: I have never given adoration to anybody except myself.
CARSON: I suppose you think that a very smart thing?
WILDE: Not at all.
CARSON: Then you have never had that feeling?
WILDE: No…

DEFENSE COUNSEL

Edward Henry Carson (1854–1935), the defense lawyer in the first Wilde trial, was born in Dublin, Ireland, became a Queen's Counsel at the Irish bar in 1880 and a Q.C. at the English bar in 1894, after serving in 1892 as solicitor general for Ireland. During 1892–1921 he was a Conservative member of Parliament. After serving as solicitor general for England in 1900–06, he really made his mark during World War I, becoming successively attorney general (1915), first lord of the Admiralty (1917) and a member of the war cabinet (1917–18). In his later years he was associated with the cause of Ulster Protestantism, vehemently opposed the 1912 Home Rule Act, and organized the Ulster Volunteers to resist by violence if necessary. He was created baron in 1921 and served as lord of appeal until 1929.

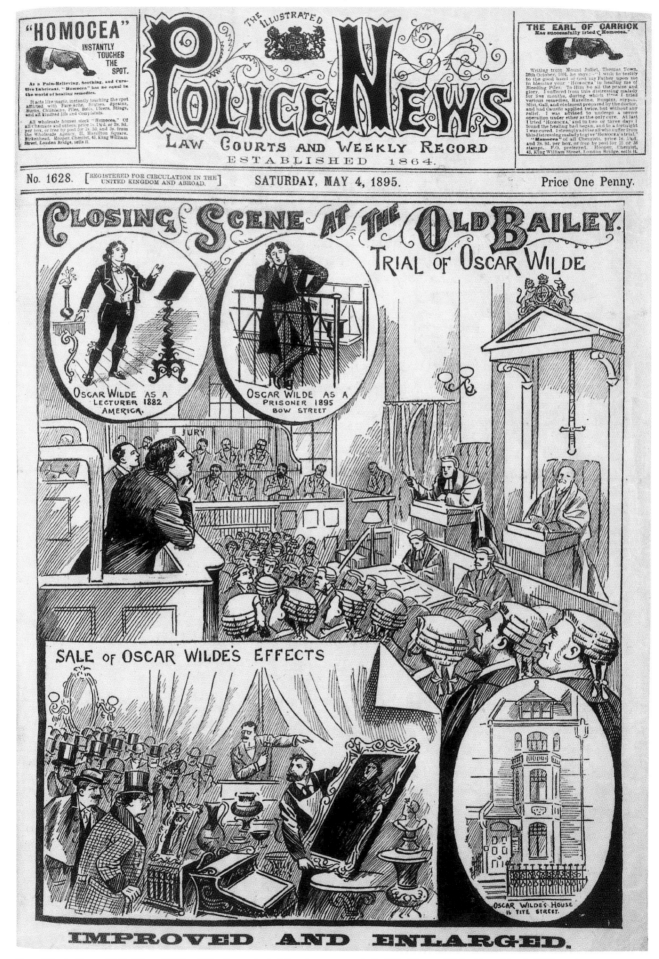

Above The decline and fall of Oscar Wilde told in pictures in the Victorian penny periodical *The Illustrated Police News*, May 4, 1895.

Despite the public's amusement, Carson soon regained the upper hand, as he shifted his questions to the list of names in the plea of justification. In particular, he asked Wilde about a boy named Walter Grainger, a servant in Oxford where Lord Alfred Douglas had rooms:

CARSON: Did you ever kiss him?
WILDE: Oh, dear no. He was a peculiarly plain boy. He was, unfortunately, extremely ugly. I pitied him for it.
CARSON: Was that the reason you did not kiss him?
WILDE: Oh, Mr. Carson, you are impertinent and insolent.
CARSON: Why, sir, did you mention that this boy was extremely ugly?
WILDE: For this reason. If I were asked why I did not kiss a doormat, I should say because I do not like to kiss doormats. I do not know why I mentioned that he was ugly, except that I was stung by the insolent question you put to me and the way you have insulted me through this hearing.

One by one, the names of men alleged to have had liaisons with Wilde were read to the court: Sidney Mavor in October 1892, Freddie Atkins on November 20, 1892, Alfred Wood in January 1893, Charley Parker in March and April 1893, Herbert Tankard and other unnamed youths in March 1893 at the Savoy Hotel, and many more. The case was lost, and privately Clarke advised Wilde to flee the country before he was arrested. Wilde refused, and Clarke asked for a verdict of "not guilty" on the grounds that Wilde was not "posing" as a sodomite. But the prosecution insisted that the entire plea be vindicated, with the implication that Queensberry had called Wilde a sodomite in the public interest. Clarke backed down, and Judge Collins instructed the jury to find in favor of Queensberry. Collins later sent Carson a note complimenting him on his performance, adding: "I congratulate you on having escaped the rest of the filth."

Below Wilde began a fashion for wearing a carnation dyed verdigris green on the opening nights of his plays. Soon green carnations were adopted by his friends as a symbol of decadence and artistic temperament.

POSTSCRIPT

On April 6, 1895, the day after his libel case against Queensberry ended, Wilde was arrested for criminal indecency and taken to Bow Street police station in London. Refused bail, he was transferred to Holloway prison outside London, where he remained until April 26. There followed two consecutive trials that scandalized observers throughout the English-speaking world. Journalists and commentators publicized evidence from servants and housekeepers in the Savoy Hotel, London, concerning Wilde's liaisons with a large number of young men. The judge, Sir John Bridge, was quoted in the papers as saying that "no worse crime than this" [criminal indecency] existed. In his first trial Wilde made an eloquent defense of "the Love that dare not speak its name," which moved the public galleries to applause and probably contributed to the fact that it resulted in a hung jury. The case was retried beginning on May 1, and this time Wilde was found guilty. After serving his sentence of two years' imprisonment with hard labor, Wilde was released in 1897—broken, bankrupt, and ill. He died in Paris at the age of 46, too poor to pay for the medical care he needed. "Ah well, then," he is reputed to have said, "I suppose I shall have to die beyond my means."

"The 'Love that dare not speak its name' in this century is such a great affection of an elder for a younger man as there was between David and Jonathan, such as Plato made the very basis of his philosophy, and such as you find in the sonnets of Michelangelo and Shakespeare."

OSCAR WILDE,
defending himself against charges of indecency and sodomy,
April 26, 1895

The Perfect Crime

THE STATE OF ILLINOIS v. LEOPOLD AND LOEB

JULY 21 – AUGUST 28, 1924

Above Bobby Franks, the 14-year-old schoolboy victim of the murder plan. Bobby was a cousin of Richard Loeb.

*M*any people have at one time or another fantasized about committing the perfect crime. In Chicago in 1924 two brilliant young students decided to carry out such a crime. They had studied the works of the German philosopher Friedrich Nietzsche, who argued that certain supremely talented individuals were "beyond good and evil" and owed allegiance to no moral law save their own will. According to the young men's simplified and bowdlerized reading of Nietzsche's ideas, such "supermen" would be justified even in taking the life of one of the "lesser breeds." In the summer of 1924, Richard Loeb and Nathan Leopold were brought to trial for turning a common fantasy into a grisly crime.

LEOPOLD AND LOEB FIRST MET IN 1918, when they were 13 and 14 years old respectively. By the fall of 1923, when they decided to put their version of Nietzsche's theory to work, they had already built a short history together of minor theft, arson, and larceny. Committing murder was just another step along an already well-trodden criminal path. As part of their plan, they decided to prolong the agony of their victim's relatives, and compound murder with extortion, by sending a ransom note. To avoid betraying themselves by their handwriting, Nathan stole a typewriter. They opened a bank account under a false name and established credit with a car rental firm. Then they practiced throwing packages off the Michigan Central train to work out a safe method for receiving the ransom money. On May 21 they rented a car, bought a chisel, a rope, and hydrochloric acid. Finally, they chose their victim. After first considering and rejecting nine-year-old Johnny Levinson, a classmate of Loeb's younger brother, Tommy, they settled on Loeb's 14-year-old cousin Robert Franks.

On May 24 Leopold and Loeb drove to the Harvard Preparatory School in the affluent South Shore area of Chicago, where Bobby Franks was a

Equality before the Law?

The U.S. Constitution states that all people are created equal and have equal rights before the law. But for many, the trial of Leopold and Loeb undermined that belief, raising a political issue far older than the Constitution. Leopold and Loeb were intelligent and articulate young men, and their families wealthy and influential. They hired a high-profile lawyer who made use of the most up-to-date theories and arguments. The defense team saw to it that the case was featured on the front page of the *New York Times* virtually every day of the proceedings, giving their leader, Clarence Darrow, a national forum for his arguments against the death penalty. If the defendants had been poor, ill-educated, or black, people asked, would they have received the death penalty? Could wealth buy off a capital charge, no matter how damning the evidence? The answer to both questions, many concluded, was yes. The controversy continues today over highly publicized celebrity trials, such as the O. J. Simpson case. With most prisoners on death row being people of color from impoverished backgrounds, and lacking the benefit of an eminent lawyer to defend them, an important question hangs over the judicial system. Are the wealthy and famous "more equal" than others in a free society?

Above The Illinois state police examine the body found beside the Pennsylvania Railroad tracks.

student. They enticed the boy into their rented car and—according to later press reports—sexually abused him. Richard proceeded to murder his young cousin, using the chisel as a weapon. Nathan then drove to a deserted spot beside the Pennsylvania Railroad tracks 20 miles away. The murderers stripped their victim of clothing and hid the body in a culvert, where they imagined it would not be found for years. They burned Bobby's clothes in a furnace at the Loeb home and buried his shoes, belt buckle, and jewelry in a field. Then they washed the bloodstains from the car.

On returning, the young men telephoned Richard's uncle anonymously and told him that Bobby had been kidnapped. They followed the call with a ransom demand the next day, asking Jacob Franks to prepare a parcel of used bank notes and to throw it from his car at a specific location by the railroad tracks. It was then that their plan began to unravel. By the time the Franks family received the ransom note, banner headlines in the newspapers were already announcing that the boy's body had been found. A railroad workman had seen a bare foot sticking out of the culvert and had called the

Below The ransom note that Leopold and Loeb sent to the boy's father, millionaire Jacob Franks. It was found later in a New York Pullman coach.

Dear Sir:

Proceed immediately to the back platform of the train. Watch the east side of the track. Have your package ready. Look for the first LARGE, RED, BRICK factory situated immediately adjoining the tracks on the east. On top of this factory is a large, black watertower with the word CHAMPION written on it. Wait until you have COMPLETELY passed the south end of the factory - count five very rap idly and then IMMEDIATELY throw the package as far east as you can.

Remember that this is your only chance to recover your son.

Yours truly,
GEORGE JOHNSON

Above Nathan Leopold's glasses, left behind at the scene of the crime, were the conclusive piece of evidence that linked the two young men to the murder.

"The killing was an experiment....It is just as easy to justify such a death as it is to justify an entomologist in killing a beetle on a pin."

NATHAN LEOPOLD
to Darrow during preparation
for the trial,
1924

police. Another workman found a pair of horn-rimmed glasses nearby. Fortunately for the investigative team, the spectacles were expensive and unusual, making them an important piece of evidence. The Chicago optical firm that made them confirmed that only three pairs had been sold: the police found one of the owners wearing her pair; a second purchaser was away in Europe; the third pair had been sold to Nathan Leopold, who was unable to explain why he could not produce them. When forced to admit that the glasses were his, he and Loeb were arrested. Leopold brazened out the intensive questioning that followed, but Loeb cracked and admitted everything.

LEOPOLD'S FATHER ENGAGED CLARENCE DARROW, the famous defense lawyer. Celebrated for his advocacy of radical causes and underprivileged defendants, Darrow surprised his admirers by accepting the wealthy young men as clients. He replied: "Even the rich have rights." At the heart of his decision was his lifelong opposition to capital punishment. He hoped that the trial would showcase his belief that the death penalty never deters criminals. Meanwhile the public, fired by the media, was baying for blood, and a rumor arose that Darrow had "sold out" for a fee of $1,000,000. In fact he received just $30,000 and incurred vast expenses over a two-month period, during which his firm took on no other work. By the end of the trial his law firm had lost money on the case.

Darrow went to work on tactics right away. He reasoned that if he entered a plea of not guilty by reason of insanity, the jury would have to decide if his clients were guilty or not. In the prevailing climate of opinion, he felt sure that this would result in both receiving the death sentence. On July 21 he entered a plea of guilty with diminished responsibility due to severe mental disturbance. This admission of guilt deprived the jury of its

---

BIOGRAPHY

Richard Loeb (1905–36) and Nathan Leopold (1904–71) were, at the time of their murder trial in 1924, the youngest people ever to graduate from college in the state of Illinois. At 19 years of age, Leopold, the son of a retired millionaire box manufacturer, had already completed his Bachelor of Arts degree at the University of Chicago, while 18-year-old Loeb, son of the multi-millionaire vice-president of Sears, Roebuck and Company, had graduated from the University of Michigan. Between them, they were heirs to a combined fortune of $15 million.

Both young men suffered from mental and physical health problems. Leopold had glandular abnormalities and

consequent irregularities of blood pressure, temperature, and metabolism, which resulted in violent mood swings. He was also physically unattractive— short of stature, round-shouldered, with prominent eyes, coarse hair, and a protruding abdomen. He was spoiled and pampered by his mother, who protected him from other boys' roughness by sending him to a girls' school. During his early youth he was educated at home where, it emerged at the trial, he was sexually assaulted by his governess.

Richard Loeb, by contrast, was classically handsome. A voracious reader of crime stories as a child, he later became obsessed with the idea of

committing the perfect murder, one that would baffle the police and establish his superiority of mind, backing up his belief that he belonged to Nietzsche's race of "supermen."

On May 24, 1924, Leopold and Loeb kidnapped and murdered Loeb's cousin, 14-year-old Bobby Franks. Arrested almost at once, they were tried and sentenced to life imprisonment for murder and 99 years each for kidnapping. In 1936, Loeb was stabbed to death in the state penitentiary by a fellow inmate. Leopold devoted his attention to prison reform and was paroled in 1958. He settled in Puerto Rico, where he married in 1961. Ten years later he died of a heart attack.

Above Schoolboy Johnny Levinson testifies before Judge Caverly (left) that he spoke to Loeb at the school on the morning that Franks was kidnapped.

usual role; the only remaining question was whether the teenagers would be executed or sentenced to life imprisonment. Darrow had deliberately calculated the effect of throwing the full burden of the decision onto a single judge, whom he thought would be reluctant to order a double execution. His strategy was risky, but proved effective when Justice John R. Caverly announced that he would listen to Darrow's case in mitigation.

FOR 33 DAYS EACH SIDE PRODUCED EXPERT WITNESSES. Psychiatrists for the defense argued that Leopold and Loeb were mentally ill. Evidence was given that Leopold was a victim of what was at the time called a "split" personality. Such was the disintegration of his personality, the experts explained, that he should be considered schizophrenic. Loeb, also described as ill, was prone to fainting fits and was proved in court to be a pathological liar. When psychiatrists for the prosecution claimed that both young men were sane and entirely responsible for their actions, Darrow attacked them as benighted representatives of a past age who would only consider a raving maniac insane. He paced the Chicago courtroom—shimmering with July heat—stripped to his shirtsleeves, big round shoulders hunched forward, a wisp of hair over his eyes, and as he strode back and forth before the judge, he defended not only his clients but his beliefs about criminal psychology and his theories on deterrence and effective punishment as well.

As in many U.S. criminal trials, a lengthy period of expert testimony was a mere prelude to the real drama, when prosecution and defense

"I know the future is with me and what I stand for here....I am pleading for life, understanding, charity, kindness, and the infinite mercy that considers all. I am pleading that we overcome cruelty with kindness and hatred with love."

CLARENCE DARROW
summing up for the defense,
August 22–25, 1924

counsel made their final pleas. State's Attorney Robert Crowe asked the court for the death penalty. He countered Darrow's speech on the evils of capital punishment by arguing for the supremacy of the law. It did not matter what Crowe or Darrow thought of capital punishment, he said. The death penalty had been ordained by the state legislature, which was elected by the people of Illinois. He also insisted that the tender age of the accused was irrelevant, arguing that most crimes were committed by young people between the ages of 16 and 24. Finally, he reiterated for the court his three-fold argument in favor of the death penalty: the boys were entirely sane and responsible for their actions; they had been motivated by the hope of keeping the ransom money to pay off gambling debts; and together they had sexually abused Franks before murdering him.

DEFENSE COUNSEL

Clarence Darrow (1857–1938) was born near Kinsman, Ohio, and, until the age of 37, enjoyed a successful but uneventful career as a corporation lawyer. He shot to fame in 1894 when he defended the American Socialist leader Eugene Debs, president of the American Railroad Union, who, together with several other union leaders, had been arrested on a federal charge of contempt of court arising from a strike at the Chicago Pullman Palace Car

Company. Although Darrow lost the case, he won a national reputation as a champion of radical causes. A brilliant orator as well as a master of reforming the law, framing pleas, and eliciting evidence, he became one of America's most renowned defense lawyers. He made use of his position to conduct a tireless campaign against capital punishment. By the time of the Leopold and Loeb trial in 1924, Darrow had already applied his skill to saving 102

Above Clarence Darrow at the bar during the arraignment with Leopold on the left, and Loeb on the right.

people from the death sentence. The following year he shattered the career of populist American politician, William Jennings Bryan, by volunteering his services to defend the right of a biology teacher to teach Darwin's theory of evolution to public school students in the state of Tennessee.

DARROW TOOK THREE DAYS (AUGUST 22–25) TO SUM UP for the defense; in the process he was dubbed "the old lion" by the press. He pointed out that in the previous 10 years, 340 people had been indicted for murder in the state of Illinois, but only one had been hanged. Of 90 men hanged in the history of Illinois, not a single person under the age of 23 had ever been hanged on a plea of guilty. "We would not have civilization except for those 90 that were hanged," he added with heavy sarcasm, "and if we cannot make it 92 we will have to shut up shop."

He scorned the idea that capital punishment could ever reform or deter murderers and urged the court not to return to the cruel and barbarous past. "Do I need to argue to your honor that cruelty only breeds cruelty; that hatred only causes hatred; that if there is any way to soften this human heart, which is hard enough at its best…it is not through evil and hatred and cruelty? It is through charity, love and understanding. How often do people need to be told this? Look back at the world. There is not a philosopher, not a religious leader, not a creed that has not taught it."

BY THE THIRD DAY DARROW'S VOICE FALTERED FREQUENTLY, sometimes becoming faint; but not a word was missed, so deep was the silence in the Chicago courtroom and so riveted the audience. He attacked his own profession: a doctor, he declared, would try to discover the causes of typhoid fever by putting water and milk under the microscope; a lawyer would simply put the typhoid patient in jail as a "deterrent" to others. At four o'clock in the afternoon of August 25, Darrow finished his speech with a verse from Edward Fitzgerald's *Rubáiyát of Omar Khayyám:*

> *So be it written in the Book of Love,*
> *I do not care about that book above;*
> *Erase my name or write it as you will,*
> *So I be written in the Book of Love.*

The press later reported that listeners hardly knew where Darrow's voice ceased and silence began. The silence lasted a full two minutes after he finished speaking. Two weeks of nerve-wracking suspense followed before Judge Caverly gave his decision on September 10. More than five thousand people packed the streets surrounding the courthouse, waiting eagerly for the verdict. At last, word was released. Because of the defendants' mental state, their age, and the Illinois precedents, Judge Caverly stated, he was sentencing both Nathan Leopold and Richard Loeb to life imprisonment. This might, he added, turn out in the end to be more severe a form of retribution than the death penalty.

Within moments of the sentencing, the two young men were on their way to the State Penitentiary in Joliet, Illinois. Twelve years later, in 1936, Loeb was stabbed to death by a fellow prisoner. Nathan Leopold was paroled in 1958, after devising an educational system for prison inmates.

"You may hang these boys; you may hang them by the neck until they are dead. But in doing it you will turn your face towards the past. In doing it you are making it harder for every other boy who in ignorance and darkness must grope his way through the mazes which only childhood knows."

CLARENCE DARROW,
summing up for the defense,
August 25, 1924

Below The records from Illinois State Penitentiary for prisoners number 9305 (Richard Loeb) and 9306 (Nathan Leopold).

Evolution on Trial
THE STATE OF TENNESSEE *v.* JOHN T. SCOPES
JULY 10 – 21, 1925

Above John T. Scopes, the high school science teacher at the heart of the debate on creationism. He was charged with violating Tennessee law, which forbade teaching evolutionary theory in public schools.

The Butler Act

When John Washington Butler, the Tennessee legislator, sponsored the 1925 act that carried his name, he claimed to be motivated by the conviction that children should not be taught to deny the existence of God. "The Bible is the foundation upon which our American government is built," he said. "The evolutionist who denies the biblical story of creation...cannot be a Christian." The Butler Act made it illegal to teach the theory of evolution in state public schools. Passed in the Senate under the slogan Save our children for God, the act was signed into law by Governor Peay on March 21, 1925. Because the act did not require public schools to teach any single interpretation of the Bible, Peay believed that it did not violate the Bill of Rights. "After careful examination," he stated to the press, "I can find nothing of consequence in the books now being taught in our schools with which this bill will interfere in the slightest manner."

On March 21, 1925, the state of Tennessee passed an antievolution bill called the Butler Act, which forbade public school teachers to include Darwin's theory of evolution in their biology curriculum. Tennessee's governor, Austin Peay, acknowledged the depth of feeling expressed by parents who were fearful for their children's spiritual welfare, by signing the bill into law. "Probably the law will never be applied," he told the legislature. "Nobody believes that it is going to be an active statute."

Over subsequent months, state authorities made no effort to monitor what biology teachers taught. Then Lucile Milner, secretary of the New York–based American Civil Liberties Union (ACLU), saw a newspaper clipping about the Butler Act. The ACLU claimed as its mission the protection of the liberties of U.S. citizens, and Milner presented the clipping to the ACLU as evidence of a likely infringement. The organization agreed to raise a special fund to finance a test case and placed an advertisement in the Tennessee papers, asking for a teacher to volunteer to be prosecuted.

THE ACLU ADVERTISEMENT WAS SPOTTED BY GEORGE RAPPELYEA, a manager in the Cumberland Coal and Iron Company in Dayton, Tennessee. In Rappelyea's view, a court case could put Dayton on the map, attracting celebrities and boosting local business. He contacted 24-year-old John T. Scopes, a science teacher from Rhea County High School. Rappelyea asked Scopes if he thought he could teach biology without mentioning evolution. Scopes said no. When Rappelyea accused him of breaking the law, Scopes replied, "So has every other teacher," and pointed to George Hunter's *Civic Biology*, the standard textbook. Rappelyea showed Scopes the ACLU advertisement. Although the young teacher was understandably reluctant, he was persuaded to take part in the test case. "It's a bad law. Let's get rid of it," Rappelyea urged. "I will swear out a warrant and have you arrested...that will make a big sensation." Four days later a Rhea County grand jury met and indicted Scopes for violating the Butler Act.

A local lawyer in Dayton sent a telegram about the forthcoming trial to the populist orator and lawyer William Jennings Bryan. A former secretary of state and a Christian fundamentalist, Bryan had built a political power base in the Bible Belt. At the center of his campaign was a crusade to secure, in each of the states, a statute outlawing the teaching of the theory of evolution. Ultimately, if antievolution acts were passed in two-thirds of the states, Bryan would have a springboard for passage of an antievolution amendment to the U.S. Constitution itself.

Although he had not practiced law for 36 years, Bryan announced publicly on May 13 that he would like to represent the World's Christian Fundamentals Association in the Scopes trial by heading the prosecution team. Bryan's decision captured the attention of one of the country's outstanding criminal defense lawyers, Clarence Darrow, a confirmed religious

William Jennings Bryan (1860–1925) was born in Salem, Illinois. He studied law, and practiced in Jacksonville and Lincoln, Nebraska, where he was elected to the U.S. Congress in 1890. He secured the Democratic nomination for the presidency in 1896 but suffered a crushing defeat by William McKinley in that year and again in 1900. He lost a third time to William Howard Taft in 1908. Bryan was appointed secretary of state by President Woodrow Wilson in 1913, but his commitment to neutrality in World War I, which erupted the following year, led him to resign in 1915. Instead, he turned his attention to promoting peace, prohibition, and traditional Christian values and beliefs.

Although he was not a great thinker, Bryan had a gift for producing the appropriate phrase. He also had a large view of his own morality. "I have always been right," he claimed. His appetite was legendary; when reporters told Darrow the news of Bryan's sudden death and accused him of breaking Bryan's heart with relentless cross-examination, Darrow allegedly muttered: "Broken heart nothing; he died of a busted belly." In fact, Bryan suffered from diabetes, which, combined with stress, may have brought on the hemorrhage that killed him.

skeptic. Fresh from his triumph in saving Leopold and Loeb from the death penalty, Darrow saw the Scopes case as a challenge to personal and religious freedom. He cabled Dayton's officials, put his talents at Scopes's disposal, and offered to waive his fee. The stage was set for a great national debate.

THE TRIAL OPENED IN THE TINY TOWN OF DAYTON, population 2,000, on July 10, 1925, in sweltering heat. Rappelyea had secured an old Southern plantation house to serve as the courtroom so that all of the lawyers, journalists, and spectators expected to attend such a sensational trial could be housed. As it turned out, from the first day of the trial all 700 seats in the main room were taken, with another 300 members of the public standing. Many of the observers were committed fundamentalists who sang hymns and prayed for a verdict of guilty. The eyes of the country, even the world,

> *"We shall take the Scopes case to the United States Supreme Court if necessary to establish that a teacher may tell the truth without being thrown in jail."*
>
> RODGER BALDWIN,
> Spokesman for the American
> Civil Liberties Union,
> May 1925

> *"I do not consider it an insult, but rather a compliment, to be called an agnostic. I do not pretend to know where many ignorant men are sure—that is all that agnosticism means."*
>
> CLARENCE DARROW
> to the court,
> July 15, 1925

were on Dayton. Journalists flocked to Tennessee to cover the case, which they nicknamed the Scopes Monkey Trial. For the first time in U.S. history, microphones were set up in court to broadcast the proceedings.

THE PROSECUTION BASED ITS CASE ON GENESIS 1 : 25–27. Bryan's team of seven included the existing and former attorneys general of Tennessee. The judge, John T. Raulston, upheld the literal truth of the Bible and refused throughout the trial to admit scientific evidence from the defense. Darrow, the star in the defense team of four, did not object to the jury, even though 11 were fundamentalists and the twelfth could not read. He hoped to convince the court that there were, in fact, no charges to answer.

The jury was sent out of the courtroom during the technical arguments on constitutional law. Darrow, already in good form, declared that the antievolution act was "as brazen and as bold an attempt to destroy learning as was ever made in the Middle Ages." Portraying the case as a confrontation between freedom of scientific inquiry and benighted barbarism, he declared that convicting Scopes would mean a return to the teaching of the Dark Ages. He pointed out the U.S. Constitution's prohibition of religious instruction in public schools. The antievolution bill, he claimed, forced public schools to accept fundamentalism, in violation of this principle.

Below Judge John T. Raulston makes a ruling to the court, July 17, 1925.

Right A bookstall erected in Dayton during the Scopes Monkey Trial offers a selection of antievolution literature. Much of the material was written by Bryan.

On July 15 Judge Raulston formally ruled in favor of the indictment, at the same time refusing to accept any argument based on the validity of Darwin's theory. The jury would be instructed, he said, simply to decide whether or not Scopes had taught the theory of evolution. When he opened his defense on July 16, Darrow did not deny that Scopes had taught his students about evolution. Instead, he contended that more than one interpretation of biblical creation was possible; that although Scopes might have violated the fundamentalist interpretation of the Bible, he had by no means contradicted the theory of creation as held by millions of Christians. Surely, Darrow maintained, it was possible for a teacher to demonstrate that humankind had evolved over a period of hundreds of thousands of years, from an infinite variety of lower organisms, without violating the story of Genesis. To back him up, Darrow had assembled a huge cast of experts to testify on every aspect of evolution.

Bryan blocked this move by claiming that it was impertinent for "foreigners" to dictate to the state of Tennessee what laws it could enact. In a powerful piece of oratory, he upheld the literal interpretation of the Bible and condemned those who doubted it. Judge Raulston then ruled to exclude Darrow's experts and their testimony. With yet another of his motions denied, Darrow lost his temper and confronted the judge:

DARROW: I do not understand why every request of the defense is overruled.
RAULSTON: I hope you do not mean to reflect on the court.
DARROW: Well, your honor has the right to hope.
RAULSTON: I have a right to do something else.

He cited Darrow for contempt and forced him to apologize.

Denied his expert witnesses, Darrow decided to turn the tables and put literal interpretation of the Bible on trial. He asked Bryan if he would take the stand as an expert on the Bible. Bryan agreed. Darrow launched a relentless battery of questions, and Bryan began to flounder on his lack of biblical knowledge. Darrow coaxed the public to laugh out loud at the embattled prosecutor. In the end, Judge Raulston intervened to save Bryan from further embarrassment and sheer physical exhaustion. One reporter remarked: "Darrow never spared him. It was masterful, but it was pitiful."

In the aftermath of the exchange, Bryan took a terrific beating nationwide from the media. The judge ruled that Bryan could not go back on the stand and that all of his remarks should be stricken from the record. Darrow asked the jury to agree to a verdict of guilty so that the case could go straight to the Tennessee Supreme Court for appeal. They accepted this reluctantly on Raulston's instructions. Scopes was found guilty and fined $100. Five days later Bryan died suddenly of a cerebral hemorrhage.

POSTSCRIPT

In 1926 the Scopes appeal was heard by the Supreme Court of Tennessee in Nashville. The same passions and prejudices that had ruled both sides of the trial surfaced once again, and members of the public thronged the courthouse and shouted aloud in court. Nevertheless, the Tennessee Supreme Court reversed the decision of the Dayton Court on the technical grounds that Raulston, instead of the jury, had fixed the amount of the fine and that the fine was excessive. Two of the justices declared the antievolution law constitutional; a third justice agreed but considered the law irrelevant to the Scopes case; another justice declared the law to be unconstitutional. "Always there is one man. Amen!" Darrow is said to have remarked.

Meanwhile, at the next county election, Judge Raulston's constituency retired him. Scopes left teaching and after further education became a geologist. Bryan's disastrous performance on the stand did not help the cause of Christian fundamentalism in the United States. After the trial, the projected Bryan University in Dayton, which was to have taught a fundamentalist view of Christianity, never progressed beyond the deep hole dug in the ground for its foundations. However, the law that prohibited the teaching of evolutionary theory in Tennessee's public schools was not repealed until 1967.

Communists and Spies

THE PEOPLE v. JULIUS AND ETHEL ROSENBERG

MARCH 6 – 29, 1951

Above An anti-Rosenberg protester displays a placard with the message "Death To All Traitors" outside the White House in Washington, D.C., on February 17, 1953.

On March 6, 1951, headlines across the United States screamed the news that traitors were being brought to trial. At the center of the scandal were Julius Rosenberg (an electrical engineer who had formerly worked for the U.S. army) and his wife Ethel. Together they faced charges of passing U.S. atomic secrets to the Soviet Union. On trial with them was Morton Sobell, a radar expert who stood accused of supplying the Rosenbergs with classified information, which he had recorded on 35mm film. A wave of apprehension had swept over the country after the Soviet Union exploded its first atomic bomb on August 29, 1949; and intelligence agents discovered that details of the Manhattan Project—the U.S. World War II operation that developed the bomb—had been divulged to the Soviets. The agents identified Klaus Fuchs, a brilliant German-born physicist working at Harwell Atomic Energy Authority in Britain, as the Soviets' source. The British intelligence agency MI-5 arrested Fuchs and allowed the FBI to interrogate him. The trail that ended at Fuchs led back to the United States and implicated the Rosenbergs, who were known Communists in an era of anxious anticommunism.

THE ROSENBERG TRIAL WAS CONTROVERSIAL from the start. The judge, Irving R. Kaufman, was Jewish, as were the Rosenbergs, but he was as conservative as they were radical. Jury selection took two days, during which 29 prospective jurors were dismissed, and five with Jewish names asked to be excused. Eventually 11 men and one woman were selected.

Irving Saypol, U.S. attorney, led the prosecution, aided by five assistants, including Roy Cohn, who played a part in Senator Joseph R. McCarthy's anti-Communist activities in the 1950s. The prosecution set out a simple case. Under questioning by the FBI, Fuchs identified his contact as Harry Gold, who implicated David Greenglass. In the summer of 1944, Greenglass had worked as a machinist at the atomic weapons center in Los Alamos, New Mexico, where the atomic bomb was developed. In January 1945 he passed to Gold rough drawings of a lens used as a detonator. In September 1945 he passed on a drawing of the bomb itself. Greenglass, the prosecution noted, was Ethel Rosenberg's brother.

After running Gold to ground, the FBI arrested Greenglass and his wife, Ruth, in June 1950. Gold was subsequently sentenced to 30 years in prison, his wife got a minor sentence, and Fuchs was sentenced to 14 years. The authorities told Greenglass that if he would

Left Wartime laboratory buildings at Los Alamos, New Mexico, where David Greenglass allegedly stole secrets.

Executive Clemency

The Espionage Act of 1917, under which the Rosenbergs were sentenced, allows for the death penalty only if the spying occurs in wartime. The court decided that if secrets had been passed to the Soviets in 1944, the severest penalty could be imposed.

Any U.S. citizen condemned to death for a federal crime has the right to appeal to the president for executive clemency. Almost the first decision that Eisenhower had to make upon coming to office in 1953 was whether to pardon the Rosenbergs. Despite pleas for mercy from Pope Pius XII and President Auriol of France, he rejected the appeal. Writing to Prof. Clyde Miller, Eisenhower gave three reasons for his refusal. First, he regretted that a woman had to be executed but believed that a commuted sentence might lead the Soviets to recruit more women spies; second, he believed that Ethel had controlled Julius as her puppet; and third, he considered it a matter of credibility to show that the U.S. would not be swayed by public opinion to favor communism.

Two Nobel Prize winners (Albert Einstein and Dr. Harold Urey, formerly of the Manhattan Project) protested that the trial was blatantly unfair. Urey sent a telegram to President Eisenhower on June 12, 1953, setting out the injustices he saw in the case: Greenglass, the key prosecution witness, was a confessed spy; his word alone pointed to the Rosenbergs; and no important information was passed to the Soviets. Although there was no proof of guilt, the Rosenbergs received the most severe penalty.

Above Harry Gold identified himself to David Greenglass at their first meeting in 1945 by producing one half of a Jell-o box. Greenglass had received the matching half from his Soviet controller.

cooperate fully with the prosecution, he would face no more than a 15-year sentence, and his wife would go free. Greenglass agreed to cooperate and identified the Rosenbergs as his spymasters. The Rosenbergs denied everything, but they were nonetheless put on trial for passing national secrets to an alien power during wartime, an offense that could carry the death penalty.

IRVING SAYPOL MADE A POWERFUL CASE FOR THE PROSECUTION based on circumstantial evidence. But his trump card was the weakness of the defense. The team was led by Emmanuel Bloch, a civil rights specialist who represented Julius Rosenberg, and his father, Alexander Bloch, a 73-year-old business lawyer, who represented Ethel. The defense could have destroyed the prosecution's case at the outset. The evidence showed that atomic secrets had been passed on, but it did not prove that the Rosenbergs were responsible. A clear link was established between Gold and Greenglass and between Gold and his Soviet controller, "John"—an alias for Vice-Consul Anatoly Yakovlev. But the link to the Rosenbergs depended on the uncorroborated word of Greenglass, backed only by implications drawn from the fact that the Rosenbergs were Communists. The Blochs failed to exploit the weak links in the prosecution's case. Judge Kaufman, for his part, not only neglected to direct the jury on these points but allowed questions from the prosecution that should have been permitted only if the Rosenbergs were on trial for treason.

The defense missed some critically relevant facts, beginning with the reliability of Gold as a witness. Both Judge Kaufman and the counsel for the prosecution had been involved the year before in a spy trial in which Gold testified. They both knew that Gold's testimony in that case contradicted his testimony in this

Below David Greenglass, Ethel's brother, is taken out of the court in handcuffs by U.S. Marshal Eugene Fitzgerald. The Rosenbergs' lawyers argued that Greenglass accused his sister and her husband because of a long-standing family feud.

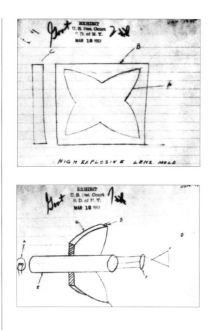

High explosive lens mold

Above David Greenglass's drawings of the high explosive lens molds used to detonate the bomb were presented to the court as evidence of espionage. Dr. Philip Morrison, an atomic scientist interviewed for a publication in 1973, described them as "a crude caricature…without enough detail to make it possible to reproduce or even understand [them]."

Below Ethel and Julius Rosenberg leave the federal court in New York in a U.S. marshal's van.

one, but the Blochs failed to discover this themselves. They also missed the fact that Greenglass changed his story 10 days before the trial, when he suddenly alleged that Ethel had typed secrets for the Soviets. David Greenglass made a full confession to the FBI admitting that he had stolen secrets and quantities of uranium from Los Alamos, but his sentence was reduced in return for testifying against the Rosenbergs. It was not normal procedure to convict on the uncorroborated word of a felon, especially in a capital case, yet Greenglass's testimony was the sole accusation against the couple.

However, the defense's worst mistake was to put the Rosenbergs on the stand. The confident manner adopted by Julius alienated the jury. Under cross-examination he denied every item of the prosecution's argument, but he harmed his own case (as Ethel did) by pleading the Fifth Amendment when asked about Communist Party membership. Meanwhile Judge Kaufman intervened to ask leading questions about the Rosenbergs' attitude toward communism. It became clear that, in his mind, Communist Party membership was synonymous with spying.

The Blochs came through for their clients on one issue, at least, when they focused on Greenglass's unreliability as a witness. In Emmanuel Bloch's words: "Not only are the Greenglasses self-confessed spies, but they are mercenary spies. They'll do anything for money…. Any man who will testify against his own flesh and blood, his own sister, is repulsive, revolting, and is violating any code of civilization that ever existed. He is lower than the lowest animal I have ever seen."

UNUSUAL CONDUCT BY LEGAL PERSONNEL was one of the hallmarks of the trial. Judge Kaufman treated the prosecution with obvious partiality, and Emmanuel Bloch, fearful of alienating public sympathy, decided not to raise objections. For example, Sobell and his wife were described in court as having been deported from Mexico, when they originally claimed that they had been kidnapped there by agents working for the FBI, making their sworn testimony illegally obtained. During the trial, counsel for the defense was fearful of the implications of accusing the FBI of misconduct, and failed to object. To prove that the Rosenbergs were about to flee the country when arrested, the prosecution produced a surprise witness, a photographer named Schneider, to whom, it was alleged, they had applied for passport photographs. The prosecution did not name him among their 102 witnesses, which should have made his last-minute testimony inadmissible. But Judge Kaufman allowed him to give evidence when the prosecution claimed that they had not known about the photographer's existence until the day before. In court, Schneider could not produce the negatives of the alleged photographs, nor any business records to support his testimony.

Kaufman directed the jury with noticeable partiality. He devoted three times as much attention to the prosecution's case as to the defense. He failed to warn jurors against convicting on uncorroborated testimony and reassured them regarding the testimony of Gold and Greenglass by stating: "In the federal court a defendant can be convicted upon the uncorroborated testimony of an accomplice whose testimony satisfies the jury of the defendant's guilt beyond a reasonable doubt." Neither did the judge mention the defense's major point—that the Greenglasses had lied to save their skins.

The jury retired at 4:55 P.M. on March 28. The next morning at 11:00 A.M. they delivered their verdict—guilty as charged. Judge Kaufman postponed sentencing for a week, while he consulted the prosecution team, the Justice Department, and J. Edgar Hoover. In a memo dated April 2, 1951, Hoover expressed doubts about executing Ethel Rosenberg on the grounds that it would reflect badly on the government after the dust of the trial had settled. However, Kaufman maintained to the end that the Rosenbergs' crime was worse than murder, since the Soviet Union's possession of the atomic bomb allowed it to unleash a war in Korea, in which over a million people were killed. Gratuitously describing the Rosenbergs as bad parents and Ethel Rosenberg as the mastermind behind the operation, he sentenced them both to death in the electric chair. Sobell got 30 years in prison.

> *"The nature and crime for which they have been found guilty and sentenced far exceeds that of taking the life of another citizen; it involves the deliberate betrayal of the entire nation."*
>
> PRESIDENT DWIGHT D. EISENHOWER
> refusing executive clemency on
> February 11, 1953

POSTSCRIPT

The Rosenbergs were the first Americans to be sentenced in peacetime to death for espionage; this and their controversial trial attracted international attention. In January 1952 they appealed to the Supreme Court, but on October 13 the court refused to review the case. They were granted a stay of execution while they petitioned for reconsideration of the refusal. When this too was denied, the original sentencing judge (Kaufman) stayed the execution to allow the Rosenbergs to appeal to President Eisenhower. Eisenhower refused to pardon them.

A third stay of execution was granted in May 1953 pending a new appeal to the Supreme Court. On May 25, 1953, the court refused to review the case, but this time two justices dissented. The execution date was fixed for June 18. The defense applied for another stay based on new evidence, but the Court of Appeals rejected this, and the Supreme Court confirmed the rejection on June 15 by a 5 to 4 vote. The Court then went into summer recess. On June 17, Justice William O. Douglas, who remained in Washington as the Court's skeleton staff and who had cast one of the four dissenting votes in the recent decision, agreed to consider new evidence and granted a stay of execution.

When the Supreme Court was recalled from summer recess, it reversed Justice Douglas's decision by a vote of 6 to 3 and set the execution for Saturday, June 20. Widespread protests erupted because this was the Jewish Sabbath. In one final act of conciliation, the Court brought the execution forward to the Friday evening. At 8:00 P.M. on June 19, 1953, Julius and Ethel Rosenberg died one after the other in the electric chair.

Above Pro-Rosenberg supporters board the "Clemency Train" to Washington, D.C., on June 14, 1953. Mrs. Sophie Rosenberg, Julius's mother, holds aloft her relatives' words.

Not since Mary Surratt was executed in 1866 for her alleged role in President Lincoln's assassination had a woman died for committing a federal offense. Never in the history of the U.S. had such an execution been carried out in daylight.

I Am Not Guilty

THE CROWN v. WILBERT COFFIN

JULY 16 – AUGUST 5, 1954

Above Wilbert ("Bill") Coffin, the 39-year-old Canadian prospector accused of murdering three hunters from the United States. At the time he was arrested he had no history of violence and no police record.

The most controversial trial in Quebec's history opened in Percé courthouse in the Gaspé Peninsula, Canada, in July 1954. Gaspé is a remote region of eastern Canada that attracts hunters from other parts of North America. In June 1953 three men from Pennsylvania—Eugene Lindsey, his son Richard, and a friend named Frederick Claar—failed to return from a hunting trip to Gaspé. When Claar's father contacted the Pennsylvania state police, they alerted police in Quebec, who sent out a search party. A month after their disappearance, the party was found murdered. An impoverished prospector, Wilbert Coffin, admitted meeting the hunters in the wilderness. He was charged with their murders.

COFFIN GAVE HIS VERSION OF EVENTS when he was questioned by police on July 20, 1953. He had driven a friend's truck into the wilderness to prospect for minerals. There he met the three men, whose truck had broken down. He drove Richard Lindsey 60 miles to the nearest town to buy a new fuel pump. When the two men returned to the camp, they found two more Americans there in a jeep. Coffin promised to look in on Lindsey and his party in a few days and continued prospecting. On June 12 he returned to find the camp deserted, though the truck was still there. He waited for five hours in the hope that the hunters would return to camp. Eventually he gave up, stole some binoculars and the fuel pump from the truck as "compensation," and drove back to his home and then on to visit his common-law wife, Marion Petrie, in Montreal. He stayed in Montreal until July 20.

Below Mrs. C. E. Claar identifies her dead son's personal possessions for the inquest, August 1953.

Circumstantial Evidence

Wilbert Coffin was convicted of murder solely on the basis of circumstantial evidence. No murder weapon or bullet was ever found, and no evidence placed Coffin in Gaspé at the time the hunting party disappeared. In a fair trial, with a proper defense, these facts should have been enough to make a conviction impossible, perhaps even to justify dismissing the case for lack of evidence. Instead, the prosecution loaded its case with inference, supposition, and, as was later revealed, falsehood. Before he was finally put to death, Coffin was reprieved seven times, and he remained confident that he could convince a jury of his innocence if given a chance to defend himself. The chance never came. When another man confessed to the murder after Coffin had been hanged, the words of the French hero of the American Revolution, Lafayette, were widely quoted in the Canadian press: "I shall ask for the abolition of capital punishment until I have the infallibility of human judgment demonstrated to me."

> *"The police had been constantly questioning me and had tried to force me to sign statements and make admissions of guilt which would have been untrue."*
>
> WILBERT COFFIN,
> referring to his arrest in a
> statement at Bordeaux jail, Quebec,
> October 9, 1955

Meanwhile, Frederick Claar's father contacted the authorities on July 8. On July 10 a search party found the hunters' abandoned truck, and while Coffin was still in Montreal, Eugene Lindsey's corpse was discovered. The next sweep of the area revealed the remains of the other two Americans. Their bodies had been partly eaten by bears, but there was a bullet hole in Richard Lindsey's shirt. Coffin, who joined the search, pointed to marks around the camp made by a second jeep as evidence of the second party of Americans, but the police ignored him and did not trace the jeep.

Capt. J. Alphonse Matte, the chief of detectives in Quebec, took over the case. He decided that Coffin was the murderer and arrested him on August 10. Using what Coffin called "Gestapo methods," Matte subjected his prisoner to 18 days of questioning. Throughout this ordeal Coffin maintained his innocence. When, on August 28, an inquest determined that Richard Lindsey had been murdered, Coffin was jailed pending trial.

It was almost a year before the trial was held, and throughout the delay pressure built from a number of sources to secure a conviction. Maurice Duplessis, attorney general of Quebec Province, worried that an unresolved murder would jeopardize the tourist trade—the mainstay of the local economy. The U.S. consul in Quebec city told the authorities that U.S. Secretary of State John Foster Dulles was taking a personal interest in the case and that decisive action was needed right away. Once Matte decided that Coffin was the murderer, Duplessis impressed on the principal prosecutors, Paul Miquelon and Noel Dorion, that their careers depended on getting a conviction. They worked unscrupulously to this end. Coffin's family accepted the inexperienced Raymond Maher as their defense counsel, simply because Maher thrust himself on them.

THE TRIAL BEGAN INAUSPICIOUSLY with a protracted wrangle over jury selection. The defense asked for an English-speaking jury, but this was ruled out because of the predominance of French speakers in the region. On the other hand, the prosecution ruled out all potential

Below Newspaper reporters, officials, and spectators crowd outside the courthouse on July 17, 1954, waiting for proceedings to begin on the second day of the Coffin trial.

jurors who opposed capital punishment for murder. Three hundred candidates were sifted and winnowed before the final 12 were chosen—6 of them English-speaking and 6 French-speaking. Judge Gerard Lacroix presided, and the proceedings were conducted in French and English.

The prosecution called a long list of witnesses: the families of the victims, the people who had found the bodies, those who gave details of Coffin's movements after June 12, the police, woodsmen, and the friend who had lent Coffin his truck. Much was made of the evidence of a man who let Coffin borrow a rifle early in 1953, coupled with testimony from another who thought he saw a rifle in the back of Coffin's truck when he emerged from the wilderness on June 12. Based on this evidence, the prosecution claimed to have established that there was a rifle in Coffin's truck.

CAPTAIN MATTE CAUSED A SENSATION in and out of court when he testified that defense counsel Maher's former clerk, Guy Hamel, had admitted that he and Maher had disposed of Coffin's rifle before the trial by throwing it off the Quebec bridge. In court Hamel denied this and was subsequently convicted of perjury. In his book *I Accuse the Assassins of Coffin*, Jacques Hébert maintains that Matte set up Maher and Hamel to dispose of the rifle, knowing that it was not the murder weapon, but ensuring that it would be impossible to prove that it had not killed Lindsey. Not only was Maher incriminated by his actions, but Coffin was too, although he had no part in it.

The prosecution called Coffin's common-law wife, Marion Petrie, to testify that Coffin had told her about the stolen goods. Contrary to due process, the judge allowed the prosecution to cross-examine Marion as though she were a hostile witness, when in fact she had been called by the Crown. Throughout the trial, the two prosecutors, Miquelon and Dorion, indulged in insult, sarcasm, and insinuation, quoted some of Coffin's words out of context, and twisted others. In a perverse summation, Dorion transformed Coffin's cries of despair during his cross-examination by Matte into an admission of guilt and reminded the jury of the effects on the tourist industry if U. S. visitors stopped coming to the region.

Behind the legal process stood a chief of detectives who had prejudged the defense. Throughout the trial, Matte held parties every night; on the wall of his apartment he hung a photo of Coffin with a noose above his head. At no time did he pursue other avenues of inquiry. Yet numerous eyewitnesses placed Coffin in Montreal with Marion Petrie on June 13, 1953, and the police had in their possession a note written by one of the hunters on June 13. That note should have been considered evidence that the hunting party was still alive when Coffin left the area; instead it was suppressed. There were other gaping holes in the prosecution's case that an able defense lawyer could have exposed in rebuttal. One of the police sergeants, who had accompanied Coffin on the search of the area immediately after the murder, admitted that he too had seen tire marks from a second jeep at the campsite. But the police continued to ignore this evidence and defense counsel did not press the point.

Below Handcuffed to a police officer, Wilbert Coffin is taken to court for a day's proceedings during the summer of 1954.

"I repeat I am innocent of this crime and feel I was not given a fair trial....I was made to look as though I was a liar...."

WILBERT COFFIN'S statement at Bordeaux jail, Quebec, October 9, 1955

IN EFFECT, THE DEFENSE COUNSEL threw away the case. When the time came for Raymond Maher to produce the hundred or so witnesses that he had promised in refutation of the prosecution and to put Coffin (who was still longing for a chance to proclaim his innocence) on the stand, Maher got to his feet and said: "My lord, the defense rests." These words, the sole defense offered for a man on trial for his life, caused stupefaction and incredulity. The effect of Maher's action, expressed later by Romuald Caron, one of the 12 jurors, was to convince the jury that Coffin's case was a tissue of lies and that his lawyer refused to collude in the proceedings. "For several days we had heard the Crown prosecutors and the Crown witnesses strive to persuade us of Coffin's guilt. But we were expecting to hear the defense lawyers and witnesses, especially Coffin himself. When Maher stood up to tell us he had no defense to offer, we decided that Coffin was guilty. A man who does not defend himself must be guilty." The jury took just 30 minutes to convict Coffin of murder. The judge sentenced him to hang, took off the black three-cornered hat worn to pronounce the death sentence, endorsed the jury's verdict, and congratulated them.

Above Following sentencing, a police car takes Coffin through the main gates of Bordeaux jail, Quebec. He remained there for most of the period leading up to his execution in February 1956.

POSTSCRIPT

Wilbert Coffin was sentenced to death on August 5, 1954, and a date of execution was set for November 26 of that year. However, his hopes were kept alive for 18 months beyond the appointed date, through seven stays of execution. The first appeal, to the Court of the Queen's Bench in Quebec, resulted in a stay of execution until March 12, 1955. When the appeal was dismissed, the execution date was moved to September 23, 1955. One month before he was due to hang, Coffin's lawyers applied for permission to appeal to the Supreme Court in Ottawa. This was refused.

On September 6 Coffin escaped from jail after wielding a fake gun that he had made from a bar of soap. Maher talked him into giving himself up, and the Quebec Superior Court granted another stay of execution until October 21, 1955. Late in September, prompted by national publicity, the Canadian Cabinet voted that the Supreme Court should review the case, and Coffin's execution was put off until February 9, 1956. The Supreme Court upheld the conviction by a majority of 5 to 2. Only one option remained, a motion for a new trial. On February 8, the motion was refused. Coffin was hanged the next day.

Three years later a 35-year-old Native American from Quebec named Francis Gilbert Thompson was arrested on a vagrancy charge in Miami. In the mistaken belief that the case could not be reopened after Coffin had been executed, Thompson confessed to the murder, explaining that he had robbed Eugene Lindsey, a moneylender who was known to carry wads of cash. When Thompson realized that he could still be prosecuted, he retracted his story.

Above Coffin used a fake gun in an escape attempt on September 6, 1955. This is the picture that appeared in the national papers.

In January 1964 Prime Minister Jean Lesage announced the formation of a Royal Commission to investigate allegations of foul play in the Coffin case. The commission concluded that there had been no wrongdoing.

To Deprave and Corrupt

THE CROWN v. PENGUIN BOOKS LTD.

OCTOBER 20 – NOVEMBER 2, 1960

On August 25, 1960, Penguin Books in London announced its intention to publish an unexpurgated edition of D. H. Lawrence's novel *Lady Chatterley's Lover*. An expensive, abridged version had been available in Britain since 1932, but Penguin maintained a commitment to publishing complete texts and pricing them for the mass market. In a test case on the same novel in the United States, federal judge Frederick Bryan had ruled in 1959 that "the language which shocks, except in a rare instance or two, is not inconsistent with character, situation, and theme." Subsequently, Penguin decided to produce an unexpurgated text in Britain to retail at three shillings and sixpence, less than the price of a pack of cigarettes. Only weeks before the publication date, the director of public prosecutions (DPP) informed Penguin Books that he might prosecute the company under the Obscene Publications Act of 1959. In reply, Penguin offered to give him 12 copies so that his department could form a reasoned judgment; the police, however, would have to collect them so that, should the DPP decide to take action, no booksellers would be prosecuted for stocking an obscene book. After reading the novel, the DPP decided to prosecute.

THE CASE OPENED IN COURT NUMBER ONE AT THE OLD BAILEY in London on October 20, 1960. Appearing before the judge, Mr. Justice Byrne, were Gerald Gardiner, Queen's Counsel for the defense, and for the prosecution, Mervyn Griffith-Jones, senior treasury counsel, who had come to national prominence as a member of the British team of prosecutors at the Nuremberg trials. Because the "prisoner at the bar" was Penguin Books, the dock remained empty; Sir Allen Lane (a respected member of the publishing world) and Hans Schmoller, both of whom were directors of Penguin Books, sat with solicitors in the well of the court.

Mr. Griffith-Jones opened for the prosecution by declaring that the proceedings were a test case for publishers all over the country. He read aloud the relevant provisions of the Obscene Publications Act of 1959: "An article shall be deemed to be obscene if its effect is, if taken as a whole, such as to tend to

Above The Penguin edition of *Lady Chatterley's Lover*, in which an adulterous relationship was depicted fully and with graphic language, much to the shock and titillation of its readership.

> *"The curtain is never drawn. One follows them not only into the bedroom but into bed, and one remains there with them. Or rather not just bed but a forest hut, the middle of a forest, a cottage, an attic."*
>
> MERVYN GRIFFITH-JONES
> opening for the prosecution,
> October 20, 1960

Above Sir Allen Lane, a director of Penguin Books, photographed outside the Old Bailey during the trial. He received a knighthood in 1952 for services to literature.

160

Obscene Publications

In 1954, during a successful prosecution of pornographic books in the British legal system, the counsel for the defense mentioned a number of other novels that, he claimed, were as bad if not worse than those being prosecuted; yet no action had been taken. The director of public prosecutions examined these other books, and five additional publishers were subsequently prosecuted.

Alarmed by these unexpected prosecutions, the British Society of Authors set up an action committee to lobby for clearer legislation on what constituted an obscene publication. After a five-year battle, the government passed the Obscene Publications Act of 1959, which put an end to the common law on "obscene libel" (an obsolete term meaning obscene writing). Among the many new protections for publishers and authors, section four of the 1959 act laid down that, although a book might "deprave and corrupt persons likely to read it," there could be no conviction "if it is proved that publication of the article in question is justified as being for the public good on the grounds that it is in the interests of science, literature, art, or learning, or of other objects of general concern." In practice, this provision meant that any trial for obscenity would depend on the testimony of expert witnesses to establish the book's literary status.

deprave and corrupt persons who are likely, having regard to all relevant circumstances, to read, see, or hear the matter contained or embodied in it." He reminded the jury that under section four of the 1959 act, an obscene book as defined by the act could still be published legally if it possessed sufficient literary merit. The jury, therefore, had to decide two things: whether the book was obscene and, if it was, whether its publication could be deemed for the public good because of its literary merit.

TO ESTABLISH A DEFINITION OF OBSCENITY, Griffith-Jones cited a precedent from 1868. This law stated that a book was obscene if it was likely to prompt lustful and impure thoughts in readers. The proposed low price of the Penguin edition, Griffith-Jones noted, would make the book easily obtainable by the majority of the population and accessible to young people. He reminded the jury that they must judge the book as a whole and not base their opinions on specific passages containing sexually explicit material, and he reiterated the definition of obscenity—having a tendency to deprave and corrupt—set out in the act of 1959.

"Members of the jury, when you have seen this book," he continued, "making all such allowances in favor of it as you can, the prosecution will invite you to say that it does tend, certainly that it may tend, to induce lustful thoughts in the minds of those who read it. It goes further, you may think. It sets upon a pedestal promiscuous and adulterous intercourse. It commends, and indeed it sets out to commend, sensuality almost as a virtue. It encourages, and indeed even advocates, coarseness and vulgarity of thought and of language. You may think that it must tend to deprave the minds certainly of some and you may think many of the persons who are likely to buy it at the price of three shillings and sixpence and read it, with 200,000 copies already printed and ready for release. You may think that one of the ways in which you can test this book, and test it from the most liberal outlook, is to ask yourselves the question, when you have read it through, would you approve of your young sons, young daughters—because girls can read as well as boys—reading this book. Is it a book that you would have lying around in your own house? Is it a book that you would even wish your wife and your servants to read?"

Above The statue of Justice at the Old Bailey, London's most famous court of law, where the *Lady Chatterley* trial was heard. The bronze figure wears a blindfold to indicate impartiality and carries in one hand a raised sword to defend the right, and holds in the other a set of scales to balance the arguments in each case.

Above Mervyn Griffith-Jones, Britain's leading prosecutor in the 1960s. His reactionary views, expressed during the *Lady Chatterley* trial, brought him ridicule in the press.

"Witnesses read the book; they do not become depraved or corrupted. Nobody suggests the judge or the jury become depraved or corrupted. It is always somebody else: it is never ourselves."

GERALD GARDINER, Q.C.,
opening for the defense,
October 20, 1960

This last statement provoked smiles from the jury. Griffith-Jones had shown himself to be remarkably out of touch with the changes in postwar society in Britain. By the 1960s feminism had begun to make a difference to public attitudes, and domestic servants had disappeared from all but the wealthiest households; certainly no one on the jury had servants at home. Undaunted, Griffith-Jones pressed on, defining the words *deprave* and *corrupt* and suggesting that *Lady Chatterley's Lover* was "a book of little more than vicious indulgence in sex and sensuality." This last remark was widely quoted in newspaper headlines and stirred considerable public interest in the trial.

Griffith-Jones conceded the literary status of D. H. Lawrence but sought to prove that this particular work did not live up to its author's greatness. He summarized the plot of the novel, going into some detail over the adulterous relationship at the center of the story and the 13 sexual encounters that the novel described. The plot, he claimed, was mere padding for the book's "bawdy conversations." He then read to the court a list of offending "four-letter words" that Lawrence had used, forcing himself to say them aloud and noting for the record that he had counted 76 usages. Having delivered this list Griffith-Jones began to quote selected passages. At this point the defense objected on the grounds that the members of the jury ought to be allowed to read the whole book and decide for themselves.

The prosecution called only one witness, Detective Inspector Charles Monahan, who reported serving the summons on Penguin Books. When the defense, in cross-examination, put it to the court that the ordinary man in the street could buy *Lady Chatterley's Lover* almost anywhere in the world except Britain and the Commonwealth, the judge interrupted to say that the availability of the book in other civilized countries did not constitute evidence of the novel's value. Gerald Gardiner protested vigorously that that was precisely what it did, but the judge brushed this aside: "I don't think that is the kind of evidence the statute contemplates. I am against you." That statement concluded the case for the prosecution.

GERALD GARDINER STOOD TO ADDRESS THE JURY FOR THE DEFENSE. He guided them through the background of the case and the intricacies of the Obscene Publications Act of 1959. He then dealt with the book itself, describing the author, D. H. Lawrence, as a "puritan moralist" who was concerned that society, for all its talk of love, had paid too little attention to the physical love between a man and a woman. He argued that the use of four-letter words, to which the prosecution so objected, was an attempt to talk about sex without shame. The members of the jury should read the book "just as though you had bought it at a bookstall," he instructed, and not make up their minds until they had heard the whole case. There followed a wrangle about where the jury should read the book. Gardiner proposed that the jurors take the book home, but Justice Byrne insisted that they read it in the courthouse. A reading room with armchairs was hastily prepared, and the court declared a three-day break during which the jury read the novel.

BEGINNING ON OCTOBER 27, THE DEFENSE CALLED 35 WITNESSES to testify to the literary merit of the book. All were distinguished and well-known academics, critics, literary editors, and journalists, including the author and academic Cecil Day-Lewis; the Reverend John Arthur Thomas Robinson, bishop of Woolwich; the author Dame Rebecca West; and the literary critic and academic Dame Helen Gardner. Although Griffith-Jones sneered as certain witnesses described Lawrence's attitude toward sex as "religious" or "sacramental," this illustrious panel of experts unanimously agreed that the book was an important work of literary merit. Referring to the prosecution's proposal that the "purple passages" (the writings on a sexual theme) should be expurgated from the novel, Dame Helen Gardner

> *"I think Lawrence tried to portray this relationship as, in a real sense, an act of holy communion. For him flesh was sacramental of the spirit."*
>
> THE BISHOP OF WOOLWICH
> giving evidence for the defense,
> October 27, 1960

Below A London commuter reads a much-sought-after advance copy of *Lady Chatterley's Lover.*

stated her opinion that they were, in fact, "the corn heart of the book's theme and meaning." On the issue of "obscene language," Dame Helen Gardner spoke for a number of literary experts when she said: "I do not think any words are brutal and disgusting in themselves. They are brutal and disgusting if they are used in a brutal and disgusting sense, or brutal and disgusting context." She went on to claim that by the end of the novel Lawrence had actually redeemed some of the words from their "low and vulgar associations."

The evidence most damaging to the prosecution's case came from the Labor Party member of Parliament Roy Jenkins. Jenkins had been the chief sponsor of the Obscene Publications Act of 1959 during its five-year preparation, and at the time that he testified he had already written an article in the political journal, *The Spectator*, in which he declared this prosecution a travesty of the real intentions of the Parliamentary Select Committee on Obscene Publications in 1958. In the witness-box he stated that part of the intention of the act had been "to provide for the protection of literature" and that he considered *Lady Chatterley's Lover* to be a work of high literary merit. It would not have occurred to him during his five years' work on the bill, he said, that such a book would be prosecuted. Before he could say more, the judge silenced him, but he had already made a telling point.

GERALD GARDINER ENDED THE CASE FOR THE DEFENSE on the fifth day of the trial, November 1, with an impressive recapitulation that ridiculed the prosecution's case. In reply Griffith-Jones closed by referring to the defense's experts as self-serving specialists. He contrasted their refined attitudes with the ones likely to be exhibited by the ordinary person on the street. "What is the story?…a woman who…before she is married, has sexual intercourse, and then, after marriage…proceeds to have an adulterous intercourse with her husband's gamekeeper." In his final push, Griffith-Jones put Lady Chatterley herself on trial as a multiple adulteress, in hopes that the jury's presumed distaste for her would influence their verdict on the book: "Ladies and gentlemen, there must be standards….There must be instilled in all of us standards of restraint."

The judge completed his summing up on the sixth day of the trial, and in instructing the jury on a point of law, he made it plain that he assumed that they were repelled by what they had read and heard. "The mere fact you are shocked or disgusted, the mere fact you hate the sight of the book when you have read it does not solve the question as to whether you are satisfied beyond reasonable doubt that the tendency of the book is to deprave and corrupt." He disparaged the expert witnesses more vehemently than Griffith-Jones had done and put more emphasis

Above Mr. Justice Byrne, arriving fully robed for a day in court. The *Lady Chatterley* trial was the last of his career.

THE NOVELIST

David Herbert Lawrence was born in Nottinghamshire in 1885, the fourth child of a coal miner. Delicate health kept him from working in the mines, so he trained as a teacher and soon began to write fiction. After the success of his first novel, *The White Peacock* (1911), he decided to earn his living by writing. In 1912 he met Frieda von Richthofen, a cousin of the German ace pilot Baron von Richthofen and wife of Professor Ernest Weekley, Lawrence's former tutor at the University of Nottingham. She divorced Weekley to marry Lawrence in July 1914. After an unhappy interlude in Cornwall during World War I, the couple embarked on a life of travel, which they pursued from a series of temporary bases in Italy, Mexico, and New Mexico. Among the international literary community Lawrence received mixed reviews, hailed by some as a great genius and liberating prophet of sexuality, and by others as a pornographer, charlatan, and fascist. His best-known works are *Sons and Lovers* (1913); *The Rainbow*—also banned for obscenity—(1915); *Women in Love* (1920); *The Plumed Serpent* (1926); and *Lady Chatterley's Lover* (1928). Although the warmer climates helped alleviate Lawrence's worsening tuberculosis, he died in a sanatorium in 1930 at the early age of 45.

on the character issue that Lady Chatterley was an adulteress than on the legal issue of whether the book's literary merit justified publication. He implied that he expected the jury to pass a moral judgment on the behavior that the novel described, but his direction was ignored. After a three-hour deliberation on November 2, the jury delivered a verdict of not guilty.

Before the case was closed, Gardiner asked that costs for his clients be reimbursed, especially since the DPP had said at the outset that Penguin Books should consider the prosecution to be a test case. "I can understand the desire of the director to obtain a decision on the construction of this new act and how it would work," he argued, "but nobody appreciated being the vehicle for such a case." Justice Byrne refused to award any costs to the defense, leaving himself open to subsequent speculation in the media that he was piqued by a verdict that he did not welcome. As a result, Penguin Books had to pay the legal fees incurred in publishing a book that had not infringed any law. But the publishers more than recouped their losses in the long run—media coverage of the trial produced enormous publicity for the novel and for Penguin Books. The trial has since come to be regarded as a watershed, marking the 1960s as the beginning of a more permissive age.

Below During November 1960, thousands stood in line to buy copies of "Lady C."

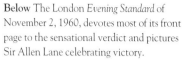

Below The London *Evening Standard* of November 2, 1960, devotes most of its front page to the sensational verdict and pictures Sir Allen Lane celebrating victory.

Fighting for Freedom

THE STATE OF SOUTH AFRICA *v.* NELSON MANDELA

OCTOBER 9, 1963 – JUNE 11, 1964

Above The ANC flag, symbol of the struggle for freedom. Its colors symbolize the people (black), the land (green), and the nation's resources (gold).

"We shall not submit and we have no choice but to hit back by all means within our power in defense of our people, our future and our freedom."

UMKHONTO WE SIZWE,
a militant offshoot of the ANC,
in its manifesto, distributed
December 16, 1961

*I*n 1961 a new black organization became headline news in South Africa. Called Umkhonto We Sizwe ("Spear of the Nation"), it was a militant offshoot of the African National Congress (ANC), an organization set up in 1912 to campaign for democratic rights for the country's black citizens. Umkhonto's 1961 manifesto pledged justice at any cost for all South Africans. "The time comes in the life of any nation," the document proclaimed, "when there remain only two choices: submit or fight. That time has now come to South Africa. We shall not submit and we have no choice but to hit back by all means within our power in defense of our people, our future, and our freedom."

On December 16, 1961, Umkhonto marked its birth with widespread acts of sabotage against government installations. December 16 was a public holiday in South Africa commemorating the Battle of Blood River in Natal in 1838, when the Boers (white settlers) defeated the Zulus (a native African people). Now at last, the black population was beginning to retaliate. The founding member and commander in chief of Umkhonto was Nelson Mandela. He had spent most of the previous five years as one of 156 defendants in a treason trial (1956–61), the authorities' largest action ever taken against black militants and sympathizers. During most of the trial, Mandela was released on bail under a banning order that confined him to Johannesburg and forbade him to attend public meetings. Within these limits he kept up his law practice with Oliver Tambo, helping others who were arrested under the apartheid laws. After his acquittal he began to work underground, redoubling his efforts against apartheid and earning the nickname the Black Pimpernel.

Apartheid

Mandela's trial drew the world's attention to apartheid, a system of segregation that had been in operation in South Africa since the Population Registration Act of 1948. Every citizen was given a racial label—white, colored, Asian, Chinese, or black—and each black person was classified according to tribe. Every inch of the country was divided into segregated districts, and it became illegal for nonwhite persons to live or work outside their allocated areas. More than 3.5 million people lost their homes and businesses through the Group Areas Act of 1950, which allowed the whites to take possession of the prime residential and business areas and to set up a system of racially segregated transportation, education, leisure facilities, and even public toilets. Some jobs were advertised as "for whites only."

The movement of blacks between areas was controlled by the notorious Pass Laws. Black workers had to carry a pass at all times and would be allowed or refused entry to a district only after showing this document. The most serious restrictions on freedom came in 1956, when black and colored voters were removed from the electoral rolls. By 1969 the government had passed a series of laws enabling it to suppress all criticism of its racial policies. The police could arrest and detain citizens without trial, withholding their right to see a lawyer and prohibiting them access to their own families.

This catalog of pro-white, anti-black legislation created an atmosphere in which violent protest became inevitable. A long, hard struggle would be fought before civil rights for all citizens were reinstated in the 1990s.

BIOGRAPHY

On July 18, 1918, a son was born to the third wife of the Tembu chief Henry Mphakanyiswa Gadla in the Qunu region of South Africa. The child's Xhosa name was Rolihlahla, "one who brings trouble on himself." He was also given a European name, Nelson, and his grandfather's name, Mandela. A bright student, Mandela enrolled in 1938 to study law at Fort Hare, an all-black university, but was expelled in 1940 for political activities. In 1941, at age 23, he moved to Johannesburg to complete his studies. There he met Walter Sisulu, who introduced him to the African National Congress (ANC). He joined the ANC in 1944 and through the organization met Oliver Tambo, another law student, with whom he opened a practice in Johannesburg in 1952. Mandela rose quickly through the ranks of the ANC. On September 4, 1953, he was banned from attending public meetings for two years, and later that year the authorities demanded that he resign from the ANC. Mandela's refusal inaugurated decades of banning and imprisonment. His first marriage, to Evelyn Mase, broke under the strain in 1956, when Mandela was arrested with 155 others for treason. They divorced shortly afterward. Two years later, still banned and on trial for treason, he married Winnie Nomzamo

Madikizela, a social worker in Johannesburg. During Nelson's 27 years of imprisonment (1962–90) Winnie Mandela supported her husband and carried on much of his work. But soon after his release in 1990, the couple separated, amid widespread controversy over Winnie's conduct.

Above Mandela, age 34, in the offices of the Johannesburg law practice that he shared with Oliver Tambo. Their partnership created the first black law practice in the city, and specialized in civil rights work, much of it undertaken without a fee. During Mandela's imprisonment, Oliver Tambo took over the leadership of the ANC.

MANDELA SPENT THE NEXT EIGHT MONTHS ON THE RUN, both in South Africa and abroad, before a tip led to his arrest. Although the authorities were able to connect him with acts of sabotage, they could not establish a link to Umkhonto. On November 7, 1962, he was found guilty of a series of less serious charges and sentenced to five years' imprisonment for incitement to strike and for traveling without a passport. Mandela was serving this sentence when, on July 11, 1963, police raided Rivonia farm near Johannesburg. They arrested Walter Sisulu, Denis Goldberg (the only white man of the group), Govan Mbeki, Ahmed Kathrada, Lionel Bernstein, and Raymond Mhlaba—all identified, with Mandela, as members of the High Command of Umkhonto. Three others were held as associates.

The Rivonia prisoners and Mandela were quickly brought to trial for high treason. The State *v.* the National High Command and Others opened in the Supreme Court of South Africa on October 9, 1963.

Above A passbook, issued to all blacks, but not to coloreds or whites. Failure to show it on demand could lead to imprisonment.

> *"A government
> which uses force to
> maintain its rule teaches
> the oppressed to use force
> to oppose it."*
>
> NELSON MANDELA,
> in his defense,
> April 1964

Counsel for the defense, Bram Fischer, pointed out that of 193 alleged acts of violence, 156 had occurred while Mandela was in prison. The judge had no choice but to dismiss the case for lack of evidence. However, the authorities regarded the men as dangerous terrorists and were determined to make an example of them. Mandela was taken back to prison, and his nine codefendants were rearrested under the Prevention of Terrorism Act. Realizing that a charge of high treason was very difficult to prove, the deputy attorney general of the Transvaal, Dr. Percy Yutar, opted this time to prosecute under the Sabotage Act. His decision increased the stakes, since a conviction would carry the death penalty.

THE SECOND MAJOR PROSECUTION OF Mandela became known internationally as the Rivonia trial. This time the state was determined to make no mistakes, and Yutar organized his case carefully. He began by dispelling any sympathy for the defendants by portraying them as vicious killers who were preparing for mass violence. He arranged for two key witnesses to appear for the prosecution—both members of Umkhonto, who turned state's evidence in return for immunity. These two men (referred to throughout the trial as Mr. X and Mr. Z) admitted they had carried out acts of sabotage, and—as was later disclosed—under coaching from Yutar, slanted their evidence to suggest that Umkhonto was linked to the South African Communist Party. The defense tried in vain to discredit them in cross-examination but failed even after establishing that Mr. X (later identified as Bruno Mtolo) had a history of petty crime and had served three terms of imprisonment for theft. The prosecution finished presenting its evidence in February 1964, after five months, during which Yutar had called 173 witnesses. At this point in the legal proceedings it seemed almost certain that the defendants would be convicted of a capital offense.

In the meantime, the Rivonia trial had attracted enormous public attention and was being closely

Above The Rivonia Eight, as they came to be known at the trial: (from left to right) Nelson Mandela, Walter Sisulu, Govan Mbeki, Raymond Mhlaba, Elias Motsoaledi, Andrew Mlangeni, Ahmed Kathrada and Denis Goldberg. They were charged with committing numerous acts of sabotage.

Right Umkhonto's first act of sabotage was to blow up power lines in December 1961. Initially Umkhonto members were under strict orders only to target property, not people; but over time the organization turned to more violent methods.

followed in the international press. When the accused arrived in court each day, they waved to the crowded black section of the public gallery, raised their fists in the ANC salute, and shouted out the slogan *Amandla* ("freedom"). The spectators responded with the traditional amen, *Ngawethu*. At the same time Mandela was drawing a significant show of international support. The U.S. secretary of state, Dean Rusk, and the British secretary of state for foreign affairs, "Rab" Butler, put pressure on South Africa's prime minister to grant clemency should Mandela be found guilty. The African population waited in suspense to hear how Mandela would defend the actions of Umkhonto.

DEFENSE COUNSEL

Above Bram Fischer, working undercover in disguise at the time of his arrest in 1965.

Bram (Abram) Fischer was born in South Africa in 1908, the son of a prominent judge and grandson of a former prime minister. As a young lawyer he had a brilliant career, but his involvement with the Communist Party, banned by the authorities, blocked his progress. He became involved with the ANC during the Treason Trial of 1956 to 1961. He sympathized with their aims, but saw the conflict as one of class, not race. The Rivonia Trial of 1963 and 1964 was the last important trial of his career. Angry and disillusioned he went into hiding in 1964 to work for the Communist Party undercover. The following year he was brought to trial for sabotage and revolutionary activities and was sentenced to life imprisonment in 1966. He died in prison in 1975.

BRAM FISCHER OPENED THE CASE FOR THE DEFENSE ON APRIL 20, 1964, by entering a plea of guilty to sabotage and to preparing for guerrilla warfare on a contingency basis and a plea of not guilty to expressly plotting a guerrilla campaign. This tactic conceded much to the prosecution, since Fischer's starting position was that he could not hope to win an acquittal. Fearful that his clients would be sentenced to death, Fischer concentrated most of his energies on securing life imprisonment. In his opinion this was the least serious of the likely outcomes. He stressed again and again that the ANC and Umkhonto were completely separate bodies and that neither of them was a Communist organization.

At the center of the defense strategy was a four-and-a-half-hour speech by "Accused Number One" (Mandela). Yutar tried every legal maneuver to prevent Mandela from speaking but in the end he had to settle for advising the court that "a statement from the dock does not carry the same weight as evidence under oath." Mandela delivered a long and eloquent speech, in which he set out his background and his commitment to his people since joining the ANC in 1944. He admitted to helping form Umkhonto and organizing sabotage, but added, "I did not plan it in a spirit of recklessness nor because I have any love for violence. I planned it as a result of a calm and sober assessment of the political situation that had arisen after many years of tyranny, exploitation, and oppression of my people."

Mandela pointed out to the all-white jury that apartheid legislation had closed all lawful avenues of opposition to white supremacy and that blacks had almost no rights at all. The ANC, he stated, was not committed to violence and was never a Communist organization. He strongly condemned and denied the treacherous testimony of his two former Umkhonto comrades, Mr. X and Mr. Z, that he was guilty of Communist involvement: "Basically, we fight against two features which are the hallmarks of African life in South Africa...poverty and lack of human dignity...and we do

CHRONOLOGY

December 1956 – March 1961
Mandela is tried for treason with 155 others. All are acquitted.

March 1960 Sharpeville shootings occur, in which 67 blacks are killed during a peaceful protest, and a state of emergency is declared. Mandela is imprisoned for five months. The ANC is banned.

1961 Mandela goes underground. Sets up Umkhonto We Sizwe.

August 1962 Mandela is arrested and charged with incitement to strike and with leaving the country illegally. He is sentenced to five years' imprisonment.

July 1963 Leaders of Umkhonto are captured at Rivonia farm.

October 1963 Mandela is brought back to Pretoria to be tried for treason in the State *v.* the National High Command and Others. The charges are dismissed, but the defendants are tried again for sabotage in the State *v.* Mandela and Nine Others.

June 1964 Mandela is convicted with seven others (two were acquitted) and sentenced to life imprisonment.

not need Communists to teach us about these things." He argued that Umkhonto had tried to avoid civil war and that its acts of sabotage were designed merely to attract attention to the cause of black civil rights and to bring the whites to their senses. He went on to describe the kinds of sabotage Umkhonto had envisioned—primarily attacks on domestic economic infrastructure that would make sanctions from abroad more effective.

"I have cherished the ideal of a democratic and free society in which all persons live together in harmony with equal opportunities. It is an ideal which I hope to live for and to see realized. But, my lord, if needs be, it is an ideal for which I am prepared to die."

NELSON MANDELA, in his defense, April 1964

Mandela also spoke of the massacre by whites of 69 unarmed Africans at Sharpeville in 1960, when police opened fire on an unarmed group of workers who were giving themselves up for arrest at their local police station. This was a key event for civil rights activists, one that convinced black leaders that direct action, including sabotage, was the only way to achieve their goals. He also explained his plans for building a nucleus of blacks trained for future military and administrative leadership. He went on to contrast the wealth and privilege of white South Africans with the poverty and misery of the blacks, who were denied education and discriminated against and whose families were broken up by the notorious Pass Laws. He reassured his audience that the democratic processes sought by the ANC would not replace white supremacy with black supremacy.

Stunned silence followed his final words. The wife of one of the other accused reported: "One could hear people on the public benches release their breath with a deep sigh as the moment of tension passed. Some women in the gallery burst into tears. We sat motionless for perhaps a minute before the tension ebbed."

Fischer later concluded by emphasizing the justice of Umkhonto's cause, but his efforts were in vain. Although two of the accused were acquitted, eight others, including Mandela, were sentenced to life imprisonment. In December 1964 Mandela returned to Robben Island, the high-security island prison off Capetown where he had formerly been held captive. Although Nelson Mandela survived to see his people triumph over apartheid, that victory would be another 30 years in the winning.

Below Headlines from a Capetown newspaper on the day the Rivonia verdict was announced. Photographs of Mandela were censored by the authorities, who feared that he would attract support nationwide.

The Cape Argus

CITY LATE

ITALIAN DAMASKS

Stuttafords

2 SKIRTS

NANNUCCI LTD.

EIGHT GUILTY IN RIVONIA TRIAL

Seven on all four charges and one on one count

BERNSTEIN FREED, REARRESTED

BERNSTEIN IN RAND COURT TOMORROW

ACTION THREAT AGAINST DRIVER

MRS. BERNSTEIN AND DAUGHTER IN TEARS

Natives shout and sing outside the court

WIFE HEARD THE VERDICT

Clearing

NEW LIFE! NEUROTONE

Judge's reasons

No sentence to-day

Kantor's discharge

PENALTY

ROADBLOCKS

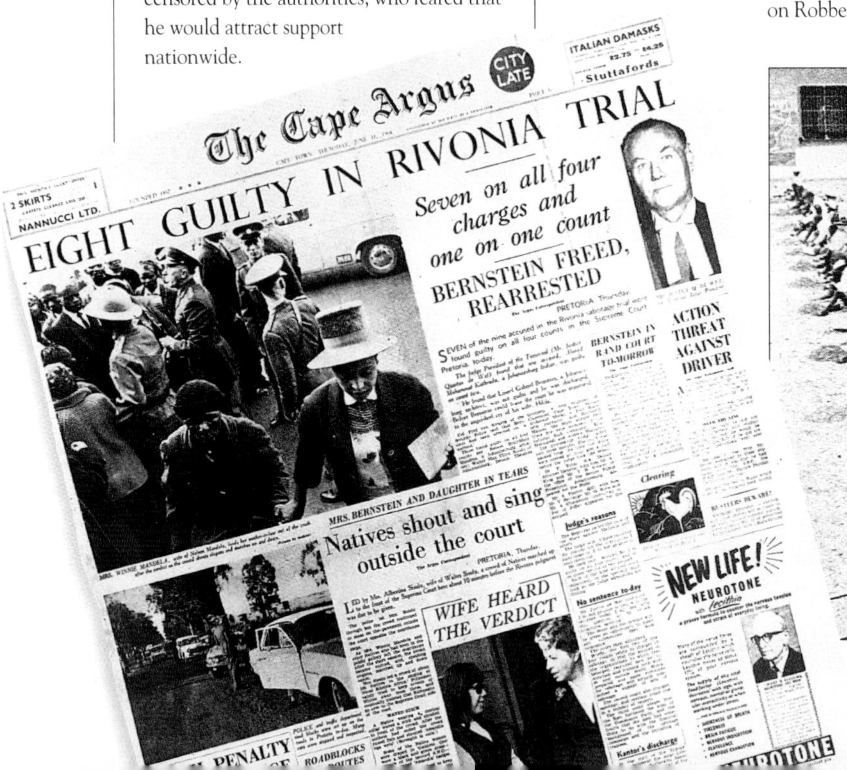

Below The Rivonia prisoners (right) sewing mailbags in the section yard on Robben Island. Other prisoners can be seen breaking rocks (left).

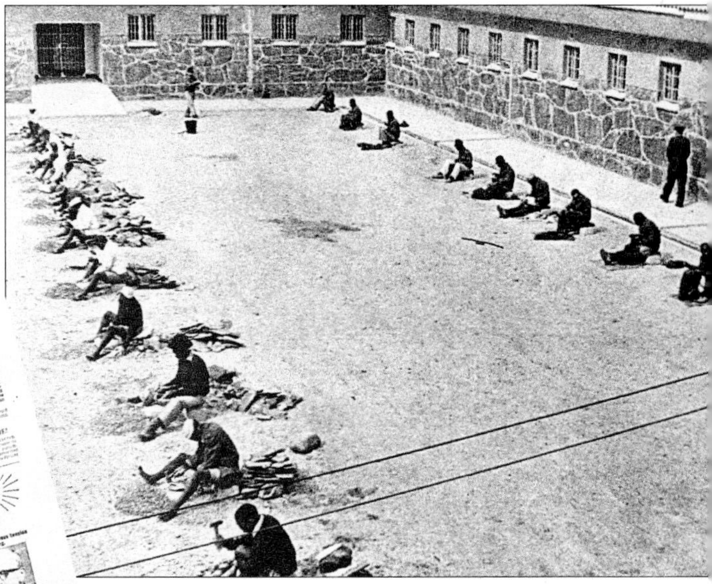

POSTSCRIPT

During the 27 years of Mandela's imprisonment, worldwide protests against apartheid gathered force. Campaigners worked for economic sanctions against South Africa, lobbied sports organizations to avoid touring there, and boycotted South African goods. In 1985, under economic and political pressure, President P. W. Botha offered all the Rivonia prisoners freedom on condition that they reject violence. Mandela refused to bargain with a regime that still denied civil rights to the majority of the population.

Three years later rock musicians from all over the world formed a group called Artists Against Apartheid to celebrate Mandela's 70th birthday with a televised concert at Wembley Stadium in London. It was seen by more than half a billion people in 28 countries. The event highlighted Mandela's status as a political prisoner and increased pressure on the government to abolish discrimination.

On February 10, 1990, South Africa's new president, F. W. de Klerk, announced that the 72-year-old Mandela and the other Rivonia prisoners would be released unconditionally.

Mandela returned to public life on a wave of hope for South Africa's black population but was dogged by personal problems. During his imprisonment, Winnie Mandela had been instrumental in the campaign to free Nelson. Shortly after his release, however, the couple became estranged when Winnie was accused of political corruption.

Finally, and with the eyes of the world upon him, former Prisoner Number 466/64 was elected the first black president of South Africa in his country's first multiracial elections, in May 1994. Scores of his ANC colleagues attended the ceremony to take their seats in the only representative sitting of Parliament convened since the state was founded in 1910. In his

Above Campaign badges from the 1980s worn at rallies and protests around the world. Their popularity showed the strength of international support for the antiapartheid movement and kept Mandela's cause in the public eye.

inaugural speech, President Mandela paid tribute to those who had given their lives or made sacrifices to win emancipation. "Their dreams have become reality. Freedom is their reward. Never, never, and never again shall it be that this beautiful land will...suffer the indignity of being the skunk of the world."

Below Mandela campaigning in Bophuthatswana during April 1994 for the presidential election held in May of that year.

Our Longest War

THE U.S. GOVERNMENT *v.* DANIEL ELLSBERG

AUGUST 16, 1971 – MAY 11, 1973

Above Protesters in the mid-1960s demonstrate outside the White House in Washington, D.C., against U.S. involvement in the Vietnam War.

Below On June 13, 1971, the *New York Times* published excerpts from the Pentagon Papers, a top secret government study on U.S. involvement in the Vietnam War. Ellsberg had leaked them the information in an effort to bring an end to the war.

Throughout the late 1960s U.S. policy on the Vietnam War was a topic of heated debate in the United States. In June 1971 it gained heightened public exposure when the *New York Times* and the *Washington Post* published excerpts from a 47-volume Defense Department study entitled "A history of U.S. decision-making process on Vietnam policy, 1945–67." This study, dubbed the Pentagon Papers, had been compiled by a team of researchers, commissioned by former Secretary of Defense Robert McNamara. (In late 1966 McNamara had begun to have serious doubts about U.S. involvement in Vietnam, and he commissioned the study without informing President Johnson or Secretary of State Dean Rusk.) The study, begun in June 1967, included classified documents—memos, position papers, field reports, and more—stretching back over 20 years. It was leaked to the media by a noted authority on Vietnam, Dr. Daniel Ellsberg, who had worked on the study in a minor capacity in 1967.

AT THE TIME ELLSBERG WAS ASKED TO JOIN THE RESEARCH TEAM in Washington, he was employed by the Rand Corporation in Santa Monica, California—a think tank specializing in military studies for the government—and was recently back from fieldwork in Vietnam. His experience there had convinced him that the war was at a stalemate; continuation of the conflict would result in only more death and destruction. Ellsberg was assigned a section dealing with Vietnam policy during the early days of the Kennedy administration. When he had made his contribution, he returned to Santa Monica.

The Pentagon Papers were finally completed in January 1969, and in June, 15 sets of the top secret document were distributed to various government offices, including one set to the

Santa Monica offices of the Rand Corporation, a Defense Department repository. There, Daniel Ellsberg read the study and became convinced that the war must be stopped. He secretly photocopied the Pentagon Papers in the belief that their disclosure might hasten the end of the war. By spring 1970, Rand considered Ellsberg unproductive and put pressure on him to leave. He moved to Massachusetts, where he became a research fellow at the Cambridge Massachusetts Center for International Studies. Ellsberg took his copy of the Pentagon Papers with him.

The *Times* began publishing the extracts Ellsberg leaked to them on June 13, 1971. It was a critical time for President Richard Nixon, who was seeking reelection to the presidency. He and Dr. Henry Kissinger, his national security adviser, treated Ellsberg's actions as a threat to national security, tantamount to treason, and tried to stop publication. A month later the U.S. Supreme Court upheld the media's right under the First Amendment to publish material in the public interest, ruling that: "The security of the nation is not at the ramparts alone. Security also lies in the value of our free institutions....There is no greater safety valve for discontentment and cynicism about the affairs of government than freedom."

A WARRANT WAS ISSUED FOR ELLSBERG'S ARREST ON JUNE 25, 1971, by a magistrate of the Justice Department in Los Angeles. The indictment brought against him by the Los Angeles grand jury charged him with unauthorized possession of "documents and writings related to the national defense," with failing to turn them in, and with converting them to his own use. Ellsberg fought to have the case transferred from Los Angeles — where the offense had been committed—to Boston, where his lawyers felt a more sympathetic trial jury might be selected. The federal court in Boston rejected all his efforts, however, and on August 16 Ellsberg appeared in Los Angeles for arraignment. He pleaded not guilty, and spelled out to the court the major question in controversy: "Was I right in my thinking that the papers deal with high crimes by officials of our government?"

Pretrial motions were scheduled for January 6, 1972; but on December 29, 1971, the grand jury returned a superseding indictment that included the additional charges of stealing and distributing Defense Department documents and of keeping national defense papers, a violation of the 1940 Espionage Act. Ellsberg stood accused of 11 federal crimes, as well as conspiracy, and if convicted could receive a maximum sentence of 115 years in jail and a $120,000 fine. Charged along with Ellsberg was Anthony Russo, with whom Ellsberg had worked at the Rand Corporation. For nearly six months Russo had refused to divulge information relating to how Ellsberg had obtained photocopies of the Pentagon Papers.

Ellsberg and Russo were committed for trial on March 7, 1972. Pretrial arguments over the precise charges against them dragged on for six months; preliminary selection of jurors did not

Left At his trial, Ellsberg declared that he was prosecuted for leaking the Pentagon Papers not because he breached national security but because of the political risk to the government.

Press censorship

In seeking to suppress extracts from the Pentagon Papers in the *New York Times* and the *Washington Post,* President Nixon and his administration challenged a fundamental right under the First Amendment of the U.S. Constitution—that "Congress shall make no law...abridging the freedom of speech, or of the press." The publication of the Pentagon Papers and Ellsberg's ensuing trial were milestones in a censorship debate that far outreaches the United States or its Constitution. At issue is the right of any government to suppress facts deemed to be in the public interest, or to prosecute individuals who feel morally bound to expose what they consider to be acts of political corruption.

Although censorship of the press is outlawed by the U.S. Constitution, the Pentagon Papers debate also raised other questions: to what extent had Ellsberg damaged U.S. security by leaking classified information to the press; and was the information really the property of the government? At the heart of the case against Ellsberg was an issue that has since been argued in cases such as the *Spycatcher* affair: how should the state balance its need for secrecy on delicate political matters with the freedom of expression guaranteed to its citizens by law? The tension is age old—freedom versus security— and only by allowing that tension between them can both be maintained.

"In releasing the Pentagon Papers I acted in a hope I still hold: that truths that changed me could help Americans free themselves and other victims from our longest war."

DANIEL ELLSBERG,
at the end of the trial,
May 1973

VIETNAM WAR

In 1945, the Vietnamese Communist leader Ho Chi Minh declared that his country's period of French colonial rule (begun in 1883) had come to an end. A bitter civil war ensued until 1954, when Vietnam was divided by a Geneva agreement into a Communist northern state and a non-Communist southern state under U.S. protection. When Communist guerrillas invaded the south, the U.S. military joined in the conflict.

In 1961 the U.S. secretary of defense, Robert McNamara, supported intervention in Vietnam. But as the death toll mounted, he struggled to find a settlement and initiated a full-scale investigation of U.S. policy in Indochina since World War II. His "task force" found documents, later known as the Pentagon Papers, that showed the government's inability over 25 years and four presidencies (Truman, Eisenhower, Kennedy, and Johnson) to end a war fueled by U.S. money and manpower. Disillusioned, McNamara resigned in 1968.

By 1971, anti-Vietnam War protests were widespread in the United States; a tide of civil disobedience caused 13,000 arrests in May alone. By 1973, when the U.S. government withdrew its troops, the war had claimed some 47,000 American lives. A peace treaty was signed that year, and in 1976 the country was united as the Socialist Republic of Vietnam.

Above Ellsberg leaving the federal court on May 11, 1973, with his wife Patricia after winning, in his own words, "A great partial victory."

begin until July 10, 1972. What had looked to government prosecutors like a clear-cut case began to change its shape. Ellsberg's sole defense was that he had acted in the public interest. He had been motivated, as he stated to the media, by "loyalties long unconsulted, deeper and broader than loyalty to the president—loyalties to America's founding concepts, to our constitutional system, to countrymen, to one's own humanity." Alongside the moral issues, Ellsberg's lawyers piled up technical arguments about government demands for secrecy and the right to freedom of expression as described in the First Amendment of the U.S. Constitution. Were the documents really the property of the government? Did the government's arbitrary classification system have the force of law? In what way had the defendants damaged U.S. interests by leaking the papers to the press?

Before these questions could be explored in court, Justice William O. Douglas of the Supreme Court ruled that the trial must wait for a Supreme Court ruling on Ellsberg's allegations that evidence against him had been illegally acquired through a government wiretap. The trial did not resume until November 13, 1972, at which point the defense applied for a transcript of the wiretap that the government admitted having made. With jury members chafing after so many delays, Judge William Byrne declined the application and ordered a mistrial.

THE NEW TRIAL OPENED ON JANUARY 17, 1973. Ellsberg explained to the jury that he had leaked the Pentagon Papers for a timely reason. President Nixon, Ellsberg said, had launched, in the first months of his presidency, three secret military actions as a warning to Hanoi that the United States was prepared to intensify the war effort. It was wrong, he continued, that Republican delegates should be asked to nominate Nixon for a second term without being apprised of his secret plans that precluded any hope of peace.

By this time the Ellsberg case had been sucked into the Watergate scandal. After his dismissal by Nixon in April 1973, presidential aide John Ehrlichman revealed that a number of Republican supporters, later known as "the plumbers," had broken into the office of Ellsberg's psychiatrist to look for incriminating material. Ehrlichman also left wiretap records from 1969 to 1971 behind in his office safe after his dismissal. Acting FBI director William Ruckelshaus discovered among these a 21-month wiretap record on Kissinger's colleague Morton Halperin that included a conversation with Ellsberg, the one he claimed had illegally been used against him. The burglary and the wiretaps made national headlines. Ellsberg's defense counsel, Leonard Boudin, described the new information as "shocking" and called for the dismissal of the government's case against his client on the grounds that Nixon had directly or indirectly authorized the plumbers.

JUDGE BYRNE, ACCEPTING THE INEVITABLE, DECLARED A MISTRIAL for the second time. On May 11, 1973, he dismissed all charges against Ellsberg and Russo because of government misconduct and "an unprecedented series of actions with respect to the defendants." He refused to grant an acquittal, which would have cleared Ellsberg and Russo of all the charges, but offered to withhold his ruling if they preferred that the jury should render its verdict. The defendants chose to accept the dismissal of the charges rather than have the case go back to the jury.

WATERGATE

In June 1972, as the Republican candidate Richard Nixon was seeking reelection as U.S. president, a group of seven Republican supporters were arrested as they were breaking into Democratic Party headquarters at the Watergate complex in Washington, D.C. The group, later known as "the plumbers," had been instructed by presidential aide John Ehrlichman to wiretap the activities of their political opponents. They were caught in the act of trying to retrieve their bugging devices. Nixon dismissed Ehrlichman. After leaving office, and in the midst of the scandal created by the release of the Pentagon Papers to the media, Ehrlichman revealed details of the plumbers' other break-in, at the office of Daniel Ellsberg's psychiatrist. The burglary had been ordered, said Ehrlichman, in the hope that Ellsberg's private files would reveal his true political and emotional motivations in leaking the Papers and also reveal the identities of his accomplices.

On top of this patently illegal activity—which destroyed the government's case against Ellsberg and Russo (on the grounds that evidence against them had been obtained illegally)—the trial that followed revealed that Nixon had also illegally taped all the conversations that he had held in his White House office. In May 1973 a special prosecutor was named, who worked with a federal grand jury to investigate. Nixon was ordered to hand over the tapes. He responded by firing the special prosecutor. Under extreme public pressure, Nixon called for a new special prosecutor. After a congressional committee adopted three articles of impeachment, Nixon was forced by the Supreme Court to hand over the tapes in July 1974. Rather than face impeachment, he resigned from office on August 8, 1974. Although he was granted a presidential pardon for his actions by his successor, Gerald Ford, a number of his high-level aides and associates served prison sentences for their roles in the Watergate affair. The scandal was so far-reaching that it overshadowed the issues raised in the Pentagon Papers court case, which ended inconclusively without conviction or acquittal.

Below Nixon, supported by his family, announces his resignation to the press in August 1974. He said that he had decided to step down because the United States needed a full-time president.

A Dingo's Got My Baby!

THE CROWN v. LINDY AND MICHAEL CHAMBERLAIN

SEPTEMBER 13 – OCTOBER 29, 1982

Above Signs warning people that wild dingoes could be dangerous were posted at Ayers Rock after the Chamberlain tragedy. They did not stipulate that dingoes can carry off very young children.

Below The Chamberlain family's campsite at Ayers Rock. Lindy saw the dingo outside the tent where Azaria was sleeping.

One of Australia's most sensational trials opened in Darwin, capital of the Northern Territory, on September 13, 1982. Thirty-four-year-old Alice Lynne (Lindy) Chamberlain stood accused of having murdered her nine-week-old daughter, Azaria, two years earlier.

On August 17, 1980, Lindy and her family—Seventh-Day Adventist preacher Michael, their sons, six-year-old Aidan and four-year-old Reagan, and baby Azaria—had gone camping at the famous Ayers Rock National Park. While the family cooked their meal at a barbecue, Azaria was left alone in a tent next to the car. Another camper, Sally Lowe, heard a baby's cry. Lindy heard it too and rushed back to the tent, just in time to see a dingo making off in the darkness with something in its mouth. There were pools of blood inside the tent, and the baby was missing. Other campers helped the couple to search the area, but they could find no trace of Azaria. Months later campers found bloodstained baby clothes some distance from the campsite, and Lindy identified them as Azaria's.

AN INQUEST OPENED AT ALICE SPRINGS ON DECEMBER 15, 1980, and Lindy's story was upheld. But rumors soon began to circulate that Lindy and her husband were religious fanatics who had sacrificed their own baby in a bizarre ritual. The press reported that the name Azaria was believed to mean "sacrifice in the wilderness," which made growing suspicions of murder all the more credible. In an effort to gather scientific evidence, researchers in a zoo in Adelaide set up an experiment; they were able to demonstrate that a starving dingo could decapitate a goat kid and extract it from a baby's jumpsuit by opening just two snaps. But the damage done to the clothes on the goat kid differed significantly from the marks found on Azaria's clothing. Deeply disturbed that the Chamberlains had been acquitted of murder, a forensic dentist named Kenneth A. Brown, whose opinion had been set aside by the Alice Springs coroner, obtained the baby's clothes from the government of the Northern Territory and sent them to Professor James Cameron, a forensic pathologist in London. Cameron concluded that Azaria's neck had not been cut by a dingo, but by scissors or a knife.

The Royal Commission

A Royal Commission is a group appointed by the British or a colonial government to investigate an issue and to recommend any necessary change to the law. In the Chamberlain case, the Royal Commission investigated the threat to humans from dingoes, for which there was no legal precedent at the time. Reports of dingo attacks in journals and newspapers were not accepted as reliable, and "death by misadventure" was the usual coroner's verdict on a suspected animal attack. However, when the commission questioned Aborigines at Ayers Rock, it discovered that Aborigine babies were in fact sometimes killed by dingoes. Because the Aborigines considered death to be a taboo subject, they did not report the deaths to the authorities, or keep records.

The commission also uncovered an incident that had occurred at Ayers Rock two months before the Chamberlain tragedy. Four-year-old Amanda Cranwell had been seized by the throat and dragged out of the family car by a dingo before being rescued by bystanders. The culprit, a semi-tame dingo known as Ding, was shot. Although the police knew of this incident, they did not mention it at the trial. Even as the commission was sitting, a dingo attacked and gashed the arm of a tourist at Standley Chasm; the victim tried to keep the incident quiet because he was "anti-Chamberlain."

Above Azaria, age nine weeks and four days, and her mother, Lindy Chamberlain, photographed on Ayers Rock by Michael Chamberlain some hours before the baby disappeared.

CAMERON'S FINDINGS PROMPTED THE POLICE TO REOPEN THE CASE. On August 19, 1981, they raided the Chamberlain house, then proceeded to recall all the original eyewitnesses. A second inquest opened in December 1981 and continued until February 1, 1982. The prosecution accused Lindy of killing Azaria in the car, hiding the body in her husband's camera bag, and disposing of it later. Police forensic biologist Joy Kuhl claimed to have found significant amounts of blood in the car and on the camera bag. She further claimed that the blood was "fetal hemoglobin," or blood from a child less than three months old. Kuhl's method of testing the blood samples was heavily criticized by other experts, but she had disposed of her records and samples by the time of the inquest, making a full investigation of her procedures impossible.

The forensic evidence presented at the second inquest led to a formal indictment against Lindy Chamberlain for murder and against her husband as an accessory to the crime. The trial was set for June 1982, but in the months leading up to it, Lindy Chamberlain became pregnant. The trial was delayed to allow her to get over the early months when she was feeling unwell, and a new date was set for September 13, by which time she was seven months pregnant. As the press continued to speculate about the case, they described Lindy's behavior as "strange" and "unnatural" and provoked national criticism about the fact that a woman suspected of infanticide was about to have another baby. As media reports continued, public opinion turned against the Chamberlains. Michael delivered a rambling, incoherent speech at the second inquest. His behavior, combined with the negative reports about Lindy, confirmed portrayals of the couple as wildly eccentric, feckless, ignorant, and fanatically religious. Besides, "everybody knew" that dingoes did not snatch babies for food.

IAN BARKER PRESENTED THE CROWN'S CASE FOR THE PROSECUTION to a jury of nine men and three women. Prosecution lawyers admitted that they could show no motive for Lindy Chamberlain's murder of her daughter. But they plugged away at the blood found in the car and the inherent implausibility of Lindy's account of dingo behavior. Only two possibilities existed in this case, they said: either a dingo had made away with Azaria, as Lindy claimed, or Lindy herself had committed murder.

> "I further find that neither the parents of the child, nor either of their remaining children were in any degree whatsoever responsible for this death. I find that the name Azaria does not mean and never has meant 'sacrifice in the wilderness.'"
>
> CORONER DENNIS BARRITT
> summing up at the first inquest,
> February 20, 1981

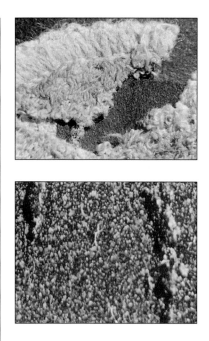

Above Court photographs submitted as forensic evidence: the damage to Azaria's jumpsuit (top), and rust-colored stains inside the Chamberlains' car. Traces of paint were wrongly identified by experts as baby's blood.

CHRONOLOGY

August 17, 1980 Nine-week-old Azaria disappears from Ayers Rock.

February 1981 The first inquest acquits the Chamberlains.

August 1981 "Operation Ochre." The police raid the Chamberlain house. A second inquest commits Lindy and Michael to trial.

Summer 1982 Lindy Chamberlain announces that she is pregnant; the trial is delayed until later in the year.

September 13, 1982 Trial begins.

October 29, 1982 The jury rules that Lindy Chamberlain is guilty.

April 30, 1983 An appeal to the federal court is turned down.

November 28, 1983 The Supreme Court upholds the trial verdict of the previous year.

February 1986 A baby's jacket is found by tourists at Ayers Rock. The case is reopened by a Royal Commission of Inquiry.

June 2, 1987 The conviction is overturned and Lindy is released from jail with a full pardon.

The prosecution could not discredit the eyewitnesses from Ayers Rock, who corroborated Lindy's story. Sally Lowe, especially, remained adamant that she had heard a baby's cry just before Lindy rushed to the tent, screaming, "A dingo's got my baby!" However, the jury remained mesmerized by the scientific evidence presented by the Crown. The statements given by Professor Cameron and Joy Kuhl seemed unshakable. Cameron insisted that the damage caused to Azaria's jumpsuit could not have been caused by a dingo, and Kuhl stated that she was certain that the Chamberlains' car was stained with the blood of a young infant. Furthermore, they both spoke in plain terms. The defense relied on two forensic pathologists, Professor Boettcher and Professor Pleuckhahn, who refuted the Kuhl–Cameron version of events; but the pathologists argued in such a pedantic way that the jury (as one jurywoman said later) could not follow their testimony.

John Phillips summed up for the defense after 73 witnesses, 145 exhibits, and a transcript of 2,800 pages had been taken into evidence. The Chamberlains' lawyers stressed the lack of motive, the spate of dingo attacks at Ayers Rock that summer, and the rapid sequence of events that would have given the Chamberlains no time to clean the car and bury the body. The defense also made its most valuable point: the prosecution had failed to prove its case beyond a reasonable doubt.

The prosecution responded with a catalog of circumstantial evidence. They reiterated their either-or view of the case—either Lindy or the dingo was the killer. Prosecutor Ian Barker exonerated the dingo because there were no known cases of dingoes attacking infants. Outside the courthouse, street vendors were selling T-shirts printed with the slogan "The dingo is innocent." Inside, Barker mocked the defense experts, calling them "mere academics." On October 28, Justice James Muirhead, who had maintained a fair and orderly court throughout, summed up strongly in favor of acquittal.

Below Reporters mob the car as Lindy Chamberlain is driven to jail in October 1982.

AT 2:20 P.M. ON OCTOBER 29 THE JURY RETIRED. At 8:33 P.M. they returned with a unanimous verdict of guilty for both Lindy and Michael. The judge condemned Lindy to life imprisonment with hard labor; Michael's sentence was suspended. Lindy was taken to Darwin prison, where, on November 17 she gave birth to a daughter, Kahlia. Remarkably, in light of the verdict of infanticide, she was released on bail and allowed to take her baby home. On April 30, 1983, the Chamberlains appealed at the federal court in Sydney. It took just three minutes for the judges to refuse to review the case. The appellants, they said, had been unable to demonstrate that the jury had made an error. Following the denial of her appeal, Lindy went to Mulawa jail to begin her sentence and Kahlia went to a foster home. Later that year the Chamberlains asked that new evidence about blood tests and dingo behavior be taken into account at the Supreme Court in Canberra. On November 28, by a 3 to 2 vote, the court held that the evidence presented at the trial was sufficient to uphold the convictions.

> *"The prosecution has had two years and three months to think of any reason, good, bad, or indifferent…but they can't supply you with a reason why this mother would kill her baby."*
>
> JOHN PHILLIPS
> summing up for the defense,
> October 1982

POSTSCRIPT

Two years into Lindy Chamberlain's jail sentence, public opinion, influenced by increased awareness of dingo attacks, began to turn. A petition, signed by 150,000 people, called for a Royal Commission of Inquiry, but the Northern Territory law officers steadfastly opposed either a review of the case or Lindy's release on parole. Then, in February 1986, during a search for a missing tourist at Ayers Rock, a baby's jacket was discovered close to where Azaria's clothes had been found. Lindy had always maintained that her daughter was wearing a jacket on the fatal night, but the prosecution alleged that this was a figment of her imagination. At the same time, a report arrived from Germany discrediting Joy Kuhl's method for detecting fetal blood.

Marshall Perron, attorney general of the Northern Territory, was forced to release Lindy and ordered an inquiry, which was quickly subsumed under a Royal Commission. The commission heard further forensic evidence, listened carefully to what Aborigine trackers had to say, recalled all the eyewitnesses, and questioned witnesses who had not been called at the trial. The Aborigines and the Ayers Rock rangers made it clear that a dingo could indeed have killed the baby. They testified that the animal is a tidy eater, quite capable, for example, of extricating the contents of a package while leaving the wrapping intact. The

dingo's teeth are sharp enough to slice through a car seat belt or standard Australian fencing wire. Human urine is effective in dingo traps, and a baby's wet diaper might have attracted a dingo. Unlike dogs, they can dislocate their jaws to hold a large object (Azaria Chamberlain weighed 10 pounds).

Before the commission closed its investigation, a Mr. Perron presented himself to give evidence. He reported that while surveying in northwestern Australia, he was asked by Aborigines to shoot a dingo that had killed an Aborigine baby. When Perron shot it, he found blood and tissue from the baby's body around its mouth. Since this was an Aborigine death, it was not

Above The Chamberlain family, reunited, celebrate Lindy's release in 1987.

reported, but Perron's family knew the story. The man's son was Marshall Perron, the attorney general for the Northern Territory who had originally opposed the judicial review and Lindy Chamberlain's release on parole.

On June 2, 1987, the Royal Commission announced its findings—that the Chamberlains' conviction was not warranted by the evidence. The Northern Territory granted a pardon and the following year released this statement: "The convictions having been wiped away, the law of the land holds the Chamberlains to be innocent."

Economical With the Truth

THE ATTORNEY GENERAL *v.* HEINEMANN PUBLISHERS & PETER WRIGHT

NOVEMBER 17, 1986 – JUNE 2, 1988

Above *Spycatcher*, the controversial autobiography banned in Britain, secretly photographed outside the Houses of Parliament in London in 1987.

In 1984, Peter Wright signed a contract with the Australian division of the publishing house Heinemann to write his memoirs of the Cold War period in a book called *Spycatcher*. When news of Wright's intentions appeared in the London *Observer* on March 31, 1985, the British government moved quickly to stop him. Sir Robert Armstrong, the British cabinet secretary, put his case in an affidavit to the Supreme Court of New South Wales, stating that Wright, as a former British intelligence officer, had signed the Official Secrets Act, which prohibited employees of the Crown from revealing sensitive information.

Heinemann hired a young Sydney lawyer, Malcolm Turnbull, to defend them. Turnbull had already acted for the Australian entrepreneur Kerry Packer in high-profile media cases. In preparing the defense, Turnbull focused on three weaknesses in the British government's case. First, *Spycatcher* contained evidence of criminal acts by MI-5 and alleged that Sir Roger Hollis, director general from 1956 to 1965, was a Soviet agent; Wright felt that this fact was so vital to the public interest that he should be granted exemption from the Official Secrets Act. Second, most of the material in the book had already been published elsewhere, without prosecution. Turnbull's third and strongest point was that international law recognized that the courts of one country are not bound to enforce the laws of another. It was high-handed and arrogant, Turnbull argued, for the British government to assume that its law applied in a former colony.

THE CASE WAS SCHEDULED FOR TRIAL IN NOVEMBER 1986, before Judge Philip Powell in the Equity Division of the New South Wales Supreme Court. In the meantime nearly 12 months of "interrogatories"—questions put by one side to another on the basis of the affidavits—were exchanged. Turnbull's interrogatories included such questions as "Did officers of the British Secret Intelligence Services…develop any plan or operation which had as its goal the assassination of Colonel Nasser, then head of Egypt?" Any attempt to reply threatened to draw attention to clandestine and arguably illegitimate operations run by MI-5. Rather than invite such exposure, Armstrong, acting in the interests of the British government, agreed that "for the purposes of the proceedings" everything written in the book would be deemed true. While this admission focused the trial on Wright's violation of the Official Secrets Act, it simultaneously damaged the reputation of the British Conservative government and its prime minister, Margaret Thatcher.

Official Secrets

From 1911 to 1920, the British government passed a series of Official Secrets Acts, which classified some types of information available to government employees as strictly confidential. Over the years, the Acts were criticized by opposition parties as a tool for suppressing any issue that would embarrass the party in power. The topic was publicly debated during the *Spycatcher* trial. To prevent publication of Peter Wright's book, and to suppress the damaging revelations it contained, Margaret Thatcher's government sought to impose British laws of secrecy on Australia—a former colony that had largely achieved legislative independence—where Wright was living. The British government was defeated in the Australian courts in 1987, and the book was published. A subsequent Official Secrets Act of 1989 attempted to close the loopholes in British law by stipulating that members of the security forces were obliged to maintain lifelong confidentiality about their work and were prohibited from revealing secrets "in the public interest."

BIOGRAPHY

Peter Wright 1916-95 was born in Chesterfield, England, and was educated at Oxford. During World War II he worked at the Admiralty Research Laboratory, specializing in antisubmarine detection. In 1946 he became principal scientific officer at the Services Electronics Research laboratory, then went to the Admiralty as a communications expert in 1949. Six years later he joined the British intelligence unit MI-5, as chief scientist, concentrating on detecting and exposing Soviet spies and acting as principal liaison officer with American intelligence officials. When he retired from MI-5 in 1976, he and his wife, Lois, bought a sheep farm in Tasmania. For eight years he lived in peaceful obscurity. Then in 1984 he gave an interview on British television about his MI-5 career, during which he referred to MI-5's head, Sir Roger Hollis, as "the spy who never was." Three years later Wright placed his autobiography, *Spycatcher,* with an Australian publisher. The court case surrounding the book ensured that it was an international best-seller.

Right Peter Wright, photographed in 1952, when he was 36 years old.

The preliminary battle switched to arguments about the "damaging" revelations in Wright's book. In fact, they were identical to those made in a previous book, *Their Trade Is Treachery,* published by the political journalist Chapman Pincher in 1981. The British government had not prosecuted Pincher; and in August 1986 Judge Powell had demanded documentation clarifying why it had not. Three days before the trial was due to begin, the lawyer acting for the British government, Theo Simos, asked for an indefinite postponement. His clients, he said, wanted to challenge Powell's ruling on the documents in the Court of Appeal. Judge Powell refused.

THE TRIAL FINALLY GOT UNDER WAY ON NOVEMBER 17. An embarrassed Margaret Thatcher had asked the Australian prime minister, Bob Hawke, to use his influence on her behalf. Hawke asked Michael Codd, Armstrong's counterpart in the Australian government, to prepare an affidavit, which was now read out in court. Codd argued that if Wright's book was published, other intelligence agencies might think that Australian law did not safeguard sensitive material provided to Australian intelligence agencies. Hawke's obligation to Thatcher was fulfilled, and the trial moved on.

Sir Robert Armstrong was sworn in, and Turnbull launched his strategy to discredit the Cabinet secretary. He produced a letter that Armstrong had

"I am extremely loyal....I have made it clear to the British government that I will take anything out of the book that would damage them. They are embarrassed because they have made a mess of it."

PETER WRIGHT,
at a press conference,
December 9, 1986

Above British Cabinet secretary Sir Robert Armstrong, returning home in December 1986 after giving evidence in the Supreme Court of Sydney, Australia.

> *"A classical fall-guy, an ambassador for Britain, in the sense that an ambassador is a man sent abroad to lie for his country."*
>
> MALCOLM TURNBULL, speaking of Sir Robert Armstrong while summing up for the defense, December 17, 1986

written to Chapman Pincher's publishers, asking for advance copies of *Their Trade Is Treachery*, saying that the prime minister had to prepare a statement in case she was questioned. Armstrong admitted that at the time the British government was in full possession of the text. Turnbull pressed his point that Armstrong had deliberately lied in his letter, trapping Armstrong into a statement that brought him international ridicule and gave Turnbull the upper hand. The media, meanwhile, gave Armstrong's humiliating evidence full, uncomplimentary coverage:

TURNBULL: So it contains a lie?
ARMSTRONG: It was a misleading impression. It does not contain a lie, I don't think.
TURNBULL: What is the difference between a misleading impression and a lie?
ARMSTRONG: A lie is a straight untruth.
TURNBULL: What is a misleading impression? A sort of bent untruth?
ARMSTRONG:…it is perhaps being economical with the truth.

ON NOVEMBER 19 THE COURT OF APPEAL rejected Simos's application to set aside Judge Powell's ruling on the documents relating to Chapman Pincher. The British government began to slide into a disaster of its own making. Pincher, it turned out, had relied heavily on Wright for the information in his book. Wright had even collected a share of the royalties. Turnbull produced Wright's correspondence with Pincher from when they were preparing *Their Trade Is Treachery*. It emerged that the intermediary between Wright and Pincher who allowed Pincher to publish sensitive material gleaned from Wright was Lord Rothschild, a pillar of the establishment closely allied to Margaret Thatcher and her cabinet. In short, the revelations suggested that the Thatcher government had leaked to Pincher the very information they now sought to prevent Wright from publishing.

Turnbull continued to press this point and piled on Judge Powell's bench a mountain of books and articles written by former British agents, all of them unprosecuted. Meanwhile, in the British Parliament, members of the Labor Party pressed the Conservative government to admit that the Wright prosecution was not some legal formality initiated by the British attorney general, but that it came straight from the prime minister. On November 27, during the regular session of prime minister's Question Time in the House of Commons, the leader of the opposition, Neil Kinnock, brought the issue under media scrutiny by asking: "In these matters, has the attorney general been a fool or a fall guy?" Under

Left Sir Robert, being grilled in Australia, appeared in *The Daily Telegraph*, a right-wing British paper, on November 26, 1986.

persistent questioning, the prime minister was forced to admit that the government initiated the prosecution and subsequently refused to compromise.

On Monday, December 8, Peter Wright, in frail health, entered the witness box and read out a lengthy affidavit. He stated that MI-5 was thoroughly penetrated by the Soviets and that following revelations in 1979 that MI-5 agents Anthony Blunt and Sir Roger Hollis were Soviet spies, Margaret Thatcher had misled the House of Commons about the extent to which MI-5 was exposed. Wright said of her statements to Parliament: "[they] were certainly not accurate. I was the senior case officer in both these matters." On December 10, Simos finally produced copies of the Wright–Pincher correspondence, complying with Judge Powell's decision, which shed a new light on what the government knew about Blunt and Hollis. The correspondence flatly contradicted Armstrong's evidence.

The prosecution made its final submission on December 15, maintaining that Wright's book was a breach of confidence that would damage MI-5 even if everything in it had already been published. Judge Powell expressed skepticism and asked why previous books had not been suppressed—a question that was not answered during the trial. On December 17, Turnbull wound up for the defense, asserting that "the real responsibility for [Armstrong's] disgraceful conduct lies with those in London who sent him here to lie and dissemble to this court." He criticized the British government for acting inconsistently and using oppressive legislation to suppress the right to question government policy. He upheld his client's right to reveal corruption in high places, in the public interest.

THE TRIAL ENDED ON DECEMBER 18, 1986. Judge Powell spent the next three months reading through every book, newspaper article, and television script that had been tendered in evidence. On Friday, March 13, 1987, he found in Wright's favor, but his judgment was mixed; on the one hand, Wright had not been employed under a contract, as the British government alleged; on the other hand, he owed a duty of confidentiality to the government. Powell did not find that Armstrong had lied to the court, but said that much of his evidence "on matters of importance" had to be "treated with considerable reserve." Powell also held that there was a public interest in revealing evidence of the many crimes and treasons in *Spycatcher*. The exposure of Britain's dirty linen to the international media during the trial was a blow to the Thatcher government.

POSTSCRIPT

Following Judge Powell's verdict, the British government petitioned the New South Wales Court of Appeal to overturn the ruling. Though *Spycatcher* could not be published in the interim, British newspapers obtained copies from the United States and published excerpts. On September 24, 1987, the appeal was rejected by a two to one majority. Faced with a British attempt to enforce its laws in Australia, the court declared the appeal a challenge to Australia's independence and territorial integrity.

The British government took its appeal to the Federal High Court in Canberra, but this time the publication ban was lifted pending the hearing. Within four months a book that would normally have sold no more than 50,000 copies worldwide sold 1 million copies. On October 14 the High Court upheld the original decision and refused to reimpose the publication ban but allowed the plaintiffs to appeal to the Federal Supreme Court. Like the other courts, this body asked why it should enforce British law in Australia or protect the public interest of Britain when doing so violated the Australian right to free speech. On June 2, 1988, it ordered the plaintiffs to pay the defendant's costs.

Right Malcolm Turnbull (left) celebrates with his client Wright (center) and former Australian prime minister Gough Whitlam at the launch of Turnbull's book *The Spycatcher Trial* in 1988. The book tells the full story of the battle to publish *Spycatcher* against the British government's wishes.

Is It Ever Too Late?

THE STATE OF MISSISSIPPI *v.* BYRON DE LA BECKWITH

JANUARY 27 – FEBRUARY 5, 1994

Above Standing in front of the Confederate flag, Beckwith speaks to the press outside his Tennessee home before being arrested for the third time for the murder of civil rights worker Medgar Evers.

edgar Evers, Mississippi field secretary of the National Association for the Advancement of Colored People (NAACP), was murdered in his own driveway in Jackson, Mississippi, just after midnight on June 12, 1963. He was shot in the back with a bullet from a high-powered rifle as he got out of his car. His wife and three children, who had waited up to see him, rushed outside to find him lying on the asphalt, covered in blood.

In 1963 racism dominated the politics of Mississippi. But the murder of a nonviolent civil rights worker forced the state's officials, all white and to varying degrees prejudiced, to take action on what was plainly a political assassination. For the first time in Mississippi's history, the murder of a black person was officially condemned. Mayor Allen Thompson of Jackson stated that he was "dreadfully shocked, humiliated, and sick at heart" and canceled his vacation. The Jackson police, many of whom maintained close links with the violently racist Ku Klux Klan, were obliged to conduct a thorough investigation, lest the black community riot in protest, especially since the murder occurred the day after President Kennedy's nationwide television broadcast endorsing civil rights activism.

A search of the area revealed the murder weapon, a 1918 vintage .30/06 Enfield rifle with telescopic sights. A clear fingerprint was taken from the rifle, and the fatal bullet was retrieved. To prevent any tampering at the local level an FBI agent took the evidence to Washington. Both the fingerprint and the rifle pointed unmistakably to a former U.S. marine, Byron De La Beckwith. Once in custody Beckwith refused to answer questions.

ON JANUARY 27, 1964, BYRON DE LA BECKWITH'S TRIAL BEGAN. His defense counsel, Hardy Lott, was lackluster, and the alibi provided by two policemen from Evers's hometown of Redwood was far from convincing. Nevertheless, prosecutor Bill Waller faced a formidable challenge. He sincerely doubted that any amount of physical evidence could damn the defendant in the eyes of the all-white jury; he also suspected that any motive he could show for Beckwith's killing of Evers would strike a sympathetic chord in them. Their acceptance as members of the jury had been determined by their response to his question: "Do you believe it is a crime to kill a nigger in Mississippi?" In fact, the prosecutor's own loyalties were torn, as some of his remarks to the jury show: "Evers was engaged in things that were contrary

Integrated Juries

The three trials of Byron De La Beckwith were heard in both state and federal courts, which together constitute the U.S. legal system. State courts include the state Supreme Court; the circuit, or district courts; county courts; and town, or Justice of the Peace courts. Federal courts include the U.S. Supreme Court and the U.S. Courts of Appeals.

Beckwith's first two trials, in 1964, were held in a circuit court before all-white juries. In the 30 years between 1964 and the third trial in 1994, however, the political and social climate changed dramatically. Before the third trial, the grand jury—which in some

states must be summoned to assess whether there is evidence to justify bringing someone to trial—was composed of 10 blacks and 8 whites. They voted for the case to go to trial.

Beckwith's lawyers appealed this decision first in the Mississippi Supreme Court and then in the U.S. Supreme Court. Both upheld the grand jury's indictment. At the 1994 trial a jury of eight blacks and four whites was asked by District Attorney Ed Peters if Evers's life goals—achieving racially integrated schools and leisure facilities—had justified his murder. In the relatively enlightened 1990s, the jurors were astonished by the question.

Above Detective Sergeant Turner of the Jackson police at the scene of Evers's murder, June 12, 1963. He stretches out his arms to determine the apparent path of the bullet that hit Evers in the back as he stepped out of his car.

to what you and I believe in." "I'm a little upset right now, with all these nigras in the courtroom—does that bother you?" "I like Mr. Beckwith. He has a pleasant way. He's a Mason, you're a Mason; he's a veteran, you're a veteran; you're a father, he's a father." The depth of the animosity at work in favor of Beckwith's acquittal was underscored in Lott's final exhortation for the defense: "I do not believe you will return a verdict of guilty to satisfy the attorney general of the United States [a reference to Robert Kennedy, who was hated by Southern racists] and the liberal national media."

On February 7, 1964, the twelfth day of the trial, the jury declared itself hopelessly deadlocked, seven to five in favor of acquittal. A mistrial was declared. After spending two months in jail, Beckwith stood trial again. With a new panel of jurors irresolvably split eight to four in favor of acquittal, a mistrial was again declared and though he had not been acquitted, Beckwith went free. On his release, the police department of Greenwood, his home town, made him an auxiliary policeman and allowed him to travel through black neighborhoods in the front seat of a patrol car, toting his gun.

SOME 25 YEARS LATER, IN THE FALL OF 1989, interest in the Medgar Evers murder case was rekindled after secret documents from the Sovereignty Commission—a prosegregation agency funded by the state of Mississippi— were leaked to the Jackson newspaper, the *Clarion Ledger*. The Sovereignty Commission had from 1956 to 1973 waged a campaign of harassment, intimidation, and disinformation against civil rights workers. In 1973, the Mississippi legislature closed the commission, and four years later sealed its secret files for the next 50 years. The *Clarion Ledger* published the leaked

Above Medgar Evers, whose stand for racial justice despite great personal danger resulted in his coldblooded murder.

Byron De La Beckwith was born in Sacramento, California, in 1920, and was brought up in Mississippi. He served in the Pacific during World War II, and was wounded in action. When he returned to Mississippi he worked as a traveling salesman. A member of the Ku Klux Klan, he soon gained a reputation as a gun freak and a racist. In 1945 he married Mary Louise Williams. By 1964 they had divorced and remarried each other two times. That year Beckwith twice stood trial for the murder of Medgar Evers. In both cases hung juries resulted in mistrials. The following year his marriage ended. As anti-Semitic as he was prosegregationist, he went to prison in 1975 for attempting to kill a Jewish regional director of the Anti-Defamation League. After his release in 1980, he married Thelma Neff and moved to Tennessee. From there he was extradited to stand trial a third time for Medgar Evers's murder in Mississippi.

Right Beckwith (center) is escorted by FBI agents to Jackson city jail on June 22, 1963.

Below On the day of Medgar Evers's funeral police and demonstrators clashed in the streets of Jackson, Mississippi. The bigotry against which the black community of Jackson protested was still burning in Byron De La Beckwith 25 years later.

information, that the commission had worked for Beckwith's defense, a clear subversion of the judicial system. Read by a much-changed community, the story stirred a public outcry, and the state of Mississippi called for a new trial of Byron De La Beckwith. Reporters who interviewed 69-year-old Beckwith at his new home in Tennessee found that he had not mellowed with age. "God hates mongrels," he told one reporter. "My people came here to take this country from the Red Man by force and violence, and that's the way we're going to keep [the country]—by force and violence."

Jackson's district attorney let his ambitious assistant, Bobby DeLaughter, take the case. While DeLaughter sought new evidence, he also built an impressive dossier of material from 1964. The official transcripts of the 1964 mistrials were "missing" from the Hinds County Court offices, but Evers's widow, Myrlie, had kept copies stowed away in a trunk. Having obtained those, DeLaughter went on to find an important lead in a 1990 publication called *Klandestine*. The author, Delmar Dennis, was a former Ku Klux Klan member turned FBI informant, who had reported the boastful remarks Beckwith had made to other Klan members: "Killing that nigger gave me no more inner discomfort than our wives endure when they give birth to our children."

THE HINDS COUNTY GRAND JURY CONVENED early in December 1990 to hear testimony from Myrlie Evers and to inspect the new evidence. On December 15 it ordered Beckwith to stand trial for a third time. He fought strenuously against extradition from Tennessee to Mississippi, raising constitutional challenges that took three years to resolve. In the summer of 1992 Beckwith's lawyers appealed to the Mississippi Supreme Court on the grounds that a hearing so long after the crime violated the defendant's right to a speedy trial. They pointed out that many key witnesses were elderly or dead and that crucial evidence was missing, including the bullet that had killed Evers. The Mississippi Supreme Court justices voted by a bare majority for the case to go forward, ruling that Beckwith's lawyers could raise the constitutional issues only after a trial and a conviction. This decision was upheld 10 months later, after an appeal to the U.S. Supreme Court.

In December 1992 the first subpoenas went out for witnesses. Jury selection took place in Panola County, 140 miles north of Jackson, where the trial would be held. It took eight days for the prosecution and the defense to agree on a jury panel of eight blacks and four whites, many of whom were infants when Evers was murdered. The trial opened on January 27, 1994, 30 years to the day after the start of the first trial. As the prosecution and defense read aloud from the early trials' transcripts, the language and ethos of a vanished era filled the courtroom. "How old are you, honey?" Bill Waller had asked one 17-year-old witness, a black waitress from a drive-in restaurant; when this was read in 1994, the public laughed in embarrassment.

As before, Myrlie Evers was the state's prime witness. All the original evidence indicated Beckwith's guilt as forcefully as it had 30 years earlier, though most of the witnesses had grown old and forgetful. The fingerprint expert was so hard of hearing that the questions had to be shouted at him. Beckwith himself was a frail old man with a heart condition, no longer a convincing symbol of white supremacy. But it was the district attorney's last witness who clinched the case against Beckwith. Mark Reiley had been watching television in Chicago when coverage of the trial appeared on his screen. He called the district attorney's office in Jackson the same day and was summoned to the trial. He testified that 15 years earlier, he had been a guard at Louisiana State Penitentiary where Beckwith was serving a sentence for attempting to bomb a Jewish regional director of the Anti-Defamation League. Reiley had befriended Beckwith: "He told me that if he was lying and didn't have the power and connections he said he had, he would be serving time in prison for getting rid of that nigger Medgar Evers."

DELAUGHTER SUMMED UP FOR THE PROSECUTION and made a passionate plea to the jury: "This assassination by a sniper from ambush is timeless. It spans the races. It is something that should sicken every decent human being regardless of race. This is about civilized society versus the vile. This is about the state of Mississippi versus Byron De La Beckwith….Is it ever too late to do the right thing? For the sake of truth and justice, I hope it's not."

The jury deliberated for five hours that evening. They returned a verdict of guilty the next morning. By their action, 31 long years after the fact, they brought Medgar Evers's killer to account. As the 74-year-old was sentenced to life imprisonment for Evers's murder, black spectators in the court shouted, "We got justice, we got justice!"

Above Bobby DeLaughter, the assistant district attorney who prosecuted Beckwith's case, outside Hinds County Court in Jackson, Mississippi.

CHRONOLOGY

June 12, 1963 Medgar Evers is murdered in Jackson, Mississippi.

February 1964 Beckwith is tried for murder. The jury is deadlocked, and a mistrial is declared.

April 1964 Beckwith is tried again, the jury is deadlocked, and another mistrial is declared. Beckwith is set free, but not acquitted.

Fall 1989 Documents are leaked from the Sovereignty Commission, showing serious misconduct in the 1964 trials.

December 1990 The grand jury hears new evidence and commits Beckwith for trial.

Summer 1992 Beckwith's lawyers appeal against the new trial. The Supreme Court rules that it should proceed.

January 1994 Beckwith is tried for a third time for the murder of Medgar Evers.

February 1994 Beckwith is found guilty of murder and sentenced to life imprisonment.

BIBLIOGRAPHY

SPECIAL COURTS

The High Priest Caiaphas v. Jesus of Nazareth
Brandon, S. G. F. *Jesus And The Zealots* (1967)
Brandon, S. G. F. *The Trial Of Jesus Of Nazareth* (1968)
Derret, J. D. M. *Law in the New Testament* (1970)
Sanders, E. P. *The Historical Figure of Jesus* (1993)
Wilson, A. N. *Jesus* (1992)

The Crown v. Sir Thomas More
Marius, R. *Thomas More* (1984)
Ridley, J. *The Statesman and the Fanatic* (1982)
Scarisbrick, J. J. *Henry VIII* (1968)

The Rump Parliament v. King Charles I
Carlton, C. *Charles I* (1983)
Fraser, A. *Cromwell, Our Chief Of Men* (1973)
Watson, D. R. *The Life and Times of Charles I* (1972)

The Committee of Public Safety v. Georges-Jacques Danton
Carlyle, T. *The French Revolution* (many edns.)
Hampson, N. *Danton* (1979)
Schama, S. *Citizens* (1989)
Schama, S. and Hibbert, C. *The French Revolution* (1980)

The Soviet Union v. Nikolai Bukharin
Conquest, R. *The Great Terror* (1968)
Getty, J. A. *Origin of the Great Purges* (1987)
Vaksberg, A. *The Prosecutor and the Prey* (1990)

Brown v. Education Board of Topeka, Kansas
Berman, D. M. *It Is So Ordered* (1966)
Hall, K. L., ed. *The Oxford Companion To The Supreme Court Of the United States* (1992)
Hyde, G. E. *Earl Warren His Public Life* (1982)
Weaver, J. D. *Warren The Man, The Court, The Era* (1968)

The State of Israel v. Adolf Eichmann
Lang, J. von, ed. *Eichmann Interrogated* (1982)
Papadatos, P. *The Eichmann Trial* (1964)
Wighton, C. *Eichmann, His Career and Crimes* (1961)

The State of Pakistan v. Zulfikar Ali Bhutto
Burki, S. J. *Pakistan Under Bhutto, 1971–77* (1980)
Wolpert, S. *Zulfiquar Bhutto of Pakistan* (1993)

The People's Republic of China v. The Gang of Four
Bonavia, D. *Verdict in Peking* (1984)
A Great Trial in Chinese History (transcripts) (1981)
Butterfield, F. *China: Alive in the Bitter Sea* (1982)

CHURCH COURTS

The Court of the Inquisition v. Joan of Arc
Duparc, P. *Procès de réhabilitation de Jeanne d'Arc* (1979)
Gies, F. *Joan of Arc: The Legend and the Reality* (1981)
Smith, J. H. *Joan of Arc* (1973)
Warner, M. *The Image of Female Heroism* (1981)
　　　　Joan of Arc (1981)

St. Julien Residents v. Local Weevils
Cohen, E. "*Law, Folklore and Animal Lore,*" *Past and Present 110* (1986) pp. 8–37
Evans, E. P. *The Criminal Prosecution and Capital Punishment of Animals* (1906)
Varlier, J. *Les Proces D'Animaux* (1970)

The Holy Office v. Galileo Galilei
Meadows, J. *The Great Scientists* (1987)
Santillana, G. de *The Crime of Galileo* (1961)

The Community v. Alleged Witches
Kittredge, G. L. *Witchcraft in Old and New England* (1929)
Rosenthal, B. *Salem Story* (1994)
Starkey, M. L. *The Devil in Massachusetts* (1952)

MILITARY COURTS

The British Army v. Wolfe Tone
Elliott, M. *The United Irishmen* (1984)
Elliott, M. *Wolfe Tone* (1989)
Pakenham, T. *The Year of Liberty* (1969)

Somerset Fry, P. and F. *A History of Ireland* (1988)
Stewart, A. T. D. *A Deeper Silence* (1993)

The State of Virginia v. John Brown
Oates, S. B. *To Purge This Land With Blood* (1970)
Villiard, O. G. *John Brown* (1910)
Ward, G. C. and Burns, R. and K. *The Civil War* (1991)

The French Army v. Alfred Dreyfus
Bredin, J.-D. (trans. J. Mehlman), *The Affair: The Case Of Alfred Dreyfus* (1986)
Burns, M. *Dreyfus A Family Affair 1789–1945* (1992)
Chapman, G. *The Dreyfus Case: A Reassessment* (1955)

The Allied Nations v. Nazi Leaders
McMillan, J. *Five Men at Nuremberg* (1985)
Neave, A. *Nuremberg* (1978)
Taylor, T. *The Anatomy of the Nuremberg Trials* (1993)

The Allied Nations v. Hideki Tojo
Brackman, A. *The Other Nuremberg* (1987)
Browne, C. *Tojo: The Last Banzai* (1967)
Minear, R. *Victor's Justice* (1971)

JURY TRIALS

Meletus v. Socrates
Chroust, A. J. *Socrates* (1957)
Guthrie, W. K. *Socrates* (1979)
Stone, I. F. *The Trial of Socrates* (1988)

The Crown v. the "Tolpuddle Martyrs"
Citrine, W. ed. *The Martyrs of Tolpuddle* (1934)
Hughes, R. *The Fatal Shore* (1987)
Loveless, G. *Victims of Whiggery* (1837)
Loveless, J., et al. *A Narrative of the Sufferings of Jas. Loveless, Jas. Brine and Thomas & John Standfield* (1838)
Marlow, J. *The Tolpuddle Martyrs* (1971)

The Crown v. Madeleine Smith
Butler, G. *Madeleine Smith* (1935)
Lustgarten, E. *The Woman In The Case* (1955)
Morland, N. *That Nice Miss Smith* (1957)

James McNeill Whistler v. John Ruskin
Conner, P. *Savage Ruskin* (1979)
Fleming, G. H. *James Abbott McNeill Whistler* (1991)
McMullan, R. *Victorian Outsider* (1973)

The Crown v. Florence Maybrick
Hartman, M. S. *Victorian Murderesses* (1985)
Irving, H. B. *The Trial Of Mrs. Maybrick* (1922)
Maybrick, F. *Mrs. Maybrick's Own Story* (1905)
Morland, N. *This Friendless Lady* (1957)
Ryan, B. *The Poisoned Life Of Mrs. Maybrick* (1977)

Oscar Wilde v. the Marquess of Queensberry
Ellmann, R. *Oscar Wilde* (1987)
Montgomery Hyde, H. ed. *The Trials of Oscar Wilde* (1948)
Montgomery Hyde, H. *Oscar Wilde* (1975)

The State of Illinois v. Leopold and Loeb
Loeb, R. *Life Plus 99 Years* (1958)
McKernan, M. *The Amazing Crime and Trial of Leopold & Loeb, 1925,* (1958)
Report of the trial in the *New York Times,* 1924.

The State of Tennessee v. John T. Scopes
Driemen, J. E. *Clarence Darrow* (1992)
Ginger, R. *Six Days or Forever* (1954)
Jensen, R. *Clarence Darrow. The Creation Of An American Myth* (1992)
Kurland, G. *Clarence Darrow Attorney for the Damned* (1972)

The People v. Julius And Ethel Rosenberg
Goldstein, A. H. *The Unquiet Death of Julius and Ethel Rosenberg* (1975)
Radosh, R. and Milton, J. *The Rosenberg File* (1983)
Sharp, M. *Was Justice Done? The Rosenberg-Sobell Case* (1956)

The Crown v. Wilbert Coffin
Belliveau, J. E. *The Coffin Murder Case* (1956)
Hebert, J. *I Accuse The Assassins Of Coffin* (1964)

The Crown v. Penguin Books Ltd.
Montgomery Hyde, H. *The Lady Chatterley's Lover Trial* (1990)

The State of South Africa v. Nelson Mandela
Holland, H. *The Struggle* (1978)
Mandela, N. *No Easy Walk to Freedom* (1990)
Meer, F. *Higher than Hope* (1988)

The U.S. Government v. Daniel Ellsberg
Ellsberg, D. *Papers on the War* (1972)
Karnow, S. *Vietnam* (1991)
Krause, P. A. *Anatomy of an Undeclared War* (1972)
Sheehan, N. *The Pentagon Papers* (1971)
Turner, R. F. *The Myths of the Vietnam War* (1972)
Unga, S. J. *The Papers and the Papers* (1989)

The Crown v. Lindy and Michael Chamberlain
Bryson, J. *Evil Angels* (1985)
Chamberlain, L. *Through My Eyes* (1990)

Attorney General v. Heinemann Publishers & Peter Wright
Fysh, M. ed., *The Spycatcher Cases, Fleet Street Reports* (1989)
Turnbull, M. *The Spycatcher Trial* (1988)
Wright, P. *Spycatcher* (1986)

The State Of Mississippi v. Byron de la Beckwith
Lord, W. *The Past That Would Not Die* (1967)
Nossiter, A. *Of Long Memory* (1994)
Scott, R. W. *Glory In Conflict* (1991)

Acknowledgments

Abbreviations
AKG   Archiv fur Kunst und Geschichte, Berlin
AOL   Andromeda Oxford Limited, Abingdon, UK
BAL   Bridgeman Art Library, London
BN   Bibliotheque Nationale, Paris
FSP   Frank Spooner Pictures, London
HDC   Hulton Deutsch Collection, London
IWM   Imperial War Museum, London
MEPL Mary Evans Picture Library, London
NG   The National Gallery, London
RHPL Robert Harding Picture Library, London
S   Scala, Italy
TP   Topham Picturepoint, Kent, UK
UPI   United Press International, New York
V & A   Victoria & Albert Museum, London

4r Boston Athenaeum 4l BAL 5t Richard Whittington-Egan 5bl American School of Class Studies 9 MEPL 10tl RHPL 12 Magnum Photos/Erich Lessing 13t Mansell Collection, London 13 S 14–15 Sonia Halliday & Laura Washington 15t NG 15b Chester Beatty Library, Dublin 16 Royal Armouries, London 17 by courtesy of the National Portrait Gallery, London 18 RHPL/Walter Rawlings 19 TM Eyston 20 © Historic Royal Palaces, Hampton Court, London 21 BAL/NG 22 V & A 23l Fotomas Index 23r Lord Tollemache, Helmingham Hall, Suffolk 24 BAL/House of Lords, Westminster 24–5 Scottish National Portrait Gallery, Collection of the Earl of Roseberry 26 Archives National de France 27 Giraudon 28 JE Bulloz 29 Roger-Viollet 30t, 30b, 31, 32, 32–3, 33, 34t, 34b, 35t, 35b David King Collection 36 Topeka Capital-Journal, Topeka, KS 37 National Association for the Advancement of Colored People, Baltimore, MD 38t Topeka Capital-Journal, Topeka, KS 38b UPI/ Bettmann 39 Associated Press/Topham 40 Range/Bettmann/UPI 41t Magnum/Burt Glinn 41b Range/ Bettmann/UPI 42t Wiener Library Ltd 42b AOL 43 Camera Press 44 Range/ Bettmann /UPI 45 Range/Bettmann/UPI 46 Range/Bettmann/ UPI 47 Popperfoto 48 AOL 49, 50t FSP/Gamma/François Lochon 50b Associated Press/Topham 51 FSP/Gamma 52 AOL 53 TP 54 TP 55 Magnum/Riboud 56 Camera Press 57 SIPA/Rex Features 58 Bibl. Des Arts Déco/Jean-Loup Charmet 59 Peabody Essex Museum, Salem, MA 60 Centre Jeanne d'Arc, Orléans 61 British Library, London 62b Giraudon 62t BN/Giraudon 64 Holt Studios International/Nigel Cattlin 65 Mansell Collection 66–7 Cephas/Mick Rock 67t AOL/Pierre Dompnier 67b AOL/Pierre Dompnier 68 Image Select/Ann Rohan 69 MEPL 70 Science Museum, Florence 70–1 BAL 71 S 72 Harvard University Art Museums 72 Archivio Segreto Vaticano, Vatican City 73 S 74 Claus Hansmann 75t Essex Institute 75b Peabody Essex Museum, Salem, MA 76t Harvard University Art Museums 76b Peabody Essex Museum, Salem, MA 77 Massachusetts Art Commission/ Douglas Christian 78 AOL 79 AOL 81t National Library of Ireland 81b Public Record Office, London 82 The Ulster Museum, Belfast 83r National Library of Ireland 84 BAL/Guildhall Art Gallery, Corporation of London 85t Trinity College Library, Dublin 85b National Museum of Ireland 86 Range/Bettmann 87 Harpers Ferry National Historical Park 88 Boston Athenaeum 89 Range/Bettmann 90 US Library of Congress 90–91 Harpers Ferry National Historical Park 92 AOL 93 AOL 94t Collection Viollet 94b Collection Viollet 95t HDC 95b John Frost Historical Newspapers 96–97 Boston Public Library 97 Bodleian Library, Oxford 2379 d.53/1 *Histoire de L'Affaire Dreyfus* 98t AOL 98b IWM 99 IWM 100t IWM 100b Range/Bettmann/UPI 101t IWM 101b IWM 102t HDC 102b IWM 103 Topham 104–5 HDC 106 HDC 106–7 National Archives, Washington, DC 108l HDC 108r Bettmann Archive 109 TP/US Army Photography 110 Popperfoto 111 Popperfoto 112 HDC 114 Ancient Art & Architecture Collection 115 S 116 American School of Classical Studies, Athens 117 AKG/Erich Lessing 118 The Mansell Collection 119 The Mansell Collection 120t TUC Library, London 120b Brooke Photographic/AOL 121t TUC Library, London 121b BAL/Guildhall Library, Corporation of London 122 Scottish Record Office/Glasgow City Council 123 inset, 123b, 124t, 124b Glasgow City Council 127 Detroit Institute of Arts 128l US Library of Congress 128r National Monuments Record Centre/AOL 128b By courtesy of the National Portrait Gallery, London 129b US Library of Congress 130 HDC 131 AOL 132t Richard Whittington-Egan 132b HDC 133tl HDC 133tr Geoff Roberts/AOL 134 Richard Whittington-Egan 135tl HDC 135tr HDC 136 BAL 137 HDC 138bl TP 138–139 TP 139 The Ulster Museum, Belfast 140 TP 141 AOL 142, 143t, 143b, 144 Chicago Tribune 145 Birmingham Public Library, UK 146, 147c, 147b Range/ Bettmann/UPI 147c Library of Congress 148 Range/Bettmann 149 Range/Bettmann 150 Range/ Bettmann/UPI 151 Range/Bettmann 152t Range/Bettmann/UPI 152b TP 153t Bodleian Library, Oxford, 300.43r 923 *The Unquiet Death of Julius and Ethel Rosenberg* 153b TP 154t Bodleian Library, Oxford 300.43r 923 *The Unquiet Death of Julius and Ethel Rosenberg* 154b Range/ Bettmann/UPI 155 Range/Bettmann 156t, 156b, 157, 158, 159t, 159b Montreal Gazette 160t AOL 160b HDC 161 RHPL 162, 163, 164 HDC 165t John Frost Historical Newspapers 165b Popperfoto 166 Trans-Africa News & Information Service/Rashid Lombard 167t Mayibuye Centre 167b International Defence & Aid Fund 168c, 168b, 169t, 170b, 170br Mayibuye Centre 171t AOL/Mike Dudley 171b Rex Features/Marcus Zeffler 172t Magnum/Leonard Freed 172–3 TP/ Associated Press 174 Range/ Bettmann/UPI 175 Popperfoto 176b By permission of the Solicitor General for the Northern Territories, Australia 177 FSP/Patrick Riviere 178t LN Smith 178c LN Smith 178b Fairfax Photo Library/Nigel McNeil 179 FSP/Patrick Riviere 180 AOL/ D Pratt 181 TP 182 TP 183 Popperfoto 184 Clarion-Ledger 185t TP 185b TP 186t UPI/Topham 186b Range/Bettmann/UPI 187 Brian A Broom

Andromeda Oxford Ltd. has made every effort to trace copyright holders of the pictures used in this book. Anyone having claims to ownership not identified above is invited to contact Andromeda Oxford Ltd., 11-15 The Vineyard, Abingdon, Oxfordshire, OX14 3PX, United Kingdom.

For Andromeda:
Project Editor Fiona Mullan
Editors & Researchers Vicky Egan, Lin Thomas, Helen McCurdy, Pamela Egan
Art Editors Chris Munday, Ayala Kingsley
Designers Frankie Wood, Jerry Goldie
Picture Research Manager Jo Rapley
Picture Researcher David Pratt
Picture Research Assistant Claire Turner
Indexer Helen McCurdy
Proofreader Lin Thomas
Editorial Assistant Niki Moores
Project Manager Graham Bateman
Production Clive Sparling
Legal Consultants
   Leo Curran M.A. (Oxon) Barrister at Law, Oxford & London
   Peter Mirfield, Fellow and Tutor at Jesus College, Oxford

For Reader's Digest:
Executive Editor James Wagenvoord
Editorial Director Deborah DeFord
Art and Design Director Michele Italiano-Perla
Managing Editors Diane Shanley, Christine Moltzen, Daniela Marchetti

Color origination: Eray Scan pte Ltd., Singapore;
   A.S.A. Litho Ltd., U.K.

INDEX

Page numbers in *italic* indicate a
caption reference. Page numbers in
bold indicate a main entry.

A

abolitionism 89
Addison, John 134
Adulatio Perniciosa (Barberini) 68
African National Congress (ANC)
    166, 167, 168, 169, 170, 171
"aggressive war" 98, 100, 103, 107, 108
Agincourt, battle of 61
allegiance, oath of 16
Allies, the 98, 99, 100, 102, 103, 106,
    107, 108, 111
Amandla ("freedom") 169
Amenet, François 64
American Civil Liberties Union
    (ACLU) 148, 149
anathematization 64, 65
animal trials **64–7**
anti-apartheid movement 171
antievolution bill *see* Butler Act
anti-Semitism 92, 94, 95, 97, 104
Anytus 114, 115, 116
apartheid 166, 169, 171
Apologia (Plato) 115
Aragon, Catherine of 16, 19
Arcetri 71, 73
Archimedes 71
Arendt, Hannah *47*
Aristophanes 114, 116
Aristotle 68, 73
Armstrong, Sir Robert 180, 181, 182,
    183
arsenic poisoning 124, 134
assize system 118
Atkins, Freddie 141
atomic bomb 152, *154*, 155
Attainder, Act of 16
Auriol, Vincent 153
Auschwitz 99, 101
Autun, bishop of 65
Ayers Rock National Park 176, 177,
    178, 179

B

Baldwin, Rodger *149*
ballot disks *116*
Barabbas 15
Barberini, Maffeo *see* Urban VIII, Pope
Barker, Ian 177, 178
Barritt, Dennis 177
"Battersea Bridge" 129, 130
Battlecrease House *133*
Beckwith, Byron de la 6, 7, 112,
    184–7
Bellone 82
Belsen 102
Ben-Gurion, David 42, 43, *45*
Ben-Zvi, Itzhak 47
Bernstein, Lionel 167
Bertrand, Petremand 64
Bhutto, Benazir 50
Bhutto, Nusrat 50
Bhutto, Zulfikar Ali 8, 10, **48–51**
Biao, Lin 55
Bible, the 14, 64, 66, 74, 148, 150, 151
Bill of Rights 148
Birkett, Sir Norman 103
Black, Hugo 39
"Bleeding Kansas" 89
Blewett, George F. 108
Bloch, Alexander 153, 154
Bloch, Emmanuel 153, 154
Blunt, Anthony 183
Board of Education of Topeka, Kansas
    36–41
Boettcher, Professor 178
Boleyn, Anne 16, 19
Boleyn, Thomas 17
Bolsheviks 30, 31, 33, 35
Bonaparte, Napoleon 82
Bonnivard, François 64
Bormann, Martin 103
"Bosie" *see* Douglas, Lord Alfred

Botha, P. W. 171
Botts, Lawson 87
Boudin, Leonard 174
Bowen, Charles 130
Bradshaw, John 22, *23*, 24, 25
Bridge, Sir John 141
Brierley, Alfred 132, 134, 135
Briggs, Matilda 132
Brine, James *118*, 119
British government 81, 180, 182, 183,
    183
British legal system 48, 74, 80, 183
British Penal Code 74
British Secret Intelligence Services 180
Brookover, Wilbur B. 38
Brown, John 6, 79, **86–91**
Brown, Kenneth A. 176
Brown, Linda 36, 37
Brown, Reverend Oliver 36
Brown v. Board of Education 8, **36–41**
Bruno, Giordano 68, 70
Bryan, Frederick 160
Bryan, William Jennings 146, 148, 149,
    150, 151
Buber, Martin 47
Bukharin, Nikolai 8, 10, **30–5**
Burgundy, duke of 61
Burma-Siam "death railway" 107, 111
Burne-Jones, Edward 128, 130
Burnett, Lena 37
Burroughs, George 77
Burton, Harold 39
Butler Act (1925) 148, 150–1
Butler, John Washington 148
Butler, R. A. B. ("Rab") 169
Byrne, Mr Justice 160, 163, *164*, 165
Byrne, William 174

C

Caesar, Julius 15
Caiaphas, Joseph 12, 13, 14, 15
Caligula 14
Cameron, James 176, 177, 178
canon law 60
capital punishment, arguments against
    142–7
Capone, Al 34
Caron, Romuald 159
Carson, Edward Henry 138, 139, 141
Carter, Robert *37*
Catholic emancipation 81, 82
Cauchon, Pierre 60, 61, 62
Cavaignac, Godefroy 94
Caverly, Justice John R. 145, 147
Chandler, Caroline 132
Chandler, Florence *see* Maybrick,
    Florence
Chamber of Deputies (France) 92
Chamberlain, Aidan 176
Chamberlain, Azaria **176–9**
Chamberlain, Kahlia 179
Chamberlain, Lindy & Michael 112,
    176–9
Chamberlain, Reagan 176
Charles I 11, **20–5**
Charles II 25
Charles VI 61
Charles VII 60, *62*
Charmides 114, 116
Chassenée, Bartholomew 65
Chilton, Samuel 90
China, People's Republic of 52–7
Chinese constitution 56
Chinese criminal code 52, 53, 54
Christian fundamentalism 148, 149,
    150, 151
Chunqiao, Zhang 52, 53, 57
Churchill, Winston 98
circuit courts (U.S.) 184
circumstantial evidence 157
civil disobedience 174
Civil Rights Act (1964) 41
civil rights movement 36–41, 185
Civil War, English 20, 21, 22
Claar, Mrs. E. C. *156*
Claar, Frederick 156

Clarion Ledger 185
Clark, Ramsey 50
Clark, Tom 39
Clarke, Sir Edward 139, 141
Clarke, Henry Jacques 82
Cleave's Penny Gazette 118
"Clemency Train" 155
Clouds, The (Aristophanes) 116
Codd, Michael 181
Coffin, Wilbert 6, **156–9**
Cohn, Roy 152
Cold War, the 180
Collins, R. Henn 139, 141
Combination Acts 118, 120
Commons, House of 20, 21, 25, 135,
    182, 183
communism 34, 154, 169, 174
Communist Party (China) 52, 53, 154
Communist Party (South Africa) 168
Communist Party (Soviet) 33, 35
Communists 99, 152, 153, 169, 170
concentration camps 99, 102, 104
Cook, John 22
Copernicus, Nicolaus 68, 69, 71
Corey, Martha 74, 76
Cornwallis, Lord 83, 84, 85
Corwin, Jonathan 74, 75, 76, 77
county courts (U.S.) 184
court-martial 78, 80, 83, 85
Court of Appeal 181, 183
Court of Criminal Appeal 133
Court of the Exchequer 128
Court of the King's Bench 85
Court of the Queen's Bench 159
Cranmer, Thomas 17
Cranwell, Amanda 177
creationism *148*
crimes against humanity 99, 100, 105
crimes against peace 98, 100, 108
Criminal Appeal Division 92
criminal code (China) 56
Criminal Evidence Act 120, 133
Cromwell, Oliver 21, 22, 24, 25
Cromwell, Richard 25
Cromwell, Thomas 17
Crose, François de la 64, 66
Crowe, Robert 146
Crown Court system (Britain) 118
Cultural Revolution (China) 52, 53,
    55, 56
Curran, John Philpot 85

D

Daily Telegraph, The 182
Danton, Georges-Jacques 10, **26–9**
Darrow, Clarence 112, 142–7, 148–51
Darwin, Charles 146, 148, 151
dauphin of France 60, 61, 62
d'Auvergne, Martial 60
David, Jacques-Louis *117*
Day, Mary Anne 88
Day-Lewis, Cecil 163
Dayton, Tennessee 148, 149, 151
death penalty, campaign against (U.S.)
    142, 144, 153
Debs, Eugene 146
DeLaughter, Bobby 186, 187, *187*
Democratic Party (U.S.) 149
Dennis, Delmar 186
Depupet, Jean 67
Devil's Island 92, 94, *94*, 96
"devil's mark" 74, *75*, 76
Dewey, Thomas 39
*Dialogue Concerning the Two Chief
    World Systems, A* (Galileo) 68–73
Dialogues (Plato) 116
dingoes 176, 177, 178, 179
director of public prosecutions (D.P.P.)
    160, 161, 165
Directory (France) 82, 84, 85
district court (Kansas) 37
district courts (U.S.) 184
"divine right of kings, the" 20, 22
Doenitz, Karl 105, *105*
Dorion, Noel 157, 158
Douglas, Lord Alfred ("Bosie") 136,
    137, *137*, 138, 139, 141

Douglas, John Sholto *see* Queensberry,
    Marquess of
Douglas, William O. 39, 155, 174
Downes, John 25
Dreyfus, Alfred 8, 78, **92–7**
Dreyfus, Lucie 94
Dreyfus, Mathieu 94, 97
Drumlanrig, Lord 136
due process 6–8
Dulles, John Foster 157
Duplessis, Maurice 157

E

ecclesiastical courts 60–3, 64–5
Ehrlichman, John 174, 175
Eichmann, Adolf 11, **42–7**
Eichmann in Jerusalem (Arendt) 47
Einstein, Albert 153
Eisenhower, Dwight D. 41, 153, 155,
    174
Ellsberg, Daniel 8, **172–5**
Ellsberg, Patricia *174*
Enclosure Acts 119
English Bar 139
Enlai, Zhou 53, 54
"equality before the law" 142
Equity Division, New South Wales
    Supreme Court 159
Erskine, Thomas 113
Espionage Act (1917) 153; (1940) 173
Esterhazy, Major C. F. 92, 94, 95, 96, 97
Euripedes 114
Evening News 138
Evening Standard 165
Evers, Medgar 7, 184–7
Evers, Myrlie 186, 187
evolution, theory of (Darwin) 146,
    148, 151
Examiner, The 131
excommunication 77
executive clemency 153, *155*

F

Fairfax, Thomas 22
Falcon, Pierre 64
Far Eastern Commission 106
Fatzer, Harold R. 38, 39
Faulkner, Charles J. 87, 89, 90
Faubus, Orval *41*
Federal Bureau of Investigation (FBI)
    152, 154, 174, 184, 186
federal court (Boston) 173
federal court (New York) *154*
federal court (Sydney) 179
federal courts (U.S.) 184
Federal High Court (Canberra) 183
federal law (U.S.) 86
Federal Security Force (FSF) 49
Federal Supreme Court (Australia) 183
Fifth Amendment 154
Filliol, Antoine 66
"final solution, the" 7, 42, 99
firing squad, execution by 80, 85
First Amendment 173, 174
Fischer, Bram 168, 169, 170
Fitzgerald, Edward 147
Fitzgerald, Eugene *153*
Fleming, Silas Hardwick 37
Ford, Gerald 175
Fors Clavigera 126
Fortnightly Review, The 138
Fouquier-Tinville, Antoine 27, 29
Frampton, Henry 120
Frampton, James 118, 119, 120
Franco-Prussian war 92
Frank, Hans 104, *105*
Frankfurter, Felix 39, 40
Franks, Jacob 143
Franks, Robert (Bobby) 142, 143, 144
French Army 82, 83, 92, 94, 96
freedom of expression 173, 174
Frick, Wilhelm 104, *105*
Frith, William 130
Fritzsche, Hans 102, 103, 105
Fuchs, Klaus 152
Funk, Walther 102, 105, *105*